Praise for **Big Conversations with Little Ch**

"As I read *Big Conversations with Little Children*, I kept thinking: 'Have I been waiting for this book for years—all my professional career?' There isn't one topic left uncovered no matter how uncomfortable or challenging. What a courageous author. Lauren Starnes understands that children need us as they try to make sense of our complex world. She thoroughly guides us through each challenging topic with practical suggestions, including reflecting on our own emotional discomfort as we find ways to talk about everything and anything with young children and their families. An important book. It makes me wish I had written it!"

—**Tamar Jacobson, Ph.D.,** early childhood development and education consultant for early childhood programs, organizations, and families, and author of *Everyone Needs Attention: Helping Young Children Thrive*

"Human relationships must have two components to survive: trust and communication. When our kids ask questions, it is imperative to be honest in our answers to preserve and build trust. But how do we communicate our answers both appropriately and effectively? *Big Conversations with Little Children* by Lauren Starnes is instrumental in providing both early educators and parents directions on how to navigate through this process. It's a game changer when it comes to building relationships! A must-have for everyone who interacts with young children."

—**Julia Cook,** international best-selling children's author

"*Big Conversations with Little Children* is one of the most important books for everyone who works with young children to read during these turbulent and uncertain times. Young children are trying to understand the world around them and rely upon the adults in their lives to answer their questions in ways that will help them feel safe and cared for. Lauren's thoughtful and thorough approach emphasizes the importance of building and maintaining relationships with the child as well as the families you work with."

—**Barbara Kaiser,** co-author, *Challenging Behavior in Young Children* and *Addressing Challenging Behavior: The Leader's Role*

"In *Big Conversations with Little Children,* Lauren Starnes offers developmentally appropriate strategies to early childhood educators on how to address fears and worries surrounding children in their ecological systems, from the microsystem (e.g., incarceration) to the chronosystem (e.g., social upheaval). A timely book that invites educators not only to affirm children's feelings but also to empower them to understand issues they care/worry about in an age-appropriate way. Dr. Starnes prepares educators to build knowledge and skills to handle the unexpected, inspires educators to scaffold children's emotionality and agency development, and invites educators to strengthen the connection among children's ecological systems."

—**Shu-Chen "Jenny" Yen, Ph. D.,** professor, child and adolescent studies, California State University, Fullerton

"Lauren Starnes has written a beautiful and much-needed resource for our field inside her new book. Early childhood educators, leaders, and parents can all utilize Lauren's wonderfully crafted communication tools for having elegant conversations with young children in challenging times. The world needs this book. Well done!"

—**Kris Murray,** founder of The Child Care Success Academy

"Research tells us in no uncertain terms that caring, responsive adults stand to play a hugely important role in helping young children learn to work through their feelings. What becomes far less certain when confronted with complex family and social issues ranging from drug abuse and deployment to death or divorce, however, is just where to begin, much less how to engage in such daunting conversations. That's where *Big Conversations* comes in. Rather than steering clear, Dr. Starnes offers clear and concise language and real-world examples to help fellow early educators confidently rise to the challenge. Complete with detailed and developmentally appropriate strategies and plenty of printable pages designed specifically to be shared with families, this book offers anyone who cares about young children's well-being a framework for respectfully supporting them and their families through tough times."

—**Laura Jana, MD, FAAP,** pediatrician, educator, health communicator, and author of *The Toddler Brain*

"We are already having big conversations with little children in the early childhood setting, but we might not be *ready* for them. Dr. Starnes's book prepares the practitioner for meaningful connection with kids on a great variety of big conversations with nearly an encyclopedia of examples. Her specific guidance for supporting social and emotional experiences in young children is spot-on and she provides clear verbiage for early educators to use with example conversations alongside supporting research and evidence-based practice. While it may not be possible to have all the answers all the time, *Big Conversations with Little Children* will light the path for thoughtful, responsive, and connected conversations when we don't know where to begin."

—**Molly Breen, M.A., E.C.E.,** preschool director, St. Paul, MN

✳ ✳ ✳

BIG
Conversations
with Little
Children

Addressing Questions, Worries, and Fears

Lauren Starnes, Ed.D.

free spirit
PUBLISHING®

Library of Congress Cataloging-in-Publication Data
Names: Starnes, Lauren, author.
Title: Big conversations with little children : addressing questions, worries, and fears / Lauren Starnes, Ed.D.
Description: Minneapolis, MN : Free Spirit Publishing Inc., [2022] | Includes bibliographical references and index.
Identifiers: LCCN 2021035819 (print) | LCCN 2021035820 (ebook) | ISBN 9781631986321 (Paperback) | ISBN 9781631986338 (PDF) | ISBN 9781631986345 (ePub)
Subjects: LCSH: Child psychology. | Social work with children. | Conversation. | Life change events.
Classification: LCC BF721 .S5796 2022 (print) | LCC BF721 (ebook) | DDC 155.4—dc23/eng/20211206
LC record available at https://lccn.loc.gov/2021035819
LC ebook record available at https://lccn.loc.gov/2021035820

ISBN: 978-1-63198-632-1

Edited by Marjorie Lisovskis
Cover and interior design by Emily Dyer

10 9 8 7 6 5 4 3 2 1
Printed in the United States of America

Free Spirit Publishing Inc.
6325 Sandburg Road, Suite 100
Minneapolis, MN 55427-3674
(612) 338-2068
help4kids@freespirit.com
freespirit.com

Acknowledgments

Sincere thanks to the early childhood professionals who reviewed
sections of this book prior to publication

Dedication

To my sons, Braden and Gavin, my two young minds who always
challenge me with big questions and big conversations

Contents

List of Printable Pages for Families

See page 218 for instructions for downloading digital versions of these family take-home pages.

Introduction

"There is no trust more sacred than the one the world holds with children."

—Kofi Annan

To work with young children is to constantly encounter the unexpected. Every early childhood educator aims to help young children make connections to what they are learning by linking something new to a prior experience, and to encourage children to ask questions about what they are curious about, wondering about, and wanting more information about. Given this dynamic, young children frequently ask questions about seemingly disconnected concepts or about topics teachers are not expecting or prepared to discuss. This may be a conversation about why cats are purple on a cartoon but not in real life, or a question about a parental argument a child overheard and a puzzling new word, *divorce*.

Building and Nurturing Trust

As early childhood educators it is our role, above all things, to build and nurture trust with the children in our care. This trust is built in many ways, but especially through:

▶ our continuous, consistent presence in children's lives

▶ naturalistic observation of the child—what motivates the child, what interests the child, how the child expresses emotions, and how the child tends to respond to situations

▶ conversation where the child is given opportunities to speak and to have us fully present and listening

▶ care for the child's emotional, social, and physical well-being

When facing an unexpected question or comment from a child, it's imperative to maintain these dynamics. A child asking a question of an adult does so because they trust the adult, feel the adult is able to help, and genuinely seek to *know*. While the emotionality of the question or the topic may cause us initial surprise, it is critical to stop, take a breath, and approach the conversation with respect, honesty, and love.

Likewise, it's critical that we maintain open, two-way communication with families. Families will frequently seek out their child's teacher or care provider as a resource, a trusted confidant and support during difficult times. Many parents* see

---

** The terms *parents* and *family adults* are used interchangeably throughout this book. Children may live with parents, stepparents, foster parents, grandparents, aunts, uncles, or other caring adults. Likewise, children may live with a mom and dad, with two moms, with two dads, with a single parent, or in other family configurations. In this book, information related to *parents* applies to whoever these adults may be in the lives of the children in your setting.*

1

the early childhood educator as an extension of the family or, at the very least, an important member of their child's community. With all the unknowns that come from raising children, many families will confide in you and seek your advice as it relates to child and family issues.

This is a lot to ask—and added to it is the reality that many of the issues children face and ponder are concerns we grapple with as adults as well. We live in a world where terror attacks, war, famine, natural disasters, and health crises are ongoing; these major world events permeate our radio, television, internet, and adult conversations. And the words of Margaret Mead from decades ago ring truer today than ever before: "The young are seeing history being made before it is censored by their elders." We have to be aware that, like their elders, young children are likely seeing, hearing, and trying to make sense of the news. More personal stressors at home or among extended family and friends can be just as unsettling and confusing: death, illness, divorce, loss of job, and military deployments to name a few. Children will inevitably ask questions and express concerns about what is going on around them.

As adults, we learn to compartmentalize. We find ways to sort the issues into likely threats, improbable threats, and impossible threats to self. We try to make peace with the world, stay steady, and live our best lives. Young children have not yet learned these skills.

Adults may be inclined to assume that young children are unaware, unfamiliar, not listening, and not wondering or worrying. This could not be further from the truth. Children learn from an early age to pay careful attention to what is said to them and around them, along with what is expressed nonverbally. Infants and young toddlers can discern tone of voice and may exhibit a stress response when the verbal and nonverbal messages of a trusted adult are misaligned. And while older toddlers and preschoolers may not know or grasp all the vocabulary of what they overhear being discussed, an adult's emotional expressions and attempts to shield the conversation from the child signal that the topic is important. This may inadvertently lead a child to try to listen or attend more closely.

Children's resulting anxieties can be exacerbated by fears derived from real-life events. A child may focus excessively upon an event or feel it is larger or has greater impact than it actually does. The reality of a divorce may lead a child to think both parents are going away. The reality of a death may lead a child to think that other people in their life are dying. The reality of terror events in places far from a child's home may lead a child to think that their own home and community are under attack. In some situations, the child's community itself may indeed be threatened, yet children still need to be helped to feel safe in such circumstances. Even when adults themselves struggle to understand and navigate events or grapple with difficult situations and experiences, children need those adults to hear their questions and provide answers and support with as much reassurance as possible.

Fred Rogers famously said, "When I was a boy and I would see scary things in the news, my mother would say to me, 'Look for the helpers. You will always find people who are helping.'" This is true, and knowing there are adult helpers can go a long way toward supporting young children's feelings of safety and validation. Even in situations and experiences that try the human spirit, children need to know that the trusted adults around them are committed to their well-being and are working to make the world as safe as it can be.

> Even in situations and experiences that try the human spirit, children need to know that the trusted adults around them are committed to their well-being and are working to make the world as safe as it can be.

Preparing for Your Role

Big Conversations with Little Children is designed to support adults in having potentially difficult or emotionally charged conversations with young children while ensuring the conversations provide children ways to express and explore their feelings. What makes some conversations so difficult to have, particularly with children?

Often the root cause is that the issue being discussed itself is socially charged or invokes very strong personal reactions. This can lead the adult to question not only what to say but how best to say it without making assumptions, oversharing, or being inappropriately opinionated.

Equally as often, the topic is difficult to discuss because it centers on an issue that activates emotion in the adult or may potentially spark emotion in the child. And as we all well know, young children are more likely than not to pipe up with an unexpected question at an unexpected time. Therefore, the adult may be mentally, emotionally, and socially unprepared to have the conversation and may lack background knowledge on the issue or about the child's particular situation.

> As the educator, you are regarded as the expert and so you can expect tough questions to arise in your regular interactions with children and families. Preparation is the key that can help you in this role.

As the educator, you are regarded as the expert and so you can expect tough questions to arise in your regular interactions with children and families. Preparation is the key that can help you in this role, and this book is intended to provide it. With thoughtful preparation, you can build the knowledge and skills needed to handle the unexpected. This book can be your resource when a child asks

Consider a Community of Practice

Difficult conversations with young children and their families don't occur in a vacuum: it's natural and expected that some discussions will evoke personal responses and sometimes intense emotions in teachers and care providers. Like the children in our care, we too experience turmoil—job loss, addiction, marriage difficulties, illness, death, violence, upheaval. Our family makeup, our culture, our race, our gender, and those of our friends and loved ones are complex and can present us with questions and worries, just as they do for children.

As you focus on answering the "big" questions raised by small children, it's wise to take time to reflect on and explore your own emotions around the topics. Doing this will help you feel more grounded and confident in supporting the children in your care. One effective way to be intentional about this exploration is by forming a community of practice to discuss the topics with other adults who work with you in your setting.

A community of practice is a group of people who work and learn together over time about a challenge or concern they all share. You and your colleagues might meet regularly to discuss how to navigate teachers' personal emotions in the face of difficult conversations with children, or you might focus on a topic that has emerged as particularly important in your setting, such as racism or food insecurity. A community of practice lets you address your own apprehensions, look back on and evaluate your actions, gain self-awareness, learn from your own experience and that of others, consider new ideas, and plan for the future. It is a safe place to have "real" conversations.

In speaking to colleagues about sensitive topics, or about situations that have occurred in your classroom, it's essential that you protect confidentiality of everyone in the group and of the children and families in your school or program.

Learn more about starting a community of practice:

★ *Growing Together: Developing and Sustaining a Community of Practice in Early Childhood* by Kathi Gillaspy, Megan Vinh, Nancy Surbrook-Goins, and Sarah Nichols

★ *Reflecting in Communities of Practice: A Workbook for Early Childhood Educators* by Deb Curtis, Debbie Lebo, Wendy C. M. Cividanes, and Margie Carter

you a difficult question and when an adult, such as a parent or another teacher, seeks your support in approaching difficult topics with a young child.

Families look to their child's school or child care setting and often to their child's teacher for support in multiple realms of child development. Early childhood education is, after all, a field that requires and relies upon interdependence among educators and families. Trust is the cornerstone of the field: trust from parent to teacher, from teacher to parent, from child to parent, and from children to teacher. This dynamic requires that a teacher evaluate and act upon a child's best interest in all situations.

Open rapport between educators and families is essential from the beginning of this relationship. Being a consistent presence in the classroom at times when families are present, asking the family open-ended questions about the child and events in the child's life, and sharing observations with the family are key ways to establish this rapport. The child is the bridge uniting the relationship, and it is imperative that anything said about the child or in the presence of the child always be respectful. This respect carries forth into answering the child's questions. A question asked by a child should be respected, honored, and answered. The goal of this book is to guide and empower you with the confidence and developmental appropriateness to have these difficult and important conversations whenever and however they occur.

> **A question asked by a child should be respected, honored, and answered. The goal of this book is to guide and empower you with the confidence and developmental appropriateness to have these difficult and important conversations whenever and however they occur.**

About This Book

Big Conversations with Little Children consists of two main parts:

Part I: Preparing for Difficult Conversations addresses how to cultivate understanding and partnership among the adults involved. Here you will find suggestions on questions to ask parents to determine the best way to approach a child's questions or concerns. Part I also helps you anticipate three types of conversations or questions to be prepared for:

▶ Conversations between a parent and teacher. This might involve the family member asking the teacher for advice, support, or suggestions (such as a father asking the teacher about how to tell his child about a miscarriage) or the teacher letting a family adult know about something the child brought up (such as a question about gender).

▶ Conversations between the teacher and the individual child (such as speaking with a child who experienced a death in the family or a child who is questioning the major illness of a family member).

▶ Conversations between the teacher and a class or group of children (such as discussing ways the community and children are affected by a natural disaster or the death of a classmate).

Part I includes an overview of need-to-know information for having important conversations with families and with young children, specifically about ensuring developmental appropriateness, maintaining neutrality, speaking with parents first, perceiving emotions, and evaluating the context of a conversation. It also offers guidance for determining what to share among other adults and staff in the school.

Part II: Conversation Topics addresses specific subjects of potentially difficult conversations you might have with a young child:

- **Family** topics cover issues that happen at home and require especially close or sensitive communication with the family.

- **Illness and death** topics include those that all children might experience, such as the death of a classroom pet or a teacher's illness, as well as those that are more personal to a given child, such as the death of a relative or a sibling's disease.

- **Social issues** topics address conversations around race, gender, and other cultural matters, such as one preschooler telling another she can't be Princess Elsa because she is Black or a child wondering why someone has a mom and a dad while someone else has two dads.

- **Upheaval and violence** topics offer ways to reply to children's concerns—whether about a crisis that is far away, such as a terror event the child has seen or heard about on television, or one that is closer to home, such as a storm that ruined people's homes or a shooting in the community or school.

Part II can be referenced by topic. For each topic you will find an overview of how families and children might respond to the issue, suggestions for discussing the subject with family adults, examples of how to reply to a child's questions and how to invite a conversation with a child as needed, and ideas for following up. Each topic also includes information for parents and other family adults with suggestions for responding to children's questions at home; ways to handle unexpected questions and concerns; and books, websites, or other resources parents may find helpful.

The topics included reflect many that are likely to emerge in conversations with young children, but the list is not exhaustive. The guidance and examples provided can help ground you in general approaches that can be extended and applied to other issues that may arise.

Each section contains **family take-home pages** with information for parents on how to talk with children about the topic. You can photocopy these pages directly from the book or download and print them to give to family adults. Be sure to read these handouts yourself—they give some additional information and can support you in your conversations with families.

Also included with the family take-home pages is an introductory letter explaining to families that this book is being used by

> Use this book as a guide, not an instructional manual. The dialogues are examples of language and approaches and are not meant to be scripts to follow verbatim. Once you become familiar with the underlying goals for a given type of conversation, you can adjust the language to the needs of a particular situation and to your own way of speaking.

their children's teachers and that information pages on various topics are available for parents and caregivers. See page 218 to learn how to download this letter and the family take-home pages.

Use this book as a guide, not an instructional manual. The dialogues are examples of language and approaches and are not meant to be scripts to follow verbatim. Once you become familiar with the underlying goals for a given type of conversation, you can adjust the language to the needs of a particular situation and to your own way of speaking.

It's not your role, or the purpose of this book, to work through a complex family or social problem with a young child or to "fix" such a problem. Rather, you are there as a trusted sounding board who allows the child space and comfort for talking about how they feel and who communicates with families about the worries and feelings children share with you. You always want to support a child emotionally in a way that gives only the information the child needs and is developmentally ready to understand.

✳ ✳ ✳

Thank you for all that you do to better the lives of young children and solidify a stronger tomorrow. Your caring and thoughtful work with children will leave a legacy.

I would love to know how *Big Conversations with Little Children* has supported you in working with young children and their families. I also welcome learning about other ideas you have or additional topics you've addressed with the children in your care. Please write to me through my publisher at help4kids@freespirit.com.

Lauren Starnes, Ed.D.

PART I

Preparing for Difficult Conversations

Preparation is key when it comes to difficult conversations. Being *emotionally* prepared and *verbally* prepared are equally important. As a trusted adult you need to be emotionally calm and approach questions young children ask with respect, caring, honesty, and objectivity. It's natural for emotions to surface in the face of a child's questions or worries, but often an adult's emotional reaction can unintentionally silence the child. With intention and practice, you can learn to take a deep breath, pause, and then answer the child with a relaxed tone and facial expression. It's also possible to prepare for what to say and how to respond to the unexpected statement or question.

Part I will guide you on how you approach challenging conversations with families, children, and other staff members in ways that are developmentally appropriate for children and with full respect for privacy. There are always two types of "big" conversations when it comes to young children:

▶ the planned conversation where the adult leads the discussion or is well prepared to address expected questions

▶ the unplanned, spontaneous question or shared information that comes seemingly out of the blue

In Part I, and throughout the book, you will find guidance on how to approach both.

Partnering with Families About Communicating with Children

"Children are the priority. Change is the reality. Collaboration is the strategy."

—Judith Billings

It is essential that early childhood teachers find a method to learn from families on a daily basis how their child is feeling and functioning, generally speaking. This best practice ensures consistent communication and provides you with critical insight that can help you support the child. Learning that "Vinnie didn't sleep well last night" or "Makayla woke up grumpy this morning" gives you information about the child's demeanor and emotions and cues you to things to be mindful of or signs and symptoms to be watching for. This daily communication also builds trust and opens dialogue for other potential topics.

General Family Check-In Questions

To invite daily information from families, you might greet family adults at drop-off, use a form that is sent home with the child, or email or text a parent. Questions like the following can foster this brief exchange:

- "How is Xavier doing at home?"
- "How was Peyton's weekend/evening?"
- "Is there anything new I should know?"
- "How did Ava sleep last night?"
- "How is Kaylee feeling today?"
- "How has Ryan's morning been so far?"
- "Malachi seems to be in a very good mood today. What is he so happy about this afternoon?"
- "How is the Rodriguez family doing today?"
- "Emma has a birthday coming up. How are you feeling about her turning four?"
- "I have not seen Mom/Dad in a few days. How is she/he doing?"

Framework for Parent Conversation Starters

Having these daily check-ins also provides an opening when family members—or you—need to have a potentially challenging conversation. Initiating a conversation with a parent or family member after an unexpected discussion with a child may feel awkward. To begin, the key things you want to do are let the family member know what the child expressed and how it was addressed, and then open a dialogue for any additional information the family may wish to provide. The following give examples of how this may be approached:

▶ "Today Jeremy asked me about where dogs go when they die. I shared what happened with my pet when she died, and I want to respect you and your family's wishes in how I respond with Jeremy. How would you like me to address this with him if the topic comes up in discussion again?"

▶ "Today Michael built a structure in the block center. His friend asked him what it was, and he said it was a jail where his uncle was going. I want to respect your family's wishes in how I talk about this with Michael. I have a conversation guide that has additional resources that might help your family talk with him about it, if you're interested."

▶ "Izzy wanted to write a letter to Grandpa today to tell him not to die in the hospital. I want to be sure to talk with Izzy about this in the way you wish me to. Is there something you'd like me to say or emphasize if Izzy brings up Grandpa again? This must be a difficult time, and I do have a resource that may help your family talk with Izzy about what's happening. Would you like a copy?"

▶ "This morning, Maggie was extremely concerned about going outside—she said she was afraid a tornado would come back. I immediately reassured her that she was safe, and I comforted her. May I share with you how I would like to approach this topic with Maggie if it comes up again, so we can discuss and plan together? I want to handle this in a way that's comfortable for your family."

Next Steps: Taking the Conversation Further

After checking in with the family, your next conversation may be between you and the child, or between you and the parent. It is important to consider the topic, the impact, and the context to determine the best way to proceed.

Conversation with a single child. Often, before or after an initial conversation with a family adult, you will find yourself having a conversation with a single child about a personal issue that is affecting that child and that child alone. It does not impact the other children in your class or group and is private to the child and the child's family. Examples would include parental divorce, death of a family member, or a major medical diagnosis of a family member.

Conversation with a group of children. There are also times when you will have a conversation between yourself and a group of children. This might come about as result of hearing from several parents that children are concerned about something at school (for example, fears after having a safety drill). It might also come about due to an issue in the community that is affecting them all, even if the effect is felt in different magnitudes. For example, you may need to speak with children about a natural disaster, a local terror event, or a teacher suddenly being gone from school.

The defining factor between the two teacher-to-child conversation types is the effect and privacy of the issue. If the issue affects and impacts only one child, the conversation should be kept private to the one child.

> The defining factor between the two teacher-to-child conversation types is the effect and privacy of the issue. If the issue affects and impacts only one child, the conversation should be kept private to the one child.

Conversation with family adults. In your role as an early childhood educator you will frequently have conversations with parents that go beyond routine check-ins and even beyond initial inquiries you might make when a child has raised an issue. A conversation with a parent might occur about a personal issue in which the parent or family member approaches you for insight, support, and guidance on how best to have the conversation with the child. Examples include separation or divorce, loss of an unborn baby, or parental incarceration. This is where you can act as a guide and resource, relying upon Part II of this book to provide targeted suggestions for the family on how they can have conversations at home with the child from a family lens. This is also an ideal time for you to discuss with the parent what the child already knows, what the parent has already shared and the language they used, and what, if anything, the parent would like you to discuss or be prepared to discuss with the child.

An ongoing parent-teacher dialogue might also be a conversation you initiate about a question or comment a child has raised or to follow up on an earlier exchange you had with the parent.

Rules of Thumb for Difficult Conversations

For any conversation about difficult or emotionally charged topics, there are some general rules to keep in mind. These guidelines will help in any of conversation related to children in your care.

1. Talk to families first. When possible, conversations with parents and families should precede conversations with young children. Questions like the examples in the "General Family Check-In Questions" (page 11) invite an open dialogue that can lead to a parent sharing important family information with you in advance.

2. Follow the family's desired approach. Parents and families should be the drivers of what is shared, discussed, and offered, as much as this is possible. Use prompts like those in the "Framework for Parent Conversation Starters" (page 12) to confer with a family member before a child presses the conversation, question, or topic further. The goal is to work with the family and within the family's desired approach to the topic at hand. Some families may be reluctant to share details of what is occurring at home even when questioned directly. Your role is to provide support for the child and the family to the degree that you are able and the family is receptive. If families are not receptive or forthcoming, continue to share with the family what the child has said and how you have responded and to offer resources (such as the take-home pages from this book and information and referrals available through your school or program).

3. Expect the unexpected. Anyone interacting with young children should be prepared for unanticipated questions at unexpected times. A young child may ask about a community terror event or question the gender identity of a classmate with little context, catching the teacher unprepared. The topics in Part II provide in-the-moment guidance and support to scaffold these conversations.

4. Be aware of your nonverbal communication. Children are watching your emotional reaction and may shut down if your face or body language hints that a topic or question is taboo. For example, the child who asks, "Is my daddy a bad guy now that he is in jail?" may read surprise or shock on the face of an adult as a signal that affirms the child's fear or as a signal to not talk about this subject any further. Try to maintain an open and matter-of-fact facial expression, and avoid sudden body movements in response to children's statements and questions.

5. Use open-ended questions. Respond to a child's question or statement with an open-ended question. For example:

> **Child:** "My Aunt Charlotte was going to have a baby but the baby died."
>
> **Teacher:** "Thank you for telling me. I did not know that. How are you feeling about Aunt Charlotte and the baby?"

Here the teacher's response affirms what the child shared, acknowledges to the child that the teacher did not know about this, and then allows the child to share their emotions. The teacher does not presume how the child feels.

It is important for children's emotional health for them to be able to consider how and what they are feeling and to find words to express that. Using emotional vocabulary takes time and practice. The more children can verbally express how they are feeling, the less likely they are to have tantrums or meltdowns, act out, or internalize. To help children recognize their emotions, encourage them to focus on what they are physically experiencing (such as tears, clenched fists, heavy breathing, a fluttering feeling in the chest). Guide them to match an emotional label to the feeling with a question such as, "I see you are holding your fists very tight. How are you feeling?" This allows you to help the child understand and verbalize emotions without making assumptions or giving unnecessary information.

> **Using emotional vocabulary takes time and practice. The more children can verbally express how they are feeling, the less likely they are to have tantrums or meltdowns, act out, or internalize.**

6. Pause. After asking your question, the next most important part of the conversation is to pause. The open-ended question allows the child to share what they are feeling, say what they know, and potentially ask additional questions. The pause also allows you a chance to center emotionally and to mentally prepare for the response, which may or may not follow.

Some young children will respond with silence. This is okay, and you should not press for a verbal response. If a child follows this pause with additional comments or questions, you'll want to answer in very simple terms until you can have a conversation with the parent.

> **Child:** "Mama says Aunt Charlotte is sad."
>
> **Teacher:** "Would you like to draw a picture for Aunt Charlotte to let her know you are thinking of her?"

The child's statement doesn't really reveal what the child is feeling or any information about what happened. That's okay. The child may be sad too, or may feel curious, troubled, worried, scared, or some other emotion. By inviting the child to draw a picture, the teacher sets the stage for the child to explore and express feelings about the situation and to then share their art with the loved one if they wish.

> **Child:** "Is my cousin Katia going to die from her cancer?"
>
> **Teacher:** "It sounds like you have some very big questions about what is happening with your cousin Katia. I do not know what is happening with her but I am sure the doctors are helping her. Would you like to make a card for Katia to let her know you are thinking of her?"

Note here that the response does not offer information; the teacher has little knowledge about Katia's illness and needs to know how the family wants this discussed. Instead, the teacher acknowledges the question, affirms what can be safely assumed from the question (that Katia is getting medical care), and prompts the child to find a way to channel their feelings about the situation.

Three A's and a B: Acknowledge, Affirm, Ask, and Be There

In your role as the teacher, you always want to avoid sharing information with a child that might not have already been shared by the family at home. An approach structured by "three A's"—*acknowledge, affirm, ask*—can help you do this. In response to a child's comment or question, offer an affirmative statement followed by an open-ended question, acknowledging and keeping an intentional focus on the emotions the child expresses. For example:

★ "I'm glad you let me know your daddy is going away to help fight a big fire. How are you feeling about Daddy going to do that?"

★ "I didn't know your doggie had died. Thank you for telling me about it. Would you like to draw a picture about you and your dog?"

This technique answers the child in a respectful way but also allows you time to communicate with the family and determine their wishes in terms of information sharing.

Following any conversation, children need you to *be there*, to continue to be available to listen and help them cope with their feelings. By remembering and practicing these "three A's and a B," you will help children share when they need to and will help yourself appropriately support them.

Other Important Considerations in Preparing for Big Conversations

"The most precious gift we can offer anyone is our presence."

—Thich Nhat Hanh

There are several other critical considerations to evaluate before engaging in potentially difficult conversations with and regarding young children.

▸ At the forefront is to gauge what is developmentally appropriate for the child at their age and individual level of cognitive understanding.

▸ It's also important to maintain confidentiality and honor the family's privacy as you involve others in a conversation. Consider your own comfort level in speaking about the topic with the child. Who else needs to know about the conversation or take part in it? Where will the conversation take place? How will you keep parents informed?

▸ The family's perspective and preferences are another key factor. What is the family context around religion? What words are the family using to discuss the topic with the child? What do you need to know about a timeline (for example, with regard to illness or military deployment)? What is the impact of the issue on the child, and what does the child know or understand about the impact?

The Child's Developmental Level

Specifically, consider both what the child is able to take in and comprehend in terms of time and future events and what and how the child communicates through actions and words.

Understanding of Time and Future Events

The following are general developmental milestones of comprehension of the concept of time and future events by age.[*] Always bear in mind that every child's development follows a unique trajectory and progresses at its own pace. Use your knowledge of the child as you consider what they are likely able to understand.

Ages 18 months to two years: Toddlers do not have a concept of time but do begin to understand routines and schedules. Toddlers understand the present and the expectation of the order that the present moment should follow.

---

[*] Adapted from Poole, Miller, and Church.

Ages three to five years: Preschoolers begin to understand temporal time, particularly *before* and *after*. Vocabulary to describe past and future events is often inaccurate, but the concept of *past, present*, and *future* begins to form. Time-telling tools such as clocks and calendars begin to be understood as a way to sequence events.

Ages six to eight years: Early elementary-age children understand and begin to use temporal words such as *before, after, next, a long time ago*, and future terms such as *in a few days* or *near Christmastime*. *Far past* and *far future* are still difficult to conceptualize.

Communication

Along with being sensitive to a child's developmental understanding of time, it is also essential to evaluate the behaviors of a child. Children will express discomfort and react to changes in their world, or perceived changes in their world, the best way they know how. Caring adults need to be mindful both of what is being *said* and what is being *seen*. Behavior is communication. When children lack the words or ability to communicate how they are feeling, they will demonstrate it through behavioral means. For example, when under emotional stress, a child who was previously toilet trained might show signs of toileting regression; a child who does not typically have tantrums may begin to have frequent meltdowns. And when children ask questions in an attempt to make sense of what they have seen or heard, vocabulary—the words used and understood—will vary significantly by child.

> **Behavior is communication. When children lack the words or ability to communicate how they are feeling, they will demonstrate it through behavioral means.**

Maintaining Confidentiality and Honoring Privacy

The respect for privacy is essential for issues related to the child and the child's family. Here are some questions to guide you in maintaining this respect.

Who needs to know and be involved? The first question of consideration is who in your school or setting needs to *know* about the issue and the questions being posed by the child. For example, in a classroom where there is more than one teacher, it may be deemed appropriate to share the topic with the other teachers to maintain transparency and consistency of language. Leadership at the school should be informed and consulted for support and to provide guidance.

There is the secondary question of who may need to be *involved*. The family should always be the first involved party, with partnership from the teacher. In a setting where guidance counseling or health services are available, a counselor or health worker may be an additional partner.

Finally, it is important to consider who needs to be kept *informed* of any ongoing conversations had with the child or questions asked by the child. This always includes the family but likely will also include other teachers in the classroom, people in leadership roles within your organization, and support staff, such as a guidance counselor.

....

Note: If there is ever a suspicion or an allegation made of child maltreatment, danger, abuse, or neglect, follow all of your program's stated regulations about mandatory reporting. Even if your geographic jurisdiction or role does not require mandatory reporting, it is important to inform parents, school leadership, and/or other authority figures if you suspect a child may be in need of intervention.

....

What's your own comfort level? Equally important to the child's comfort is your own comfort in having the discussion. Often the difficult conversation topic may be one that activates an internal response or one that is not intended to be discussed or heard by other children in the classroom. It's important for you to determine where you are comfortable talking with the child and whether you want to talk with the child alone, be joined by a co-teacher, or have a colleague carry out the conversation without you. Respectful teacher-child interactions require a teacher to be internally aware. It is important to ask yourself the following questions:

▶ "When faced with this topic, what do I feel?"

▶ "What is it about this topic that sparks something in me?" Perhaps it is a community-wide issue or perhaps it is an issue that you have personally faced.

▶ "How can I answer the child in a respectful way, independent of my experience, to empower the child to feel comfortable and trust me at this time?"

How will you communicate with parents? In addition to considering who should be kept informed, you should also think about the most appropriate and preferred mode of communication. While many parents prefer in-person communication for conversations, questions, and any follow-up discussions, others may wish to communicate via phone calls, texting, or email. A verbal, face-to-face conversation should always be the initial mode of communication if possible. Directly ask parents how they wish to communicate regarding any future conversations you overhear or have with their child.

If the parent prefers phone follow-up, ensure that this is manageable within the school or program's structure. Discuss with the parent which staff member will make the call and when this person will be able to call. Verify that the phone number on file is the correct one to use. If email is what the parent prefers, again confirm that this communication method is manageable and accessible within the structure of your setting. Discuss with the parent which staff member will email them and when, and verify that the email address on file is correct.

Where will the conversation take place? When a child asks a question or makes a statement regarding a socially or emotionally charged topic, it's always important to approach them with respect and reassurance. One element to evaluate is where you will speak with the child. While stepping out of the classroom to talk may be more private, this setting may not help the child feel comfortable. In fact, being removed from the room may inadvertently communicate that the question was wrong or that the child is now in trouble. Instead, consider a more private area of the classroom, still well within lines of sight, that the child will find comfortable and natural. This could be sitting in the class library, at a table, in a cozy corner, or in a less busy area of the classroom or playground, such as at the handwashing sink or on a stoop or bench in the outdoor play area.

> One element to evaluate is where you will speak with the child. While stepping out of the classroom to talk may be more private, this setting may not help the child feel comfortable.

Family Considerations

With any conversation related to family dynamics, social issues, or world events, there are other familial preferences to remain aware of and consider carefully when speaking with a young child.

What is the religious context? While religion and religious teachings are not openly discussed in many early childhood education settings, when there is going to be a "big" conversation with a child, it is important to know what the family's teachings, beliefs, and practices are in relation to the topic. A family's religion and beliefs will influence whether and how some parents wish issues to be addressed. This decision is a very private one and further demonstrates the need to approach child-initiated topics of conversation about sensitive issues open-endedly and with family input. For example:

> **Teacher to parent:** "Jade told me today that her Aunt Nariah has died."
>
> **Parent:** "Yes. My sister-in-law, Nariah, passed away over the weekend. We've explained to Jade that Aunt Nariah is in heaven now and that we can still talk about her because we miss her. She may bring this up again."
>
> **Teacher:** "I see—thank you for explaining. You mentioned telling Jade that Aunt Nariah is in heaven now. Can you share with me a little of what Jade knows about heaven and how she has reacted to the news so far? I want to be sure I stay consistent with what you have told her and with your family's faith beliefs."

This example shows how a teacher or child care provider can respectfully ask a family about their religious beliefs, particularly regarding the idea of afterlife or about specific religion-based explanations of life events. Here the teacher repeated the parent's language and then asked an open-ended question to learn more about the family's faith teachings in order to give appropriate and caring support to the child.

What words are the family using? Families have vocabularies—ways of talking about sensitive subjects. With this in mind, you'll need to be familiar with how the topic is being explained to the child and what language is and is not being used at home. This is important to ensure consistency and continuity for the child. For example, a parent may have told a child about a family member's diagnosis of cancer by saying that the family member is sick and needs special medicine. If the word *cancer* has not already been used, you do not want to introduce a new term, which may lead to confusion, anxiety, or further questions.

Among the other children, a child may still hear a new word that hasn't been used in the child's home. For example, one child may talk about *chemotherapy* and you know another child's family does not use that word. If this happens, define the term very simply for children in the moment. Then follow up with the family to let them know what occurred and how you explained the term to their child.

What is the timeframe of the concern? Also critical to explore is how the timing of the topic is being discussed by the family. When does the child think the topic is going to happen or did happen? What language is being used around this? For example, if a child is questioning a terror event that occurred years before, a parent may have already framed it as "a long time ago before you were even born." Comparatively, if a family member or friend is in hospice with little time remaining to live, a parent may have told the child objectively that the loved one will die before Thanksgiving or may have used more abstract language without any time constraint.

What does the child understand about the issue's impact? Be sure to ask the family about how the impact of the issue is being discussed. What has been shared with the child already? Does the child know and understand how this topic will impact them? Is the child *able* to understand this? For example, a child who overhears parents talking about divorce may not realize that this will result in any changes for the child themself.

✳ ✳ ✳

The family is the guiding light. It is critical that the family serve as the decision maker regarding what to share with a child and how to talk about the topic in terms of wording and timelines. Always keep the family informed of any questions, comments, or emotions shared by the child as these relate to a topic of concern.

PART II

Conversation Topics

Part II provides additional guidance and preparation for specific difficult conversations around topics in four broad areas: family issues, illness and death, social issues, and upheaval and violence. Each topic starts with an overview of the issue as it relates to children and family adults and then follows a consistent framework:

▶ examples of suggested ways to initiate a conversation with parents and responses for when a parent lets you know about a concern in the family

▶ conversation starters you can use when children comment or ask a question about the topic

▶ recommended ways to follow up with the family after a discussion with a child

▶ examples of suggested responses to children's further or unexpected questions and remarks

▶ parent information pages with suggestions for talking with their young child about the topic

Keep in mind that the sample conversations included in Part II are *examples* of responses that are appropriate and respectful and that can invite children to share more if they wish. No two children are alike, and there are numerous possible situations related to each topic. Use the examples to guide your choice of words and adapt them to the particular child and circumstance. These are not intended to be used verbatim. As you become familiar with the underlying goals for a given type of conversation, you can adjust the language to the needs of a specific situation and to your own way of speaking.

Big Conversations About Family Issues

"Family is not an important thing. It's everything."
—Michael J. Fox

At one time or another, all families go through stress and disruption. When a family has a crisis—a lost job, a separation or divorce, addiction—the issue is highly personal and painful for everyone involved. While there are many possible "big" conversations you may face with young children and their parents, issues around family turmoil are some of the most personal and therefore the most sensitive ones to address. And because young children may see you as a trusted caretaker and thus an extension of their own family, it is likely that they will share information and ask questions about family events that are confusing or troubling to them. While it's essential to share with parents any concerns children bring to you, it's equally important that you show sensitivity in your conversations with family adults, because as family members they are directly involved.

Families encounter a variety of domestic challenges, and no two situations are the same. Family events affect every person and family unit differently. Adults and children, in turn, are also affected and respond differently depending upon the family dynamics and the specifics of the stressful situation.

If possible, sensitive topics are best discussed with parents before a child brings up the subject to you. When parents provide teachers a sense of the situation and the perspective from the family, they help teachers be prepared to respond respect-fully, appropriately, and in a way that is helpful without making assumptions or oversharing. Some parents may do this readily, while others may tend to hold back and protect their privacy.

Either way, whether parents have spoken to you ahead of time or not, con-versations with young children about sensitive family topics should occur when a child asks a question or offers information about the life event. Let the child cue the conversation. Keep in mind your goal of supporting the child to know it is safe to talk with you about the topic and to recognize and share what they are feeling.

Also keep in mind that the family topics included here reflect many—but certainly not all—that are likely to emerge in conversations with young children. You can extend and apply the guidance, examples, and general approaches to other issues that may arise.

Unemployment

Unemployment is usually a scary time for any adult working to support a family, and its impact can be severe on every family member. The financial impact causes stress and may be devastating. It may impact the family's ability to maintain the child's enrollment in child care, school, and extracurricular activities. For some families, it may affect meeting basic needs such as paying for housing, heating, or food.

Beyond the financial impact, there is often a pronounced social and emotional strain. The unemployed adult may have a diminished sense of identity or capability in the midst of feeling intense pressure to find work. Family members may be called upon to provide support for the family. Those who were not previously working outside of the home may quickly attempt to enter the workforce. Other family members may be resentful or feel added pressure to succeed or to work longer hours. These are some of the many factors that make unemployment a time of high anxiety and uncertain social support, as friends and family struggle to know what to say and how best to help.

Unemployment in the family can be emotional and confusing for children as well as adults, and young children will have questions and concerns. Even though they have a very limited concept of what adults do for a living or that working is a means by which families make money, young children will notice the different social and emotional dynamics in the home.

The initial recognition may come as the daily home routine shifts for the child. Perhaps it was typically Dad who got up and got the children ready for school, while now Grandma is taking on this routine. Or maybe now two parents are home at dinnertime when one used to be away at work.

A child may, in a typical young-child fashion, ask for a new toy or game and be met with a sharp response, leaving the child puzzled, worried, or upset. A young child may overhear adult conversations about looking for a new job or frustrations over not getting an interview or a call back, about being unable to pay bills, about whether the child will stay involved in an activity, or about altering child care and school arrangements.

Talking with Family Adults About Unemployment

Often, a parent will tell you about a job loss. A simple, sensitive response from you can help you appropriately acknowledge the news and also provides a chance to determine what the parent expects from you in terms of supporting the child. Possible responses might include:

- "Thank you for sharing this news with me. I understand that this is a difficult time right now for your family. If Jenny brings this up, how would you prefer I respond?"

- "I am very sorry to hear this. Is Kai aware of it? What has his reaction been to the news so far?"

- "I understand this is a difficult time. I do have a resource here at school with information that may help you talk with Jayla about this in case she has questions at home. I can email you a copy if you like, and we can talk again after you've had a chance to read it."

Talking with Children: Conversation Starters

When a family adult becomes unemployed, young children will inevitably see, hear, or sense the grown-ups' anxiety and tension and develop their own questions and worries. You can manage the emotional charge of conversations with children by being prepared. The examples of responses here offer some language you might use.

> **Jamie, to another child:** "My daddy used to work at a big office but he doesn't have a job anymore. Does your daddy still have a job?"
>
> **Teacher, Ms. Julia (later):** "I heard you talking to Cyrus about your daddy not working at his job anymore. Do you want to talk with me about this?"

The goal is to let the child know the teacher is present, aware, and available to talk. Here the teacher, Ms. Julia, acknowledges what Jamie said to another child and then reassures him that it is acceptable to talk about it with her. She offers verbal comfort to reaffirm her emotional support. Note that the teacher does not say "losing his job," as this metaphor may be difficult for a child to understand. The objective language of "not working at his job" is more concrete and therefore easier for the child to understand.

> **Kelly, to teacher:** "My mommy doesn't have a job. She said I might not be able to keep going to ballet. I want to keep doing ballet!"
>
> **Ms. Julia:** "I know how much you enjoy ballet. I did not know that your mommy does not have her job. Can you tell me more about Mommy not working and how that feels for you?"

The goal is to allow the child to identify and safely express feelings. Note that Ms. Julia doesn't offer additional information. She acknowledges what the child has shared, indicates that the topic is acceptable to discuss, and responds with an open-ended question, allowing Kelly to focus on their emotions.

> **Jamie, to teacher (later):** "Is Daddy going to get a new job?"
>
> **Ms. Julia:** "That is a big question and I know your daddy is very important to you. Can you tell me more about your daddy maybe getting a new job?"

The goal is to affirm the question and guide Jamie to label his emotions. Ms. Julia does not make an assumption or offer any information about job searches. Rather, she acknowledges the question, affirms how important Jamie's dad is to him, and then asks an open-ended question to learn more. Based upon the response, she can follow by asking how Jamie is feeling about Daddy looking for a job and then offer ways to express his feelings such as painting, drawing, or writing. This reassures Jamie that it's okay to talk about the topic and helps him label and channel his feelings into something tangible. Ms. Julia might also offer a hug.

Following Up

Following any conversation with a child about unemployment, it is appropriate and strongly advised that you connect with the family or families of the children involved in the conversation. Share with the family what the child said or asked and how you responded. Ask the family how they would like the conversation handled if their child asks another question or further discussion takes place. This forges a partnership between school and home and also gives families appropriate notice to prepare for follow-up conversations the child may wish to have with them. (For examples, see "Framework for Parent Conversation Starters" in Part I, page 12.) Offer the family handout "Talking with Your Child About Unemployment" (page 30).

A child may approach you for further discussion. If a child seeks you out again, allow them to lead the conversation and try to keep it focused on how they are feeling. For example:

> **Jamie:** "I'm still sad about Daddy not having a job."
>
> **Ms. Julia:** "Thank you for telling me how you are feeling, Jamie. Can you tell me more about why you still feel sad?"

A child may also offer a statement or a question during a group interaction, such as:

> **Bree:** "My mommy and Quinten's mommy don't have jobs anymore. I want Mommy to stay home with me!"

Ms. Julia: "Thank you for telling me that, Bree. It sounds like your family has some changes happening. After we finish circle time, let's talk in the reading corner more about this and how you feel about it. I want to make sure I can give you all my attention."

The goal is to open the conversation up for further dialogue in a way that helps the child focus internally on emotions. In the first example, Ms. Julia prompts Jamie for more information to help focus in on the sadness he has expressed. With the focus on the emotion, Jamie may be more readily able to communicate, learn to begin to manage his feelings, and be further guided in ways to safely and appropriately express them. In the second example, Bree makes a statement in a group setting. The teacher's response here is to acknowledge the statement and affirm to Bree that they can discuss it together in private following the group interaction. If the topic becomes a group conversation, Ms. Julia should acknowledge, affirm, label emotions, and move beyond the discussion.

Talking with Your Child About
Unemployment

Unemployment can be an emotional time for a family, and your child is likely to overhear conversations and sense family tensions. Even if your child has a limited understanding of what family members do for a living or that working is how families make money, it will help to talk with your child about the situation. Use the following examples as a guide to start a conversation and answer your child's questions.

Start with a simple statement to let your child know it is okay to discuss the topic. For example:

▶ "Asha, I know you heard Mommy and me talking in loud voices about jobs. I do not work at the restaurant anymore, so we are talking about me looking for a new job. We both love you, and we know that I will find a new job soon."

▶ "Henry, I think you heard Daddy and me talking about your school. I am not working at the office anymore, so Daddy and I are trying to make the best decisions for all of us while I find a new job. While I'm not working, you might stay home with me for a while. Then when I go back to work, you can go back to school. How do you feel about that?"

The goal is to offer reassurance that what the child heard wasn't about them. The very simple explanation of unemployment provides needed information. Then you can reassure your child that your love and care for them hasn't changed. The second example also asks the child to share emotions about the pending change in routine.

Next, whether you've simply shared information or asked about your child's feelings, it's important to pause. The words are new, there is a lot of emotion to understand, and it may take your child a few moments to process what you've said.

If your child's response is silence, that's okay. A simple follow-up question— "Are you okay? Do you have any questions for me?"—allows them to respond if they wish.

Additional Questions and Answers to Consider

Your child may have questions, in the moment or later, that you will want to be prepared to answer. Here are some examples of questions and potential answers:

Question: "Will Daddy find a new job?"

Answer: "Daddy will have to spend time looking for a new job, but we are hopeful that he will find something he likes just as much or maybe even more than his old job."

The goal is not to get too detailed and to provide reassurance. Though as an adult you know that job searches take time, what young children need is reassurance of their parent's confidence. Keep the conversation upbeat, optimistic, and future-focused.

Question: "Do we have enough money?"

Answer: "Daddy and I will always make sure that we keep you and our family safe. We may need to make some small changes while I look for a new job. We don't have as much money as we did, but we will take good care of you."

The goal is to reassure your child with a simple, honest answer. Questions about money can be uncomfortable, but avoid acting defensive or saying a question is inappropriate.

Question: "What did Mommy do wrong to not have her job?"

Answer: "Mommy did not do anything wrong. Mommy worked very hard at her job. She is sad about not working at her old job because she liked it. She hopes to find a new job that makes her even happier. Will you help me make a card to let her know how much we love her?"

The goal is to acknowledge that Mommy is sad about the job change but reassure the child that Mommy expects to find a new job and be happier again. This approach gives your child "feeling words" to use and empowers them to express empathy. Suggest a way the child can encourage the parent during this time.

Preparing for Unexpected Responses

Young children aren't always aware of what "should" and "should not" be said. This lack of life experience can lead them to make statements that are unexpected and may feel hurtful. Preparing for such remarks and considering why a young child might respond that way can help you support your child and buffer yourself from an emotional reaction.

Child: "I'm happy Mom doesn't have a job."

Adult: "I understand you like it that Mom isn't working. You're happy and that makes Mom and me both happy too."

Child: "I like that she makes me scrambled eggs."

Adult: "It's nice to have Mom home in the mornings for breakfast. Mom likes that too. Let's remember that Mom is sad because she liked her job and she did not know it was ending. Mom hopes to start a new job and then things will be a little different again."

These remarks may be your child's way of telling you that they're okay. A young child may also be sharing the joy of having a parent around more of the time. Either way, remind the child how Mom feels and end the conversation by stating her intent to find a new job (if this is the case), so your child is not surprised if the home routine changes again.

Child: "I don't want to stop piano lessons! Why can't we get more money?"

Adult: "I know this is a hard time and you are feeling sad and angry. Let's do piano lessons together for now—and maybe Nana can help."

This child is expressing unhappiness and anger with the situation. This is not necessarily a personal statement directed at you, so it's important to pause and not respond defensively. It often helps, too, to simply offer a hug.

Child: "Can Daddy stop working at his job too?"

Adult: "It would be fun if we could all be home together. But we work so we can buy food, clothes, and other things for our family, so Daddy needs to work, and I hope to work again soon."

This reaction may indicate that the child enjoys the extra time with the nonworking parent and would like to have the same experience with the parent who is still employed. It reflects how little the child understands about the situation. This naiveté should be respected and honored.

When it comes to talking with your child, the overarching goal is to acknowledge their questions and feelings and answer with truthful reassurance. Use your own understanding of your child and take care not to jump to conclusions about how they are feeling. Talking together again at different times will help you better understand how your child feels and what support is needed.

....

Additional Resources for Families

"Explaining Unemployment to Kids" at Parents.com. This article offers brief but helpful suggestions for talking with children of different ages about a job loss and what it means for the child and the family. (parents.com/parenting/work/explaining -unemployment-to-kids/)

"How to Explain Job Loss to Your Concerned Child" at Scholastic.com. This web page for parents describes a six-year-old boy's struggles at home and at school after his father becomes unemployed and suggests how adults can work together to help him understand and cope. (scholastic.com/parents/family-life/social-emotional-learning /social-skills-for-kids/when-are-you-going-to-work.html)

No-Job Dad by James Hiram Malone. Through a simple storyline and colorful illustrations, this book depicts a young boy's experience with his father's loss of employment.

Substance Abuse and Addiction

The Substance Abuse and Mental Health Services Administration reports that 8.7 million children in the United States, or roughly 1 in 8 children, live in homes where a parent has or had a substance use disorder (Lipari and Van Horn 2017); 1 in 3 children placed into foster care are there as a result of parental substance abuse (Sepulveda and Williams 2019). In Canada, 1 in 10 children live with a parent who has a substance disorder (*Children's Mental Health Research Quarterly* 2014). Homes dealing with substance abuse and addiction are often unpredictable. Substance abuse may lead to gaps in communication between parents, anger and resentment among the adults in the home, cycles of sadness or depression in the family member facing addiction, and financial impacts due to the cost of supporting a substance habit and work performance issues. Parents who have substance abuse or addiction challenges are more likely to divorce, experience higher rates of physical abuse, and face a higher prevalence of legal issues, adding further stress at home (National Association for Children of Addiction 2021).

For young children, substance abuse at home is often very confusing and tumultuous. Lacking predictable structure and routine, children may experience conflicting emotions, feel higher levels of anxiety, struggle with insufficient sleep, have behavioral outbursts, become fearful about otherwise regular routines, and be overly clingy. Children may also assume more adult behaviors at home, such as helping care for younger siblings or preparing meals. Furthermore, compared to their peers, young people living in homes with substance abuse and addiction show higher prevalence of suicide attempts, attempt running away from home at higher rates, are more likely to suffer from depression, and are more likely to be physically, emotionally, or sexually abused.

In some cases, the family may have explained something about the abuse or addiction to a child; in other cases, the child may notice changed behaviors or feel tensions at home but not have much understanding of what is going on. A child may feel protective of a family member or may seem to reject the person. Young children may also become increasingly insecure about relying on adults and may exhibit defiance and disrespect for authority figures.

Naturally, you will want to be sensitive in talking with families where a parent or other family member is abusing alcohol or other drugs and be alert to what children might be experiencing.

Talking with Family Adults About Substance Abuse or Addiction

While not all families will share information about family drug or alcohol abuse readily or comfortably, a parent might tell you that it's occurring, providing an opportunity for you to learn how the family wishes the topic be addressed. Talking about this is likely to be coupled with some feelings of embarrassment and shame. A simple, sensitive response from you appropriately acknowledges your appreciation that the information was shared and provides an opportunity for you to encourage the parent to let you know how the family expects and wants you to support the child. Possible responses might include:

- ▶ "Thank you for letting me know this is happening. If Maya brings this up, how would you prefer I respond?"

- ▶ "I'm so sorry your family is dealing with this. How aware is Leo of what's going on?"

- ▶ "This must be a very difficult time. Please tell me what you would like me to do here at school to support Jack. I have some printed sheets I can provide to you that may help you talk with him about this if he has questions at home. Would you like a copy?"

Substance abuse and addiction may not be readily disclosed by a family. During interactions with parents, you may observe behaviors that give you concern. As noted earlier, if you see evidence of child mistreatment or neglect, follow all of your program's stated regulations for mandatory reporting to protect the child.

Talking with Children: Conversation Starters

As always in any "big" conversation with a young child, you will be best able to manage your own feelings and support the child by being prepared. Your role at this moment is to follow the lead of the child. The examples here offer some language you might use.

> **Ruby, to another child:** "My big brother drinks lots and lots of beers and falls down. My mommy gets so mad and so sad and yells at him! She took his keys away again."
>
> **Mr. Austin (later):** "Ruby, I heard you telling Takoda about your brother drinking beers and falling down. I care a lot about you and your whole family. If you want to talk to me, I am here. Would you like a hug?"

The goal here is to let the child know the teacher is available to talk. Mr. Austin acknowledges what Ruby said to Takoda, using Ruby's exact language. The teacher does not defend the brother's behavior, nor does he add information or interpretation. He acknowledges how special Ruby and her family are and offers verbal and physical comfort to reaffirm his emotional support.

It would then be appropriate to ask Ruby how she is feeling, attempting to guide her to use emotional vocabulary (feeling words) to express herself. This helps

Mr. Austin more clearly understand Ruby's perspective and gives him important information to pass on to family adults.

This conversation demonstrates the importance of not making assumptions and of immediately following up with the parent to avoid inconsistency and ensure the child receives needed support.

> **Elijah, to teacher:** "Did you know my mommy takes lots of little pills? My daddy told her she was an *attic*. He couldn't wake her up so he called an ambulance on her."
>
> **Mr. Austin:** "I did not know that happened at your house. Thank you for telling me. How are things feeling at home for you now?"

The goal is to allow the child to identify and express feelings. In this scenario, Mr. Austin does not offer additional information to Elijah's statement. Importantly, he doesn't correct Elijah's mispronunciation either, because correcting it could introduce terminology—and a label—that may be unknown, inaccurate, or undesired by the family. Mr. Austin acknowledges what Elijah has shared and responds with an open-ended question focused on the boy's emotions. He asks about home in general, not strictly about the mother. Given the amount of information shared, it is possible that Elijah has various feelings regarding his mother, his father, and what he may have seen or heard at home.

Following Up

Following any conversation with a child about substance abuse or addiction, it is appropriate and strongly advised that you connect with the family or families of the children involved in the conversation. Share with the family what the child said or asked and how you responded. Ask the family how they would like the conversation handled if their child asks another question or further discussion takes place. This forges a partnership between school and home and also gives families appropriate notice to prepare for follow-up conversations the child may wish to have with them. For example:

> **Mr. Austin (to Ruby's mom):** "Ruby shared today about her brother having too much to drink. We discussed her emotions about this, and I wanted you to know she shared her observation. If she brings this up again, is there a specific way you would like me to address this with her?"
>
> **Mr. Austin (to Elijah's father):** "Elijah told me some of what has been happening at home with his mother going to the hospital. I am sorry your family is dealing with all this. What can I do to support Elijah here at school?"

For other examples, see "Framework for Parent Conversation Starters" in Part I (page 12). Offer the family handout "Talking with Your Child About Substance Abuse or Addiction in the Family" (page 39).

A child may approach you for further discussion. If a child seeks you out again, allow them to lead the conversation and try to keep it focused on how they are feeling. For example:

> **Elijah:** "My mommy came home from the hospital last night."
>
> **Mr. Austin:** "How does it feel to have Mommy back home?"
>
> **Elijah:** "I hope she doesn't take those pills anymore!"
>
> **Mr. Austin:** "You can always talk to me about this. Would you like a hug?"

The goal is to continue to offer support. Note in this example that the teacher is opening the conversation up for further dialogue but is doing so in a way that helps the child focus internally on his emotions. Mr. Austin is reassuring Elijah of his availability and helping the child focus on ways to cope and manage the big feelings.

> **Christina:** "When Mommy gets sick from wine, I can help her feel better."
>
> **Mr. Austin:** "You are a big helper, and I understand you want to help Mommy feel better. Do you have someone who can help you or Mommy at home?"

> **Victor:** "I'm afraid of my daddy sometimes."
>
> **Mr. Austin:** "Can you tell me more about why you are afraid of Daddy sometimes, Victor?"
>
> **Victor:** "Sometimes he has so many beers that he gets mad and throws things at the wall."
>
> **Mr. Austin:** "Thank you for telling me this. I understand how that could make you feel afraid. Do you have another grown-up in your house that you can go to when you are feeling scared?"

The goal in both examples is to offer comfort and determine whether the child has a supportive adult at home. If they do, be sure to follow up with that person to disclose what the child shared and find out what more you can do to support the child in your setting.

> **Lin, to Mr. Austin (in a group setting):** "Sometimes my mom drinks so many alcohol drinks that she gets sick and falls asleep on the couch."
>
> **Donny:** "Your mom is a drunk! My mom says that when somebody drinks too much and acts crazy, they're a drunk."

Mr. Austin: "We need to always use respectful words in our classroom. Lin shared something personal, and we treat our classmates with kindness. This means that we will not use name-calling."

Mr. Austin (to Lin, privately): "Thank you for sharing about your mom with me. I am sorry that Donny used name-calling. You can always come talk to me. Can I offer you a hug?"

The goal is acknowledge Lin kindly within the group and to emphasize the importance of kindness and respect among the children. It's also important to follow up with Lin, as Mr. Austin does here, to make sure he knows he's been heard and can talk with his teacher more if he wishes, and to offer comfort.

Talking with Your Child About
Substance Abuse or Addiction in the Family

Many families experience substance abuse or addiction, and everyone in the home is affected. For small children, the less predictable daily routines and interactions that occur can be confusing and scary. Children may feel anxious or depressed, experience sleep interruptions, or become overly clingy. Children may revert to past behaviors like bedwetting or thumb-sucking. They may feel embarrassed or angry or become defiant.

Some children attempt to care for a family member who is struggling with addiction. It is important that young children know the person is being cared for and that acting as caretaker is not their job. It may help a child to have another family member, such as a grandparent, take an active and consistent role in their life. Family counseling and support groups can also help children cope and can help the family heal too.

Circumstances around substance abuse and addiction vary. You know your own situation best. While children can't understand much about drugs, alcohol, and addiction, they do need a basic explanation of what is happening and reassurance that any problems at home are not their fault. Start with a simple statement to let your child know it is okay to discuss the topic. Here are examples:

▶ "Lucas, I think you heard me talking on the phone. I am concerned that Mommy is drinking a lot of alcohol and I do not like how the alcohol makes her act. I am talking with Uncle Jordan about how we can get Mommy some help."

The goal here is to acknowledge the overheard conversation and reassure the child. The parent acknowledges what Lucas heard and offers a simple explanation of Mommy's alcoholism. Then the adult expresses care and concern for the family and lets the child know Mommy will have help.

▶ "I know you are scared. I called the ambulance to help Daddy. Daddy has a disease and he takes some drugs that make him act mean and say things that aren't nice. We care about Daddy, and we are going to help him. This is not your fault, and you can talk to me about it."

This example demonstrates the main elements a young child needs to hear. First, the child needs to be told honestly what is happening—that the parent has a disease that is causing him to behave badly. Second, the child needs reassurance that Daddy is getting help. Finally, the child needs to clearly hear that this is not their fault and that it's okay to talk about what is happening.

After your statement, it is important to pause. The words are new, there is a lot of emotion to understand, and it may take your child a few moments to process what you've said.

If your child's response is silence, that's okay. A simple follow-up question—"Are you okay? Do you have any questions for me?"—allows them to respond if they wish.

Additional Questions and Answers to Consider

Your child may have questions, in the moment or later, that you will want to be prepared to answer. Here are some examples of questions and potential answers:

> **Question:** "Why does Daddy take those pills if they make him sick?"
>
> **Answer:** "Daddy has a disease that makes him want to take those pills. He still loves us, and none of this is your fault."

The goal is to reassure the child and help the child see Daddy's behavior separate from Daddy himself. Avoid trying to explain addiction to your child. Referring to a *disease* helps a young child understand why the behaviors do not match the person. It is important to reassure your child that this situation has nothing to do with them. Equally important is reminding your child that they are loved.

> **Question:** "Why does Mommy act mean when she gets drunk? I don't like it!"
>
> **Answer:** "When Mommy drinks too much alcohol, it changes how she acts. I know you get scared when she acts that way. She is not angry with you or me, but the alcohol makes her behave differently. None of this is your fault, Lucas. Mommy loves us. Uncle Jordan and I are going to try to help her stop being sick."

Again, the goal is reassure the child and help him see the behavior separate from the person. Young children have a hard time understanding how a substance can change behavior. This response reassures Lucas that the substance abuse and behavior are not related to him. The parent acknowledges his fearful feelings and reminds him that adults are attempting to improve the situation.

> **Question:** "When is Mommy going to get better?"
>
> **Answer:** "We are trying to find doctors to help Mommy get better. We are going to do everything we can to help her because we love her and she loves us too."
>
> **Question:** "But what if she can't get better?"
>
> **Answer:** "We'll keep trying to help Mommy. Mommy loves you and I do too. You and I can always be together, even if we are feeling sad about Mommy."

The goal, as always, is to affirm loving family relationships. Questions about treatment for substance abuse and addiction are difficult to answer. Do not promise treatment or recovery. As long as you're committed to trying to help the adult who is challenged by addiction, assure your child of this. Here, the parent does that and then reaffirms the child's relationship with Mommy, reminding the child of their love for her.

Preparing for Unexpected Responses

Young children aren't always aware of what "should" and "should not" be said. This lack of life experience can lead them to make statements that are unexpected and may feel hurtful. Preparing for such remarks and considering why a young child might respond that way can help you support your child and buffer yourself from an emotional reaction.

> **Child:** "I don't want Mommy to be my mommy anymore."
> **Adult:** "It sounds like you have some very big feelings. This is a hard time for all of us. You can always talk to me and tell me how you are feeling."

This child may be trying to make sense of Mommy's behavior not fitting with what they want or expect from her. The child may mean they do not like how Mommy is acting. The remark might also reflect that the child is fearful of or angry at their mother. In replying, the adult does not label the child's feelings but allows the child time to think about and try to identify for themselves what they're feeling. Tell your child that the conversation is okay and you are always there to talk. You might also offer a hug or invite your child to sit on your lap or snuggle.

> **Child:** "I want to live with Grandma! I don't want to live here!"
> **Adult:** "I know you're angry. That's okay. How about a hug?" (pause)
> **Child:** (silence)
> **Adult:** "Would it feel better to go run and play at the park for a while?"

This outburst may reflect how unhappy and angry the child is with the situation. It's not necessarily a statement about the adults at home, but may instead be about the current happenings. An adult receiving these harsh words from a child may feel the need to defend the struggling parent or the way people are coping at home. It's natural to feel this way, but not necessarily helpful. It could make the child hesitant to share feelings further, which might put a deeper wedge in the child's relationship with the struggling parent or the rest of the family.

Stay calm and remind your child that they're cared for. If possible, you might also offer, "It sounds like you would like some time at Grandma's. Why don't we call her and see if you can go visit her next weekend?"

Child: "I hate those pills" (or "that whiskey" or "those drugs").

Adult, while offering a hug: "I do not like those pills and what they are doing to Daddy either."

This child's remark may show that the child is separating the substance and its effects from the person. The child sees the pills as the problem—not the parent. It's important to affirm this. Reassure your child and reemphasize this separation of the behavior (the effects of the pills) from the person.

Keep in mind that your goal is always to acknowledge your child's questions and feelings and answer with truthful reassurance. Children need to know it is not their fault, they are loved and cared for, and all their feelings are okay. Use your own understanding of your child and take care not to jump to conclusions about how a child is feeling. Talking together again at different times will help you better understand how your child feels and what support is needed.

Additional Resources for Families

Floating Away: A Book to Help Children Understand Addiction by Andrew Bauman, illustrated by Wahyu Nugroho. Read this book, geared to children ages eight and older, together to help a child understand the complexity of addiction through a simple metaphor.

National Association for Children of Addiction (NACoA). This comprehensive website includes videos, information, and support resources specific to different types of addiction helpful to all family members. (nacoa.org)

Sesame Street in Communities: Parental Addiction. This website portrays a character whose mother is in recovery from addiction. The portal provides a variety of videos and activities to support children and families. (sesamestreetincommunities.org /topics/parental-addiction/)

Timbi Talks About Addiction by Trish Healy Luna and Janet Healy Hellier, illustrated by Mackenzie Mitchell. A rhyming picture book, told from the perspective of a young character whose father is addicted to alcohol. The book is appropriate to help young children feel less alone and begin to find words to express the emotions they are feeling about the impact of addiction in their home.

Separation and Divorce

When children are involved, separation or divorce can be difficult and complex. Many couples fight to stay together amidst strong personal discord, creating emotionally charged and tense home environments. When couples decide that divorce is the best option, there is an additional onslaught of emotion. Adults struggle with a mix of emotions—sadness, anger, anxiety, fear for themselves and for their children—and young children are naturally affected by all this. Forty to 50 percent of marriages in the United States end in divorce (APA 2021). This means that many children in your care could experience separation or divorce in their families.

Family for young children is both identity and belonging. A child's identity includes their role in the family and the key family members involved in their life. Marriage is not a concept well understood to young children, but for a child in a two-parent family the presence of both parents in the home is familiar, comfortable, and assumed. A shift in this dynamic leads to increased emotions, as well as parental stress—both of which affect the child. The young child, who recognizes the absence in the home, often requests or shows preference for the "other" parent, whichever parent that is at the moment. This emotional charge, coupled with the loss of routine, can lead young children to exhibit higher degrees of emotionality, become increasingly clingy, revert in toileting, or have meltdowns.

Talking with Family Adults About Separation or Divorce

Parents will often let you know when a separation or divorce is occurring, and they might have a change in schedule or even legal issues you will need to know about. It is likely to be emotional or difficult for a parent to share this news, so being ready with a simple, empathetic response can help you acknowledge the sensitive topic and also provide a chance to determine what the parent expects from you in support of the child during this transition. Possible responses might include:

- ▶ "I appreciate your telling me about this. It must be a very hard for you and your family. What would you like me to say if Analee speaks to me about it?"

- ▶ "I am so sorry. Does Omar know about it? How has he reacted?"

- ▶ "That's hard news. Have you talked with Ty about what's going on? I have a family take-home sheet about divorce and talking about it with children. Would you like to have a copy?"

If there are legal issues that impact custody and care of the child, you will need official documentation to meet the requested needs. See your director or local resource office for more support on this.

Talking with Children: Conversation Starters

When parents are separating or divorcing, difficult conversations are inevitable when working with young children. The emotional charge of such conversations can be handled by being prepared. The examples of responses here offer some language you might use.

> **Olivia, to another child:** "My mommy and daddy don't want to be married anymore. My daddy is moving to an apartment."
>
> **Ms. Mary, later:** "I heard you talking to Kylie about your mommy and daddy. I care a lot about you and your family. If you want to talk to me, I am here. Would you like a hug?"

The goal is to affirm and reassure the child. Note that Ms. Mary acknowledges what Olivia said to Kylie. She then reassures her that it's acceptable to talk about this with her. To reaffirm her emotional support, Ms. Mary offers Olivia both verbal and physical comfort.

> **Evan, to teacher:** "Mommy won't let Mama live at home anymore. They are getting *dah-borsed*."
>
> **Ms. Mary:** "I did not know that your parents were getting divorced. Thank you for telling me that was happening. How do you feel about Mama not living at home anymore?"

The goal is to follow the child's lead. Ms. Mary does not offer additional information to the child's statement. She acknowledges what Evan has shared, responds with an open-ended question based on that sharing, and then turns the boy's focus to his emotions.

> **Olivia, to teacher:** "Is my daddy going to divorce me too?"
>
> **Ms. Mary:** "That is a big question. Your daddy will always be your daddy. Would you like to draw a picture for your daddy of something you like to do with him?"

Again, the goal is to follow the child's lead. Note that the teacher does not make an assumption or offer any information about the divorce. Ms. Mary focuses on reassuring Olivia of the consistency of the parent's role in relation to her and not on trying to explain the concept of divorce. She then provides a developmentally appropriate way for Olivia to channel her feelings into something tangible by making a picture for her father. The reassurance of the continuation of the parental role may be enough to satisfy the question, or Olivia may ask further questions.

Following Up

Following any conversation with a child about separation or divorce, it is appropriate and strongly advised that you connect with the family or families of the children involved in the conversation. Share what the child said or asked and how you responded, and ask how the family would like any future conversation handled with their child. This forges a partnership between school and home and also gives families appropriate notice to prepare for follow-up conversations the child may wish to have with them. (For examples, see "Framework for Parent Conversation Starters" in Part I, page 12.) Offer the family handout "Talking with Your Child About Separation and Divorce" (page 46).

A child may also approach you for further discussion. If a child seeks you out again, allow them to lead the conversation and try to keep focused on how they are feeling. For example:

> **Olivia:** "I want Daddy to come home. I don't want a divorce."
>
> **Ms. Mary:** "I know you don't. I am sure you have a lot of feelings about what is happening at home. Do you want to talk to me more about it?" (pause) "Or can I give you a hug to remind you that I care about you?"

> **Evan:** "I don't want Mommy to put me to bed. I want Mama. Why doesn't Mommy love Mama anymore?"
>
> **Ms. Mary:** "I understand that you have a lot of big feelings. You have some changes at home and that can make you feel lots of things at one time. Can you tell me more about how you are feeling?"

The goal is to offer support and help the child express feelings. In this example Ms. Mary opens up the conversation for further dialogue, but does so in a way that helps Evan focus internally on his emotions. If he struggles to express himself or responds with silence, the teacher might offer a hug or invite Evan to draw a picture or write a simple story.

Talking with Your Child About
Separation and Divorce

Marriage is not a concept well understood by young children, but the presence of two parents in the home is familiar, comfortable, and assumed. A child's identity and sense of belonging are shaped by the child's role and interactions with both parents and other key family members. You might see this in many situations: A child meets someone new and immediately looks to a parent to nod or assure them that the interaction is okay. A child mimics the behavior or mannerisms of a family adult. A child uses a phrase one parent says often or announces that they're going to be just like you when they grow up. Young children come to know and expect that family routines and events involve parents taking part in expected ways: *Daddy and I walk the dog together. All three of us make pizza together on Friday nights. Dad gives me my bath. Mommy reads to me before bed.*

Separation or divorce creates a big change in this dynamic and leads to confusion and worry for young children. As difficult and painful as this is for parents, it's important to recognize that children are struggling too. Young children feel your heightened emotions and worry about how life will change for them. They may become increasingly clingy or even revert to earlier behaviors such as bedwetting, tantrums, or bad dreams. This stress reaction is to be expected, though it is difficult for everyone. One thing that can help is to maintain prior routines, schedules, and activities as closely as possible.

Talking with children at a level they can understand is also important. Use the following statements as a guide to start a conversation and answer your child's questions. Begin with a simple statement to let your child know it is okay to discuss the topic. For example:

▶ "I know you heard Daddy and me talking in loud voices. Daddy and I are getting divorced. This means that Mommy and Daddy will live in different houses, but we will both still see you. This isn't your fault. You are still my child and Daddy's child too. We both love you very much."

▶ "I think you heard Mommy and me arguing. She and I are going to get divorced. This means Mommy and Daddy will live in different homes, but we will both spend time with you. None of this is your fault. We love you very much."

▶ "I think you heard Daddy talking on the phone about his new apartment. Daddy and I are going to get divorced. That means we will not be married anymore. I will live here in this house, and Daddy is going to live in a different place. You will stay here with me some of the time and you will spend some time with Daddy at his apartment. We both love you very much and that is not going to change at all."

The goal is to affirm the care and love from both parents. If this is not possible, the parent can affirm their own love of the child. These examples start by acknowledging what the child heard and explaining what it means. In each case, the parent offers a very simple explanation of divorce, which may be a new term for the child, and then reassures the child of love, security, and care. Children very often conclude that a divorce is their fault, so it is important to reassure them that this is not true.

Next, it's important to pause. The words are new, there is a lot of emotion to understand, and it may take your child a few moments to process what you've said.

If your child's response is silence, that's okay. A simple follow-up question— "Are you okay? Do you have any questions for me?"—allows them to respond if they wish.

Additional Questions and Answers to Consider

Your child may have questions, in the moment or later, that you will want to be prepared to answer. Here are some examples of questions and potential answers:

> **Question:** "Do you still love Mommy?"
>
> **Answer:** "Mommy and I do not want to be married anymore. We are glad we have you, though, and we love you very much. We want you to always feel happy, safe, and loved, and that will never change."

The question about a parent's feelings for the other is usually an indication of the child's own feelings of insecurity or unease. Do not try to explain marriage and relationships to your child, and avoid phrases like "grown apart" or "not in love anymore." These phrases are confusing for young children and may lead to more anxiety. What is needed is reassurance that your feelings toward your child are not changing.

> **Question:** "Where is Papa going to live?"
>
> **Answer:** "Papa and I have a lot of big decisions to make, and we will decide where the best place is for him to live. We will tell you as soon as we know. No matter what, we are going to make sure that you are safe."

What's most important is to reassure your child that you both will have a place to live and that your child will be safe and secure. It might not be possible to answer questions about specific living arrangements. If possible, try to decide on these details prior to any conversation about them with your child. Then you can share simply by saying, "Papa will live with Granddad until he can find his own place to live," or "Papa is going to live in his own house and he will make sure you have a special room there just like you have here at Mommy's."

> **Question:** "What did Mommy/Daddy do?"
>
> **Answer:** "Mommy and Daddy decided it was better to live in two different homes. We won't change our minds about this, but it's not your fault, and we are both still your parents."

The goal is to assure your child they do not need to choose one parent over another. Young children may feel the need to take a side. This response emphasizes that the child is not the reason for the decision. Even if a transgression did occur, it should not be discussed with a child. The decision to divorce is about the parents, and what's needed is reassurance that both of you love your child and will continue to do so.

Preparing for Unexpected Responses

Young children aren't always aware of what "should" and "should not" be said. This lack of life experience can lead them to make statements that are unexpected and may feel hurtful. Preparing for such remarks and considering why a young child might respond this way can help you support your child and buffer yourself from emotional reaction.

> **Child, to Mommy:** "I don't want a daddy anymore."
>
> **Adult:** "This is a hard time for all of us. You still have a mommy and a daddy. How about a hug?"

A young child responding this way may be trying to make sense of the change and the separation from one parent, or they may be expressing some anger or resentment toward Daddy. This statement is likely the child's way of letting Mommy know that they are okay or of expressing care and concern for Mommy. It's important for children to have their relationship with the other parent affirmed, and so it's usually best to reassure a child that their role with each parent remains.

It is also very helpful to invite your child to talk about their feelings. To do this, you might reply, "It sounds to me like you are having some very big feelings right now. Tell me more about how you are feeling." Your child may not be able to verbalize their feelings, but your response affirms that whatever your child is feeling is okay and lets your child pause to be aware of their emotions. Take care not to label the feelings for your child. Do not assume that a child feels a certain way unless they specify that they do. Continue to ask questions and allow your child time to attempt to name what they're feeling.

> **Child:** "I don't want to live with you! I want to live with Daddy!"
>
> **Adult:** "It sounds like you are angry. Is that right?" (pause for response) "It's okay to be angry. I love you very much."

This reaction may reflect how unhappy or angry the child is with the situation. This is not necessarily a statement about the parent who is present (in this case, Mommy), so it's important to pause and not respond emotionally. Instead, reassure your child of when and how they will see the other parent. Remind the child that they're loved by both of you and that you are both trying to make the very best choice for your child and the family.

A parent receiving these harsh words may feel the need to prove themself to their child, but that's not what's needed. While it may seem helpful in the moment to offer a gift or a treat, your child actually needs reassurance and emotional security. A child who expresses feelings like this to you shows how much they trust you. It's a time to reassure your child and offer a hug or a cuddle.

> **Child (when told about divorce):** "That's okay."
>
> **Adult:** "Let's have a hug, okay?"

It's likely here that the child does not understand the implications of the change ahead. This response should be respected. It is important for both parents to remain aware of questions that may emerge in the future. Saying "That's okay" may also be a child's way of attempting to dismiss the conversation, so respect that your child may want or need some emotional space.

> **Child:** "I hate you both!"
>
> **Adult:** "I know how angry you are about this. Why don't we get out a playground ball and you can bounce and kick some of those big feelings away?"

This reaction reflects the child's discontent with the pending change. The child does not truly hate either parent but does have strong feelings about the change. It's important to encourage your child to tell you how they are feeling and to acknowledge and suggest outlets for those feelings. Other suggestions could be to draw a picture about their feelings or to read books about what's happening in the family. These options help your child find a more appropriate way to express themself; they're not left to feel they have done or said anything wrong or improper. And while the words may be hurtful, keep in mind that your child may not have any other way to express how they're feeling. Offer comfort, love, and reassurance.

Additional Resources for families

Living with Mom and Living with Dad by Melanie Walsh. This children's book is designed to help young children understand that even though living arrangements may change, love and support from family is constant.

Sesame Street in Communities: Dealing with Divorce. This website has an assortment of parent resources, child activities, and video shorts to help young children navigate divorce. (sesamestreetincommunities.org/topics/divorce/)

Why Do Families Change? Our First Talk About Separation and Divorce by Dr. Jillian Roberts, illustrated by Cindy Revell. Share this picture book to help young children identify emotions that they may be feeling now or as the changes occur in the home.

Military Deployment

Any military family knows and understands that deployment is an expected part of the job. Many families have a perpetual sense of anxiety with their loved one being away from home or preparing to be away from home. In some cases there are strong or conflicting political feelings among the public as to whether troops should be involved in a particular place; while this does not change the reality of a family member being deployed, it may alter the family's inclination to discuss it.

For young children, a parent's deployment generates a sense of loss and, at times, confusion. Young children lack a well-developed sense of time, so days, weeks, and months can seem like years to a young child, and a deployment of 3–15 months can be hard to conceptualize.

Families frequently discuss military deployment in advance with young children, but the reality of the experience is still difficult to prepare for. A child's identity includes their role in relation to the key family members involved in their life, so any absence of a regular family member can leave a child feeling unsettled. Strong feelings of sadness, loneliness, and anger are common reactions in young children. Children are also keenly aware of shifts in their home routine. The family adult who once had a partner is now parenting the child alone, and this can result in heightened emotions for the parent and thus a general increase in stress at home.

This emotional intensity felt by the child and parent, coupled with the perception of loss of routine, can lead young children to exhibit more emotions and act out or become increasingly clingy to the parent and teacher. Some children may revert to previous behaviors, such as bedwetting, tantrums, or bad dreams. The familiarity and reliability of the routine in the child's school or program can help them feel more settled.

Talking with Family Adults About Military Deployment

Adults will often share information about military deployment with a teacher or caregiver, providing an opportunity to talk with families about how they wish the topic to be addressed with their child. It may be emotional for a parent to share military deployment orders with you, so being ready with a simple, sensitive response can help you appropriately acknowledge the situation and also provide a chance to determine what the parent expects from you in support of the child during deployment or during a transition to deployment. Possible responses might include:

▶ "Thank you for your service to our country and for sharing this news with me. I understand this is a transition time right now for your family. If Gracie brings this up, how would you like me to respond?"

▶ "I appreciate your service and understand this is going to be hard for your family. Does Daniel know about this, and what has his reaction been to the news?"

▶ "Thank you for letting me know. I have some information pages and can suggest some children's books that may help you talk with Hannah about this in case she has questions at home. Would you like a copy?"

Talking with Children: Conversation Starters

While military deployment is frequently something that families have come to expect or know well in advance, conversations about it are still likely to come at unexpected times, and the emotional charge of such conversations can be handled by being prepared. The examples of responses here offer some language you might use.

Mina, to another child: "My mama is in the army and now she went far away for a long time. Is your mama away too?"

Mx. [miks] Gerry (later): "I heard you talking to Taylor about your mama going away for her job in the army. I care a lot about you and your family, and I want you to know you can always tell me how you are feeling. If you like, we can make something special for you to send to your mama. Do you think she would like that?"

The goal is to acknowledge what the child said and to reassure her that it is acceptable to talk about this with the teacher. Mx. Gerry expresses caring for Mina and her family and offers her an opportunity to discuss her feelings. They then guide Mina toward a tangible way to express the emotions she feels.

Julio, to teacher: "My daddy is a Marine. He has to go to war. My mommy said he's going to be *deployed*. She and I are very sad."

Mx. Gerry: "I did not know that your daddy was being deployed. Thank you for telling me that. I know you and your mommy love your dad very much. I understand that you feel sad about Daddy going away to do his job. Would you like to draw a picture of your favorite thing to do with Daddy? We could hang it in our classroom. Maybe seeing it would make you feel happier while Daddy is away."

The goal is to acknowledge and affirm the news and the emotion the child has expressed. Note that Mx. Gerry does not offer additional information about Julio's reference to war but does repeat the child's use of the neutral term *deployed*. The teacher then offers an age- and classroom-appropriate idea to help Julio cope with his feelings. Saying "while Daddy is away" offers Julio a sense that the deployment is temporary without stating definitely that he'll return, or when that might be.

Following Up

Following any conversation with a child about military deployment, it is appropriate and strongly advised that you connect with the family or families of the children involved in the conversation. Share with the family what the child said or asked and how you responded. Ask the family how they would like the conversation handled if their child asks another question or further discussion takes place. This forges a partnership between school and home and also gives families appropriate notice to prepare for follow-up conversations the child may wish to have with them. (For examples, see "Framework for Parent Conversation Starters" in Part I, page 12). Offer the family handout "Talking with Your Child About Military Deployment" (page 54).

A child may approach you for further discussion. Again, allow the child to lead the conversation and try to keep focused on helping them identify their emotions and find ways to channel them appropriately. For example:

> **Mina:** "Some soldiers got hurt where my mama is. I don't want her to be gone anymore. I want her to come back now!"
>
> **Mx. Gerry:** "It sounds like you have some scared feelings and maybe some sad feelings inside too. Is that how you are feeling?" (waits for child to respond) "Why don't we find a photograph of you and Mama to keep near you while you are at school, so you can keep her picture close."

> **Julio:** "Is my daddy going to die while he is away in the war?"
>
> **Mx. Gerry:** "That is a big question. It sounds like you have some questions about your dad going away to do his job in the Marines. Your dad has done a lot of training and he is going to do all he can to keep himself and the other marines safe. That's his job. I know you love your Dad very much. Would it make you feel better if we recorded a special message on the iPad for your family to send to him?"

The goal is to provide comfort and gentle reassurance while helping children understand and express their feelings. In these examples, the teacher does not make assumptions or offer any assurances of the parents' safety. With Mina, Mx. Gerry gently probes to be sure they understand what Mina is feeling. With Julio, they focus on reassuring him that his father is prepared for his role and that his job is about keeping people safe. Mx. Gerry then provides the children appropriate ways to channel their feelings into something tangible: a photo to keep near or a message that can be both sent and saved. Mina or Julio may respond with follow-up questions or seek more reassurance, or these conversations and activities may be enough to satisfy any questions for now.

Talking with Your Child About
Military Deployment

For a young child, the experience of a parent's military deployment can generate a sense of loss and, at times, confusion. Even if your child knows about the deployment in advance, the reality is still difficult to prepare for. Children's identity includes their role in relation to the key family members in their life, so any absence of a regular family member can leave a child feeling unsettled. A child may not grasp or be able to express this, and so strong feelings of sadness, loneliness, and anger are common reactions in young children.

Your child may become increasingly clingy or may revert to previous behaviors, such as bedwetting, tantrums, or bad dreams. You can help your child by maintaining familiar routines, schedules, and activities as closely as possible. Do what you can to keep your child connected to the deployed parent through video chats and phone calls, by sending letters and drawings, and by placing a photo of the faraway parent in a prominent place. A doll, a stuffed animal, or an action figure can become special and remind your child of the parent's love.

Talking with children at a level they can understand is also important. Use the following statements as a guide to start a conversation and answer your child's questions. Begin with a simple statement to let your child know it is okay to discuss the topic. For example:

▶ "Zoe, I know you heard Daddy and me talking about a place called (name of place). Daddy found out today that he needs to go there to help keep people safe. This means that Mommy will stay home with you while Daddy goes away to do his job. Daddy will be gone from us for a few months, but we will still be able to call him and write to him. It will be sad sometimes to not have Daddy here, but we'll put his picture right by your bed so you can see him every time you go to sleep or wake up until he comes home."

The goal is to give clear, appropriate information and reassure the child. In this example the mother first acknowledges what her daughter has heard and follows with a simple explanation of military deployment. Note that she used the name of the region where Daddy will go. While Zoe probably won't know where this actually is, having a named place makes her father's situation less mysterious. The mother labels the emotion that she herself is feeling and then describes different ways that the family will cope.

Next, it's important to pause. The words are new, there is a lot of emotion to understand, and it may take your child a few moments to process what you've said.

A simple follow-up question— "Are you okay? Do you have any questions for me?"—allows them to respond if they wish.

Additional Questions and Answers to Consider

Your child may have questions, in the moment or later, that you will want to be prepared to answer. Here are some examples of questions and potential answers:

> **Question:** "Is Mommy going to shoot bad guys?"
>
> **Answer:** "Mommy's job is not to hurt people. Mommy's job in the army is to keep people safe. Mommy will do all she can to keep people safe and to be safe herself."

A child asking this question is grappling with a limited concept of war, the military, and the parent's job. Avoid trying to explain military conflict. Focus on the role of the military to keep people safe and reiterate the role the parent plays in maintaining safety.

> **Question:** "I'm worried Daddy is going to get bombed. Is Daddy going to get bombed?"
>
> **Answer:** "Daddy is a military helper. He has had lots of training and the military will keep him as safe as they can while he helps lots of people. I know this is a hard time and it is scary for me too, but we have each other and we will be together. Can I give you a hug?"

A child making this statement understands some of the risk and danger involved in the parent's job and where the parent is going. Do not promise safety and security. Instead emphasize the training the parent has had to prepare for the job and remind your child that they are safe and have support.

> **Question:** "Who'll take care of us while Daddy's gone?"
>
> **Answer:** "I will take care of you while Daddy is gone. Grandma and Grandpa will come help sometimes too. We are lucky to have a family that loves us. We will miss Daddy a lot, but we are going to be just fine at home."

Questions about care arrangements usually reflect that a child recognizes there will be changes in the routine. Reassure your child that things will be all right and that they will be well taken care of. Emphasize the family's love.

Preparing for Unexpected Responses

Young children aren't always aware of what "should" and "should not" be said. This lack of life experience can lead them to make statements that are unexpected and may feel hurtful. Preparing for such remarks and considering why a young child might respond this way can help you support your child and buffer yourself from emotional reaction.

> **Child:** "I want to go to (name of place) with Daddy! I don't want to stay home with you!"
>
> **Adult:** "It sounds like you have a lot of big feelings. I understand that this is a big change for our family. You can talk to me about how you are feeling."

A reaction like this may reflect how unhappy or angry your child is with the situation. This is not necessarily a statement about you, so it is important to pause and not respond emotionally. Instead, reassure your child that you will also miss the deployed parent and that you know it's a big change to have them go away for a while. Remind your child that they can always talk to you about how they're feeling. This may be an opportunity to provide a countdown calendar of when the other parent will return or to give the child a marker such as, "Daddy will come home right before your next birthday."

The parent receiving these harsh words may feel the need to prove themselves to their child, but that's not what's needed. While it may seem helpful in the moment to offer a gift or a treat, your child actually needs reassurance and emotional security. A child who expresses feelings like this to you shows how much they trust you. It's a time to reassure your child. You might offer a hug or a snuggle. Or, if your child needs help managing angry feelings, suggest an outlet like running outdoors, squeezing a pillow, or drawing a picture of the feelings.

> **Child:** "That's okay that Mommy is going to (name of place)."
>
> **Adult:** "We are going to really miss Mommy, but we are a strong family and we love each other."

It's likely here that the child does not understand the implications of the change ahead. Respect this response. It's important to remain aware of questions that may emerge in the future as the child begins to understand deployment more clearly. This may also be a child's way of attempting to dismiss the conversation, so recognize that your child may want or need some emotional space.

Additional Resources for Families

Deployment: One of Our Pieces Is Missing by Julia Cook, illustrated by Tamara Campeau. This is a story about the challenging (and fun) changes a family experiences when a father is deployed and eventually returns home. It focuses on the social and emotional reaction a child may have while also helping the child understand and appreciate the service the family member is providing.

Hug-A-Hero. An online store that allows families to order customized dolls in the likeness of a parent who's deployed or working abroad. The doll may be a strong comfort for a child who is missing a faraway parent. (hugahero.com)

I'll Lend You My Daddy: A Deployment Book for Kids Ages 4–8 by Becky King, illustrated by Valerie Valdivia. This children's book helps children identify and manage the many emotions, from goodbyes to missed birthdays, experienced during parental deployment.

Military OneSource. This Department of Defense–operated website provides a wide assortment of articles, activities, and family resources for all military families facing deployment. (militaryonesource.mil)

Incarceration

The *Family History of Incarceration Survey* (Enns et al. 2018) revealed that 45 percent of Americans will experience incarceration of an immediate family member in their lifetime. Approximately 1 out of every 14 children in the United States will experience parental incarceration at some point in their childhood (Gotsch 2018).

Incarceration of a spouse or coparent is not something ever planned for within a relationship. The partner who remains home is suddenly thrown into single parenthood, often with little or no warning. A job and income may be lost. The family dynamic is radically shifted, and one adult is left to carry alone responsibilities that had been shared. Parents who remain home experience intense feelings: sadness, anger, loss of control. Social conversations and situations outside the home become awkward and uncomfortable. There is almost always a pervasive sense of shame and embarrassment, and the adult at home is often left with little social or emotional support.

A child's identity includes their role in the family and the key family members involved in their life. When a key family member is removed from daily life for reasons that the child is not fully able to understand, there is a sense of loss and emotional insecurity. Emotions are higher in the home and parental stress increases. This is a time of confusion and emotional turmoil for a young child. A child whose parent has been incarcerated may become anxious and clingy, revert in toileting, have meltdowns, or act out. You can support the child by keeping school routines predictable and reassuring them that they're safe and you are there to listen and offer comfort. Young children may seek a comfort item such as a photo of the incarcerated parent, a blanket, or a stuffed animal for physical comfort. Starting and/or maintaining small rituals, such as a special hello or goodbye handshake, will also help young children cope with the change.

Talking with Family Adults About Incarceration

It may be difficult and emotionally painful for a parent to share news that a family member is incarcerated, and the parent may fear judgment. Being ready with a simple, sensitive response can help you appropriately acknowledge the news and also provide a chance to determine what the parent expects from you in support of the child. Possible responses might include:

▶ "Thank you for trusting me enough to share this with me. I am sure this is a very tough time right now for your family. If Max brings this up, how would you like me to respond?"

▶ "I am sorry to hear this. Is Shania aware of what is happening with Mom? What has her reaction been to the news?"

▶ "I am sorry that your family is dealing with this. I do have some pages of information I can provide to you; it may help you talk with Kobe when they have questions at home. Would that be helpful for you?"

Talking with Children: Conversation Starters

Difficult conversations are inevitable when working with young children, but the emotional charge of such conversations can be lessened by being prepared. Whether the parent has spoken to you first or the child initially brings up the incarceration, take your cue from the child when you respond. The sample conversations here give some examples of how this may be approached.

> **Brooklyn, to another child:** "My daddy got locked up. That means he has to go away to be in prison, but he's not a bad guy. He's not!"
>
> **Ms. Amanda, to Brooklyn (later):** "I heard you talking to Dylan about your daddy being sent to prison. I care a lot about you and your family. If you want to talk to me, I am here. Let me know what I can do to help you during this change. Would you like a hug?"

The goal is to affirm and reassure the child. Note that the teacher acknowledges what Brooklyn said to Dylan and uses this to prompt the conversation. Ms. Amanda reassures Brooklyn that it is acceptable to talk about this with her and acknowledges how special Brooklyn and her family are to her. She offers verbal and then physical comfort to reaffirm her emotional support.

> **Kiki, to teacher:** "Did you know my mommy is at jail? She drank too many drinks and she killed somebody with her car. Daddy said she has to go to jail for maybe a long time."
>
> **Ms. Amanda:** "I did not know that. Thank you for telling me that. How are you feeling at home now?"

The goal is to acknowledge what the child shared and invite the child to focus on their emotions. Ms. Amanda does not offer any additional information. She asks about home events, not strictly about the mother. Given the amount of information shared, it's possible that Kiki has various feelings toward her mother, toward the other parent, and about what she may have seen or heard at home.

> **Charlie, to teacher:** "My daddy is going to jail. What did he do?"
>
> **Ms. Amanda:** "That is a big question. I don't know why your daddy is going to jail, but I know your family loves you and I know your mommy will talk with you and answer your questions. Would you like to draw a picture to bring home to show your family how much you love them too?"

The goal is to reassure the child that he is safe and loved. Note that Ms. Amanda does not make an assumption, or offer any information about the father's incarceration. She respectfully admits to not having the answer and directs Charlie back to his mother. She then focuses on reassuring him of the consistency of his parents' love and provides a way for him to channel his feelings into something tangible by making a picture for his family.

Following Up

Following any conversation with a child about incarceration, it is appropriate and strongly advised that you connect with the family or families of the children involved in the conversation. Share with the family what the child said or asked and how you responded, and ask the family how they would like any future conversation handled with the child. This forges a partnership between school and home and also gives families appropriate notice to prepare for follow-up conversations the child may wish to have with them. (For examples, see "Framework for Parent Conversation Starters" in Part I, page 12.) Offer the family handout "Talking with Your Child About Incarceration" (page 61).

A child may also approach you for further discussion. If a child seeks you out again, allow them to lead the conversation and try to keep focused on how they are feeling. For example:

Kiki: "I want Mommy to come home from jail. Mommy misses me!"

Ms. Amanda: "I know you and Mommy miss each other. Do you want to draw a picture of something you and Mommy both like to do so you think about happy times with her?"

Note in this example that the teacher opens the conversation up for further dialogue but does so in a way that helps the child focus internally on her emotions. The teacher also provides the child an outlet to express her emotions and focus on positive memories of her absent mother.

Brooklyn: "I want to visit my daddy. We have to visit him at the prison."

Ms. Amanda: "That will be a new experience for you. I am happy you will be able to see your daddy, and I am sure you have a lot of different feelings about that. How do you feel about visiting Daddy?"

The goal is to acknowledge, affirm, and help the child express her feelings. Ms. Amanda acknowledges the visit as a new experience. Since Brooklyn said she wants to visit Daddy, Ms. Amanda affirms the positive in the situation. Suggesting that Brooklyn might have many feelings invites her to think and talk more about emotions she has about the upcoming visit.

Talking with Your Child About
Incarceration

A child's identity and sense of belonging are shaped by the child's role and interactions with key family members, especially parents and caregivers. When a key family member is removed from daily life for reasons a young child is not fully able to understand, there is a sense of loss and emotional insecurity. Children may become increasingly clingy or even revert to previous behaviors, such as bedwetting, tantrums, or bad dreams. This stress reaction is to be expected. It's important to reassure your child that you are still there for them—that they're loved and supported—and to provide opportunities for visits with the incarcerated parent, if this is safe and permitted.

Having a parent go to prison is a major change for a young child, and for you and the rest of your family as well. Do all you can to surround your child with people who love and care for them. As much as possible, continue clearly established routines. Your child needs to be told frequently that they are loved and secure. Young children may seek a comfort item such as a photo of the absent parent, a blanket, or a stuffed animal. Starting or maintaining small rituals—a favorite bedtime song, a morning wake-up routine, a special goodbye handshake—can also help your child cope with the change.

Talking with children at a level they can understand is also important. Use the following statements as a guide to start a conversation and answer your child's questions. Begin with a simple statement to let them know it is okay to discuss the topic. For example:

▸ "You saw the police at our house tonight. Today Daddy made a bad decision and the police are taking him to the police station to talk about it. I am feeling sad and angry right now, but I am not sad or angry with you. I love you very much, Lucas."

The goal is to offer simple information and reassure the child that he is loved. In this example, the parent first acknowledges what the child, Lucas, saw and offers an age-appropriate explanation of what has happened. Note that the parent does not immediately offer specific information about what Daddy did that led to the arrest. This would depend on the crime he's accused of, what the child witnessed, and the child's maturity. This parent does *not* say that Daddy "was bad," but rather that he "made a bad decision." This helps Lucas see Daddy, who he loves and values, distinct from the bad choice he made. This parent also carefully labels their own emotions and makes sure Lucas knows that those feelings are not directed at him.

▸ "Madeline, I know you notice that Mommy is not here, and I think you heard me talking on the phone with Grandma tonight. Mommy is not home and will not be coming home for a while. Mommy made a bad choice and the police took her to jail. This was a big bad choice, and I am very sad about that. We do not know how long Mommy will be in jail, but it will be for at least three months. I am going to find out when we can see her."

The goal is to give the child clear and simple information and demonstrate that talking about the situation is okay. This example specifically points the child to an observation and a conversation she overheard. The parent explains in simple terms that Mommy made a bad choice (this is about the behavior, not the person). The parent tells Madeline how long her mother will be gone and specifically uses the word *jail*. The word may be new to her and may need to be explained. The parent labels their own emotions, which models for Madeline how to express herself.

Next, it's important to pause. The words are new, there is a lot of emotion to understand, and it may take your child a few moments to process what you've said.

If your child's response is silence, that's okay. A simple follow-up question—" Are you okay? Do you have any questions for me?"—allows them to respond if they wish.

Additional Questions and Answers to Consider

Your child may have questions, in the moment or later, that you will want to be prepared to answer. Here are some examples of questions and potential answers:

> **Question:** "Is Daddy a bad guy?"
>
> **Answer:** "Daddy is a good dad, but he made a bad choice."

The question may reflect that the child is trying to reconcile Daddy's bad action with Daddy himself, whom the child sees as generally good. Try to help your child see their parent and the behavior as separate and distinct. This is not to make light of any crime that was committed, but rather to focus on the love the parent has for your child. Your child's age, developmental level, and exposure, as well as the nature of the crime itself, will influence how and when you discuss it with them. You might share it in small bits over time, have an open honest conversation in the moment, or avoid discussing the specifics until your child is older. This is a personal family decision.

> **Question:** "What is jail?"
>
> **Answer:** "Jail is a place where grown-ups go to live when they have made bad choices. Mommy will live there now. She will probably live in a very small room with a roommate. Mommy will go to classes to learn how to make better choices when she comes back home."

While jail and prison should not be glamorized, be mindful to not create fear or anxiety. Questions about jail need to be answered carefully. A simple definition that jail or prison is the place where the parent will live will suffice for most young children. Additionally, explain the services and support the parent will receive, such as classes, medical treatment, or schooling.

> **Question:** "Can I visit Daddy in prison?"
>
> **Answer:** "We will have to find out the rules. I do not know but I can find out. I know you can write Daddy letters and draw him pictures. How do you feel about that?"
>
> *Or:*
>
> **Answer:** "We are not allowed to visit Daddy. It's against the rules. We can send him pictures and letters though. Would you like to send Daddy a picture?"

Young children asking about visiting an incarcerated parent may be truly asking if they can *visit or may be asking if they* have *to* visit. Rather than jump right into a response, determine how your child is feeling about visiting the parent in jail. In some situations, prison rules or a court order may prevent visits. If this is the case, you will need to explain it to your child. In either situation, offering a method of communication, such as letters and drawings, may help alleviate any immediate need for contact your child may feel.

Preparing for Unexpected Responses

Young children aren't always aware of what "should" and "should not" be said. This lack of life experience can lead them to make statements that are unexpected and may feel hurtful. Preparing for such remarks and considering why a young child might respond this way can help you support your child and buffer yourself from emotional reaction.

> **Child:** "I don't want Daddy to be my daddy anymore."
>
> **Adult:** "I know you have a lot of feelings right now. I do too and that is okay. You can talk to me about it." (Offer a hug.)

A young child responding this way may be expressing anger or trying to make sense of the change and the separation from one parent. The statement could be the child's attempt to tell the adult that they are okay. If possible, affirm the love of both parents for your child and offer reassurance that it is okay to be angry or sad, or to miss the parent.

> **Child:** "I don't want Mommy to come back from jail. I want her to stay there!"

> **Adult:** "It sounds to me like you are feeling angry." (pause) "Should we find a way to let our angry feelings out?" (Offer a ball to throw, a pillow to jump on, or crayons for drawing.)

This reaction tells you how unhappy and angry your child is with the situation. It also may be an indication that your child understands that something wrong occurred and accepts the parent's punishment. Avoid scolding the child for the statement.

With statements such as these from a child, it can help to bring the focus to your child's emotions: "It sounds to me like you are having some very big feelings right now. Can you tell me more about your feelings?" Your child may not be able to verbalize their feelings, but your response affirms that it is okay for them to feel as they do and lets them pause to be aware of their emotions. Notice that this sample response does not label the feelings for the child. Some children may feel sadness; others may feel anger or confusion. It is a respectful exchange to allow your child time to attempt to find their own words to tell you how they are feeling.

> **Child:** "That's okay."
> **Adult:** "Shall we have a hug?"

It's likely here that the child does not understand the implications of the change ahead. This response should be respected. It is important for other family members to remain aware of questions that may emerge in the future. This may also be a child's way of attempting to dismiss the conversation, so respect that your child may want or need some emotional space.

Additional Resources for Families

Missing Daddy by Mariame Kaba, illustrated by bria royal. Share this storybook to help your child identify and label many of the emotions that come with having an incarcerated parent and to guide conversations about the experience of visiting a parent in jail.

The Night Dad Went to Jail by Melissa Higgins, illustrated by Wednesday Kirwan. This picture book helps young children understand what is happening in their home and addresses common emotions a young child may be feeling.

Sesame Street in Communities: Coping with Incarceration. This multimedia assortment of resources includes printables, videos for children, and resources to help families establish consistency and routine to help young children during this transition. (sesamestreetincommunities.org/topics/incarceration)

Big Conversations About Illness and Death

"You may not control all the events that happen to you, but you can decide not to be reduced by them. Try to be a rainbow in someone's cloud."

—Maya Angelou

Serious or chronic illness and death are difficult topics for adults to grapple with, and the challenge is amplified when children are directly affected by illness themselves or by the illness or loss of someone important to them. Adults struggle to know what to tell a young child, how to explain sickness or death in a way that is accurate yet not scary, and when to share information. Anxiety about the questions a young child may ask can be as unsettling and uncomfortable as the conversations themselves.

Adults process death through a multiphasic grieving process (Kübler-Ross and Kessler 2014)—denial, anger, bargaining, depression. and, ultimately, acceptance—and they cycle through a similar wave of responses to major illness, particularly a disease or condition requiring long, protracted care. Children are attuned to the tensions and feelings of adults, which are often confusing to young children and can unintentionally create high levels of anxiety.

Young children have no context or ability to comprehend serious or chronic illness in themselves or in others. The child's own experiences with visiting the pediatrician or being sick with a cold may lead to some major confusion. To most young children, a doctor is a helper who is always able to make them feel better. Likewise, an illness is understood by most children to be short-term, curable with medication and rest, and nothing to be afraid of.

For a child grounded in this understanding, the idea of an illness that is long-term and debilitating is likely to be unfamiliar, puzzling, and scary. In supporting the child, the positive early experience with doctors and medical care needs to be carefully honored. Children need to know that the doctors are helping. Even for diagnoses that are terminal or incurable, young children need the reassurance that the adults are helping and are in control. This is not the same as promising a child that the loved one will get better; instead, it is telling them that the doctors, other health workers, and family are all supporting the loved one—thus bolstering the child's sense of security.

The experience of death is notably different for children than for adults. Death is something abstract that somehow became a reality, and most children have a very difficult time making sense of the information. Young children generally lack a defined concept of death and most often relate to death from what they have seen in cartoons or with fictional characters in movies. This often leaves a very fantastical idea of death as something that happens to other people or things or even as something that is temporary or reversible. While death is abstract and difficult to process, young children do comprehend and sense the emotions exhibited by the adults around them. Like adults, children will also go through stages of grief (Boelen, Spuij, and Reijntjes 2017). While these stages may not be as clearly defined due to a lack of full understanding of what has occurred, it is important to recognize that many children will also cycle through emotions.

All these underlying factors punctuate your critical role in talking with children and families about the serious illness or death of a significant person or pet in a child's life. As with all challenging topics, it's best if you are able to talk with family adults before addressing an issue with the child. Parents are likely to tell you when someone close to the child is seriously ill or when a death has occurred or is imminent.

Whether families have spoken to you ahead of time or not, when a conversation with a child comes up, always allow the child to lead it. Check back with parents after you and a child have spoken, and ask them how they want the topic approached. Children need simple, honest, respectful replies that are appropriate to their developmental stage. They need to be able to express their feelings about what's happening and to be reassured and comforted. They need to know you are always there to talk with them.

As with all the topics in this book, the examples here reflect only some of the many topics that might emerge in discussions of illness or death with young children. Use the dialogues and suggestions as a starting point to guide your approach to other issues that may arise.

Be sure to pay attention to your own feelings as you converse with children or families, and look for ways to reflect on and process any intense responses that may be evoked. See page 4 for information about forming a community of practice where you and other adults in your setting can work and learn together about topics that concern you all.

Major Illness of an Adult

As much as we value and celebrate good medicine, there are few words that will stop an adult faster than those of major illnesses. Cancer. Stroke. Alzheimer's. These are not unknown conditions, but their treatment and management are largely unfamiliar. The human instinct to turn away from the source of discomfort is unavoidable, and anxiety, fear, and anger mount quickly. As adults, we question why the illness happened, what could have been done to prevent it, and then, most pressingly, how to persevere and support the loved one affected. Prescription drug commercials and popular media have led many of us to feel just knowledgeable enough to work ourselves into a panic. A quick search on the internet adds to this anxiety.

The emotions that accompany long-term illness for grown-ups can unintentionally create anxiety in young children. Adults often mask sadness, anger, and fear with a heightened level of care, comfort, and optimism, leaving a child confused and uncertain.

Talking with Family Adults About Major Illness

It will likely be emotional for a parent to share the news of a family member or close family friend being diagnosed with a major illness. A simple, sensitive response from you can help you appropriately acknowledge the topic and also provides a chance to determine what the parent expects from you in terms of supporting of the child. Possible responses might include:

▶ "I appreciate your sharing this news with me. What a hard time for your family. If Fergus says something to me about it, how would you like me to respond?"

▶ "I'm so sorry to hear this. Is Skylar aware of it? How has she reacted?"

▶ "I understand this is a challenging time. I do have an information sheet with ideas that may help you talk with Cami about this if she has questions at home. I can give you a copy, or email one to you if you'd like."

Talking with Children: Conversation Starters

As always in any "big" conversation with a young child, you will be best able to manage your own feelings and support the child by being prepared. The examples of responses here offer some language you might use. Remember to let the child lead the conversation and ask questions.

> **Kenji, to teacher:** "My grandma has *olds-himers*."
>
> **Ms. Thea:** "I did not know that, Kenji. Thank you for telling me. How do you feel about Grandma having Alzheimer's?"

The goal is to allow the child to identify and safely express feelings. Note that the teacher does not offer Kenji additional information. Ms. Thea acknowledges what the boy has shared and responds with an open-ended question, allowing him to focus on his emotions. The teacher also echoes Kenji's label for the illness, stating it correctly, but does not offer additional information about the illness or prognosis.

> **Mabel:** "Is my Uncle Micah going to die?"
>
> **Ms. Thea:** "That is a big question. Why are you wondering if Uncle Micah is going to die?"

The goal is to understand the reason for the child's question. The teacher does not make an assumption and does not affirm or deny the possibility of Uncle Micah dying. She first focuses on finding out more information from Mabel. She can then respond by attempting to focus on the girl's emotions if and when Mabel shares more. For example:

> **Mabel:** "He doesn't talk. He takes lot of medicine and sleeps all the time. Will he die?"
>
> **Ms. Thea:** "I do not know what kind of sickness your Uncle Micah has, and I don't know what will happen. It sounds like the doctors are helping take care of him. How does it feel to see Uncle Micah right now?"

The goal is to be honest and reassuring while also inviting the child to share her feelings. Be mindful to not make assumptions; rather, respond to what the child has said. Ms. Thea might also suggest that Mabel make Uncle Micah a card or draw him a picture to focus on ways to help herself and show her concern for her uncle.

Following Up

Following any conversation with a child about an adult's illness, it is appropriate and strongly advised that you connect with the family or families of the children involved in the conversation. Share with the family what the child said or asked and how you responded. Ask how they would like the conversation handled if their child raises another question or if further discussion takes place. This forges a partnership between school and home and also gives families appropriate notice to prepare for follow-up conversations the child may wish to have with them. Check with the parent on the exact language they've used with the child at home so that any discussions at school use consistent vocabulary. Offer the family handout "Talking with Your Child About an Adult's Illness" (page 70).

Here is one example of how you might approach this; for more, see "Framework for Parent Conversation Starters" in Part I, page 12:

▶ "I wanted to make you aware that Mabel talked to me about her Uncle Micah today. She told me that he sleeps a lot, and she asked me if Uncle Micah was going to die. I did not answer her directly because I do not know, but I did reassure her that I believed doctors were helping Uncle Micah, and I suggested she make him a card. If Mabel brings up her uncle again, is there anything in particular you would like me to say to her?"

A child may also approach you for further discussion. If so, allow the child to lead the conversation and try to keep it focused on how they are feeling. For example:

Nadya: "Mommy said Aunt Fatima may lose her hair because of her cancer."

Ms. Thea: "I am glad you and Mommy are talking about your Aunt Fatima. Can you tell me how you are feeling about Aunt Fatima being sick?"

The goal is to reassure the child and help her identify and express her feelings. Here, Ms. Thea opens up the conversation for further dialogue and does so in a way that helps Nadya focus internally on her emotions. The teacher's words also assure Nadya that the topic is acceptable for discussion.

Kenji: "Grandma said swearwords to my daddy! He said it's because of her *olds-himers.*"

Ms. Thea: "How did it feel when Grandma swore like that?"

Kenji: "She was loud and mean!"

Ms. Thea: "Alzheimer's sometimes makes people act that way. Would you like a hug?"

The goal is to listen with understanding and offer comfort. In this situation, the teacher does not overexplain the illness or assume that Kenji feels a specific emotion. This conversation acknowledges what the child shared, affirms for him that it's okay to discuss the swearing, and invites him to share feelings if he chooses to. Offering physical comfort is a simple way for Ms. Thea to support Kenji and let him know she cares about him.

Talking with Your Child About
an Adult's Illness

For a young child, a serious medical condition in a parent or another important grown-up can bring up many emotions. Young children have no context or ability to comprehend long-term illness, but their own experiences with visiting a health-care provider or being sick with a cold mean that they most likely view a doctor as a helper who is always able to make them feel better. Likewise, they may see an illness as short-term, curable with medicine and rest, and nothing to be afraid of.

As you talk with your child about a serious illness, it is wise and helpful for you to carefully honor this positive early experience with doctors and medical care. A child needs only to know that there is an illness, what it is called, briefly what it means, and—most important—that the doctors are helping. Even for diagnoses that are incurable or terminal, a child needs the reassurance that the adults are helping and are in control. This is not the same as promising your child that the loved one will get better. Rather, it reassures them that the medical professionals and the family are all supporting the loved person. Knowing this will bolster your child's sense of security.

Because a child is likely to hear some medical terms, defining these simply is key. Keep the definition basic, child-friendly, and objective:

▶ "Grandma has cancer, which is a disease on the inside of her body. You can't see Grandma's cancer. She has doctors to help her, and we will help her too."

When talking about this with your child, try to remain emotionally calm. Start with a simple statement to let your child know it's okay to discuss the topic. If your child saw or overheard you being emotional, explain your feelings in child-friendly terms. For example:

▶ "I know you heard me talking with Uncle Paul on the phone tonight. I was talking with him about Grandpa. Grandpa had a stroke, which is a boo-boo inside his brain. That made me feel scared and sad because Grandpa lives far away and I want to be there with him. We love Grandpa very much."

▶ "I think you heard Daddy talk to me in a loud voice. Daddy is not upset with me or you—Daddy is angry because MiMi is sick. She has cancer, which is a disease inside of her body. Daddy loves us very much."

▶ "I want to tell you something about Mommy. Mommy has something called MS. It makes her tired and makes her muscles slow down. The doctors are helping Mommy, and she loves us all very much."

The goal is to explain the situation in simple terms and reassure your child. In these examples the parents name and briefly describe the illness. They mention medical care and remind the child of the family's strength and love.

It's equally important to label the emotions you yourself feel in simple terms and explain briefly why you are feeling that way. Doing this demystifies the emotional atmosphere so your child can begin to understand the complexity of feelings connected to the situation. For example, "I am sad today because I do not want Aunt Deedra to be sick. I am sad that she has cancer, but I am grateful that she has doctors and nurses and our family to help her."

Next, it's important to pause. The medical words are new, there is a lot of emotion to understand, and it may take the child a few moments to process what was said.

If your child's response is silence, that's okay. A simple follow-up question— "Are you okay? Do you have any questions for me?"—allows them to respond if they wish.

Additional Questions and Answers to Consider

Your child may have questions, in the moment or later, that you will want to be prepared to answer.

> **Question:** "Is Uncle Quinn going to die?"
>
> **Answer:** "Uncle Quinn is very sick, and the doctors are helping him feel better. The doctors are doing everything they can. I hope that Uncle Quinn gets better soon, and I know you do too. We will make sure to call him and check on him a lot."

The goal is to reassure your child in an uncertain situation. Avoid metaphors and abstract phrases such as "fighting this illness" or "it is out of our hands." These phrases are confusing for young children and may lead to unintentional anxiety. Explaining in simple, straightforward terms will make it easier for your child to process the information.

Some families may choose to offer faith-based responses, such as "We will trust in God" or "We need to pray for him." Keep in mind the child's age, ability to understand, and familiarity with the faith concepts being offered.

> **Question:** "Will Pop-Pop forget me?"
>
> **Answer:** "Pop-Pop has Alzheimer's, so he will forget a lot of things. He may get confused and he may call you the wrong name sometimes, but he loves you and we love Pop-Pop."

The goal is to answer the question about long-term prognoses objectively and honestly. Confirm the likely prognosis, but balance this with a strong affirmation of what will not change. This parent expresses their love for Pop-Pop and reminds the child that Pop-Pop loves them too. This is an important reminder particularly as the interactions with Pop-Pop are likely to evolve and change.

Question: "Why can't the doctors make Aunt Nina better?"

Answer: "The doctors are smart, and they are working very hard to make Aunt Nina better. Aunt Nina has a cancer on the inside of her body, which is hard to make better. The doctors are going to use the best medicine they can and do their very best to make sure that Aunt Nina can be as healthy as possible."

The goal is to emphasize the use of medicine, the commitment to care, and the effort. Young children may feel disappointed or panicked at the idea of doctors not being able to heal an illness. It is important to remind the child of the doctors' ability and commitment to helping people.

Unless you know a death is really imminent, this is not a time to mention that some illnesses do not have a cure or are beyond the scope of modern medicine. These are abstract concepts that may elicit fear in a young child. Instead remind your child that the person is being cared for and given comfort during this time.

Preparing for Unexpected Responses

Young children aren't always aware of what "should" and "should not" be said. This lack of life experience can lead them to make statements that are unexpected and may feel hurtful. Preparing for such remarks and considering why a young child might respond this way can help you support your child and buffer yourself from emotional reaction.

Child: "I know Granny is going to die."

Adult: "We all love Granny, and she loves us very much too. Everything that is living will die one day, even Granny. That is true. Right now she is still with us and that makes me happy." (Offer a hug.)

A young child who says this may be trying to make sense of serious illness and death. The statement may be the child's way of self-soothing and attempting to portray a larger understanding of the situation. It's also possible they are worried that the loved one will die from her illness. It is important here to reassure the child that Granny is getting all the care possible and to emphasize the family's love for her. Explain death as universal, in that everything alive will indeed die one day—plants, animals, and people.

If your child makes a statement like this, you may have an urge to scold them and tell them not to say such a thing, but doing so will make the illness seem scarier and more mysterious. Keep in mind that your child may immaturely be trying to show wisdom and grapple with reality. Instead, state your own feelings, such as "I would be very sad if Granny did die. Right now we can think about how much we love her. Thinking about that love helps me feel happier."

> **Child:** "I hate cancer."
>
> **Adult:** "I am very upset that Ms. Bonnie is sick too, and it makes me sad to know that she has an illness. I know it would cheer her up a lot if we did something nice for her to help her think of something else. What do you think we can do to help Ms. Bonnie feel better and help us feel better too?"

This statement may be a true reflection of a child's anger and resentment, or it may be a response to their discomfort with lots of emotion and discussion about the illness. Either way, it's important to affirm the feelings and help your child label them. This reply lets the child know that their feelings are acceptable and the parent shares them. At the same time, by shifting the focus onto being a healing presence for Ms. Bonnie, the parent helps the child think of more positive things to focus on. This shows a way to navigate through big emotions.

> **Child:** "Maybe I can have cancer too, like Nona."
>
> **Adult:** "I am glad you do not have cancer like Nona, but I understand how much you love her. You are a lot like Nona with your happy laugh and your curly hair and big brown eyes. I wish Nona was not sick, and I do not want you to be sick. What if we called Nona so you can talk to her? I think it might be nice for both of you to talk to each other."

Here the child is likely trying to show empathy and genuine concern for their grandparent. Most likely the child doesn't truly want to be ill but instead wishes to be closer to their Nona who is sick. It's important to acknowledge that for a child. Here the adult's reply helps the child find a more appropriate way to express themself without making them feel that they have said anything wrong. It also helps the child find the deeper feelings they may not be able to express: love, care, concern, and a yearning to help.

It is also possible that this child is worried they may have or get cancer. The adult's response here can also help reassure the child and affirm that they are healthy.

When it comes to talking with your child, the overarching goal is to acknowledge their questions and feelings and answer with truthful reassurance. Use your own understanding of your child and take care not to jump to conclusions about how they are feeling. Talking together again at different times will help you better understand how your child feels and what support is needed.

Additional Resources for Families

Mom Has Cancer! by Jennifer Moore-Mallinos, illustrated by Marta Fabrega. Honest, simple information helps ease a young boy's fearful and anxious feelings about parental cancer. The story follows the boy as he comes to understand why his mother needs medical attention and continues on to depict the family resuming familiar routines after treatment.

Our Mom Has Cancer by Abigail and Adrienne Ackermann. Two sisters share their honest and hopeful story of their mother's treatment for breast cancer. The story can help young children understand what cancer is and learn about the many associated emotions.

The Tide by Clare Helen Welsh, illustrated by Ashling Lindsay. The young girl in this picture book spends a day at the beach with her grandpa, who has dementia. Carefully crafted, the story can help young children relate to Grandpa's memory loss and the feelings of both the grandfather and his granddaughter.

Worries Are Not Forever by Elizabeth Verdick, illustrated by Marieka Heinlen. This title comes in two versions: a simple board book for toddlers and young preschoolers and a lengthier paperback for children ages four to seven. The books help young children see what it means to worry and offer ideas children can use to cope with worry and anxiety.

Major Illness and Medical Conditions in Children

Major illness is scary as it requires prolonged treatment; may involve hospitalization or permanent changes in lifestyle, diet, or activity; and often has an unknown prognosis. As difficult as this can be to accept in adulthood, it is all the more so when it impacts the life of a young child. Childhood is characterized as carefree, lively, and healthy, so when major illness strikes a child, it can be difficult to understand and accept. Yet there are many major and chronic medical conditions that are notable for emerging in early childhood, such as type 1 diabetes, sickle cell disease, asthma, epilepsy, and a variety of childhood cancers, most notably leukemia (Beacham and Deatrick 2015).

When a parent or caregiver sees another family coping with the diagnosis of a serious health condition in their child, it is difficult to know what to do or say. There is an outpouring of love and support and, at the same time, a feeling of relief and accompanying guilt that it is not one's own child who is facing a major illness. And a family whose child has been diagnosed with a serious illness does not immediately know what kind of support they may need.

When illness strikes a child, it is a pervasive topic of conversation. Adults' anxiety and fear, along with a combination of guarded conversations and attempts to keep things upbeat and optimistic, can be stressful and confusing to young children.

Talking with Family Adults About a Child's Major Illness or Medical Condition

It will likely be emotional for a parent to share the news of a diagnosis of a major illness or critical condition of their own child or a child close to the family. Keep in mind the parent's emotional reaction and likely anxiety. A simple, thoughtful response from you can help you appropriately acknowledge the sensitive topic and also provides a chance to determine what the parent expects from you in terms of supporting their child. It is also critical for you to learn what to do if the child needs medical assistance and to be able to offer appropriate support for the child's family. Possible responses might include:

▶ "Thank you for telling me about this. I understand it's a stressful time right now for Sami and for your family. Is this something that you think Sami will bring up? If he does, what would you like me to say to him or to his classmates?"

▶ "I am very sorry to hear this. Is Ari aware of the diagnosis? What has their reaction been?"

- ▶ "This sounds like a big adjustment for your whole family. I want to support Olivia, and you as well, in whatever way is most helpful. Is there something I can do right now to help her here at the center?"

- ▶ "I'm sure this is a difficult time. Would you like a family information sheet that might help if Brendan has questions at home? I can give you a copy if you'd like."

Talking with Children: Conversation Starters

Children may talk with you about their own medical condition or that of another child. You can manage the emotional charge of such conversations by being prepared. The examples of responses here offer some language you might use.

> **Gabrielle, to teacher:** "Mr. Tom, do you know I have sickle cell anemia now?"
>
> **Mr. Tom:** "Yes, your parents told me about it. I know you have some great doctors and nurses who are working to help you feel better. How do you feel about having sickle cell anemia?"

The goal is to reply to the child's direct question and encourage her to share her feelings. Mr. Tom does not offer additional information but acknowledges what Gabrielle asked and confirms that her parents had let him know about the sickle cell anemia. The teacher also emphasizes the medical team working to help Gabrielle feel better. He then asks an open-ended question, inviting Gabrielle to focus on her emotions.

> **Aiden, to teacher:** "I don't understand why Paris has leukemia. Is she going to die?"
>
> **Mr. Tom:** "That is a big question. I know that Paris is a special friend to you, and she is special to me too. It sounds like you are worried about her. Paris's family and her doctors do not know why she has leukemia, but they are doing everything they can to help her get better. I know it would make Paris happy to hear from you. Do you think you could make her a card telling her that you are thinking about her and hope she feels better soon?"

The goal is to reassure the child, help him clarify and express feelings, and put a focus on positive, constructive ways to support his friend. Note that Mr. Tom does not affirm or deny the possibility of death. Rather, he focuses on helping Aiden connect with his emotions. The teacher also suggests a friendly and appropriate way Aiden can express those emotions and help support Paris as well.

> **Russel, during circle time:** "What's wrong with Lauren?"
>
> **Mr. Tom:** "Lauren has diabetes. This means she will have to be careful with what she eats and take medicine to help her body stay healthy."

The goal is to offer a simple response in keeping with your understanding of what the family and the child want shared. For a group that includes a child who is coping with major or chronic illness, a basic explanation such as this one can help alleviate anxiety. Teachers and parents should speak with a child in advance to determine what they would like to share, if anything. If Lauren were present during the group discussion, the teacher should invite her to share any information she would like with her peer group.

Following Up

Following any conversation with a child about a childhood illness or medical condition, it is appropriate and strongly advised that you connect with the family or families of the children involved in the conversation. Share with the family what the child said or asked and how you responded. Ask the family how they would like the conversation handled if their child asks another question or further discussion takes place. This forges a partnership between school and home and also gives families appropriate notice to prepare for follow-up conversations the child may wish to have with them. (For examples, see "Framework for Parent Conversation Starters" in Part I, page 12.) Offer the family handout "Talking with Your Child About a Major Childhood Illness or Medical Condition" (page 78).

A child may also approach you for further discussion. If a child seeks you out again, allow them to lead the conversation and try to keep it focused on how they are feeling. For example:

> **Gabrielle:** "Why do I have sickle cell anemia? Am I going to stay sick?"
>
> **Mr. Tom:** "You have some big questions, and you can always talk to me about this. I do not know why you have sickle cell anemia. You will most likely always have it. The doctors will take care of you and help you and your family understand how to help you feel better and keep you strong. How are you feeling about all of this?"

You may also need to follow up with your class or group when a child returns after an absence from school. Again, what you tell the group will rely on what you have discussed with the family. For example:

> **Mr. Tom, to all children:** "Lauren is coming back to school today and she will need to do a few extra things to stay healthy because of her diabetes. Before we eat, one of the teachers will check Lauren's blood to see if she needs any medicine. You will also see that she has a special plastic machine that she will wear on her arm to make sure she is healthy. This is not a toy and is very important to keep Lauren healthy."

Talking with Your Child About
a Major Childhood Illness or Medical Condition

Young children have no context or ability to comprehend major or chronic illness in themselves or in others. Their own experiences with visiting a healthcare provider or being sick with a cold mean that they most likely view doctors and other medical professionals as helpers who are always able to make them feel better. Likewise, young children may see an illness as short-term, curable with medication and rest, and nothing to be afraid of.

As you talk with your child about their own illness or that of another child, this positive early experience with doctors and medical care needs to be carefully honored. If your child has a serious health condition, or knows another child who has one, they need to be reassured that the family is giving love and support and—very importantly—that the doctors are helping. Even for diagnoses that are debilitating or incurable, a child needs the reassurance that the adults are helping and are in control. This is not the same as promising that a child will get better. Rather, it tells the child that the doctors, nurses, and family are all giving support. Knowing this will bolster your child's sense of security.

Children will sense adults' tensions about the illness of a child. They may overhear hushed or guarded conversations. They may be confused when caring adults try to keep things upbeat and optimistic. Young children may also feel left out or jealous of a sibling who is the focus of a family's attention due to a serious illness or condition. All of this is natural, but it's important to bear in mind that the emotions accompanying major and chronic illness can be confusing to young children and can unintentionally create high levels of anxiety.

Because your child is likely to hear some medical terms, defining these simply is key. Keep the definition basic, child-friendly, and objective:

▶ "The doctors told us you have asthma. Do you remember how it felt yesterday when you had a hard time breathing at the park? That was your asthma making it hard for you to take in enough air. You are going to start taking some special medicine to keep that from happening."

It's equally important that you label your own feelings in simple terms and explain briefly why you feel as you do:

▶ "I am sad today because I do not want Devon to be sick. I am sad that he has leukemia, but I am happy that he has doctors, nurses, his family, and our family to help him."

▶ "You saw me talking with Mrs. Porter in the hallway at school today. She was telling me Paul found out last week that he has type 1 diabetes. That's why he wasn't at school. Diabetes doesn't hurt Paul, but it does mean that he will have to take special medicine to stay healthy. The medicine is called *insulin*. I am happy that Paul is feeling better and has special medicine now. How do *you* feel?"

▶ "I know you heard me talking to Daddy about your visit to the doctor today. I was telling him what Dr. Ozolski told us about your epilepsy and how this medicine is going to help you not have seizures. Do you remember how Dr. O explained epilepsy to you? Can you tell Daddy what he said?" (Give your child ample time to explain.) "Now we know you have epilepsy, and I am very glad that we have medicine to help you. How do you feel about it?"

By labeling your feelings and giving a brief, child-friendly explanation, you demystify the medical condition and the feelings surrounding it. This allows your child to more easily consider their own feelings and begin to better understand some of the complex or confusing emotions.

Following statements like these, it is important to pause. The words are new, there is a lot of emotion to understand, and it may take your child a few moments to process what you've said.

Your child may be able to label how they feel but will likely need help expressing it. If your child's response is a shrug or silence, that's okay. A simple follow-up question—"Are you okay? Do you have any questions for me?"—allows them to respond if they wish.

Additional Questions and Answers to Consider

Your child may have questions, in the moment or later, that you will want to be prepared to answer.

Question: "Is Isabella going to die?"

Answer: "Isabella has a type of illness called cancer. The doctors are helping her feel better, and they are doing everything they can. I hope that Isabella gets better soon, and I know you do too. We will make sure to call her mom and check on her a lot. Would you like to paint a picture to send to her?"

The goal is to reassure your child in an uncertain situation. Avoid metaphors and abstract phrases such as "fighting this illness" or "it is out of our hands." These phrases are confusing for young children and may lead to unintentional anxiety. Explaining in simple, straightforward terms will make it easier for your child to process the information. Share with your child what the illness is, affirm that medical professionals are helping, and then guide your child to focus on how they feel and what they can do to express those feelings.

Some families may choose to offer faith-based responses, such as "We will trust in God" or "We need to pray for her." Keep in mind the child's age, ability to understand, and familiarity with the faith concepts being offered.

> **Question:** "Will I get sickle cell like Evie?"
>
> **Answer:** "Evie has sickle cell disease, Cameron, but that does not mean you will have it too. Evie takes special medicines to help her body and to help her feel better. I am happy that she has that medicine, and I am also happy that you are healthy."

The goal is to answer honestly and offer reassurance. Questions about having a similar diagnosis are to be expected. Of course, it's impossible to know if another child can or will develop a similar medical condition, so it's important not to affirm *or* deny the likelihood. Here the parent affirms that Evie is getting needed medical help and that Cameron is healthy. The parent also expresses their own feelings about the situation.

> **Question:** "Why can't the doctors make Prachi better?"
>
> **Answer:** "Prachi has a strong cancer on the inside of her body that is hard to make better. The doctors are very smart, and they are trying hard to make the cancer go away. The doctors are going to use the best medicine they can and do their very best to help Prachi be as healthy as possible."

The goal is to emphasize healthcare providers' expertise and efforts and the use of medicine. Young children may feel disappointed or panicked at the idea of doctors not being able to heal an illness. It is important to remind the child of the medical workers' ability and commitment to making people better.

Unless you know a death is really imminent, this is not a time to mention that some illnesses do not have a cure or are beyond the scope of modern medicine. These are abstract concepts that may elicit fear in a young child. In most cases, focusing on the care and comfort being given will help reassure your child.

Preparing for Unexpected Responses

Young children aren't always aware of what "should" and "should not" be said. This lack of life experience can lead them to make statements that are unexpected and may feel hurtful. Preparing for such remarks and considering why a young child might respond that way can help you more effectively support the child and buffer yourself from an emotional reaction.

> **Child:** "I know Gia is going to die."
>
> **Adult:** "I would feel very sad if Gia died. The doctors are working to help her, and I think she might like to know we are thinking about her and we care about her. Gia likes birds. Shall we make her some paper birds to hang in her window?"

A young child responding this way may be trying to make sense of serious illness and death. This statement may be the child's way of self-soothing and attempting to portray a larger understanding of the situation. It's also possible they are worried that their friend will die from her illness. Particularly in serious health scenarios, it is not a time to affirm or reject the statement. Instead, this parent offers reassurance that Gia is getting all the care she can.

If your child makes a statement like this, you may have an urge to scold them and tell them not to say such a thing, but doing this will make the illness seem even more mysterious and scary. Keep in mind that your child may be trying to show maturity and grapple with reality. Instead, state your own feelings and suggest an appropriate way to show care and concern, such as with a letter, a phone call, or a homemade gift.

> **Child:** "I hate diabetes!"
>
> **Adult:** "I am mad that you have diabetes too. I'm happy because I know you are a strong little girl and we have a special family. We all love you, and we are all going to help you through this. It's okay to be angry about it. Is there something I can do to help you feel better?" (Offer a hug or a cuddle.)

This statement may be a true reflection of a child's anger and resentment, or it may be a response to their discomfort with all the restrictions, emotions, and discussion about the illness. Either way, it's important to affirm the feelings and help your child label them. In giving a reply like this one, you can let your child know that their feelings are acceptable and that you share those feelings. At the same time, by shifting the focus onto the support and love of the family, you can help your child know that they're not alone and give open permission to express big emotions.

> **Child:** "Maybe I can have leukemia too like Trevor. I don't care if my hair falls out."
>
> **Adult:** "I am glad you do not have leukemia like Trevor, but I understand how much you care about him and want him to know you are a good friend. Would you like me to see if you can talk on the phone to Trevor? It sounds like it might help both of you to talk to each other."

Here the child is likely trying to show empathy and genuine concern for the friend. Most likely the child is not truly wishing to be ill. It's important to acknowledge that for a child. The adult's reply helps the child find a more appropriate way to express themselves without making them feel that they've said anything wrong. It also helps the child find the deeper feelings they may not be able to express: love, care, concern, and a yearning to help.

It is also possible that, with a statement like this, your child is worried they may have or get cancer. The response here can also help reassure your child and affirm that they are healthy.

When it comes to talking with your child, the overarching goal is to acknowledge their questions and feelings and answer with truthful reassurance. Use your own understanding of your child and take care not to jump to conclusions about how they are feeling. Talking together again at different times will help you better understand how your child feels and what support is needed.

Additional Resources for Families

If your child has received a clinical diagnosis, the medical team should be able to provide your family with resources to help your child understand their condition more thoroughly. Beyond that, here are some books that may help your child cope and offer opportunities for further conversations together about their own or other children's serious or chronic conditions.

Diabetes Doesn't Stop Maddie! by Sarah Glenn Marsh, illustrated by Maria Luisa Di Gravio. This heartwarming story provides a firsthand look at a young girl's diagnosis and successful management of her type 1 diabetes. Maddie knows she can live well with diabetes, though she's nervous to tell her schoolmates about her newly diagnosed condition.

I Have Asthma, What Does That Mean? by Wendy Chen, illustrated by Izzy Bean. This simple picture book written for children ages four to eight offers a message that asthma is treatable, controllable, and does not need to be a source of fear.

Just Ask! Be Different, Be Brave, Be You by Sonia Sotomayor, illustrated by Rafael López. The author shares her own childhood experience of being diagnosed with diabetes in a book that promotes acceptance while providing simple explanations for a variety of challenging conditions children face, including asthma, nut allergies, Tourette's syndrome, ADHD, and others.

A Sickle Cell Coloring Book for Kids by Elle Cole, illustrated by Kate Hamernik. Written for children ages five to eight, this coloring book serves as an educational activity guide for parents and children as it defines terms simply and offers an easy-to-understand explanation of how sickle cell anemia affects the body.

When a Kid Like Me Fights Cancer by Catherine Stier, illustrated by Angel Chang. This book offers a touching storyline of a young boy diagnosed with cancer who learns that cancer is not his fault, that some things change while fighting cancer, but most important that he has a supportive network around him who are also helping him fight cancer.

Worries Are Not Forever by Elizabeth Verdick, illustrated by Marieka Heinlen. This title comes in two versions: a simple board book for toddlers and young preschoolers and a lengthier paperback for children four to seven. The books help young children see what it means to worry and offer ideas children can use to cope with worry and anxiety.

Miscarriage

The loss of an unborn child is an emotional wound felt deeply by parents. Along with the physical loss or trauma experienced by an expectant parent, there is the loss of parents' hopes and dreams for the child that will not come to be. Understandably, miscarriage precipitates a grieving process for parents and can be an emotionally and psychologically challenging time for them. The parents have few established memories or experiences with the unborn baby and are frequently unable to go through the culturally comforting process of a funeral. Moreover, family and friends may not even know of the life that was and is no more or may not grasp the depth of impact the parents feel. This does not lessen the loss but instead may minimize the degree of social and emotional support from others. Partners may struggle to support each other as well. There may be feelings of loss of control, guilt over not knowing what to say or do, and self-doubt about the possibility of more family in the future.

Young children have little to no concept of how a baby comes to be, but for a young child, the news of a baby on the way is often received with excitement, curiosity, and joy. The child may tell others, "We're having a baby" and be met with smiles, encouraging words, and statements celebrating the change on the horizon. When suddenly the baby is no more and the joyful atmosphere is now dull and sorrowful, the child may feel confusion, sadness, anger, and even guilt or resentment.

Talking with Family Adults About a Miscarriage

It will likely be emotional for a parent to share the news of a miscarriage. A simple, sensitive response from you is important. This is an opportunity for you to determine what the parent expects from you in terms of supporting their child. Possible responses might include:

▶ "Thank you for sharing this with me. I am very sorry. Is this something you think Hiromi will bring up? If she does, what would you like me to say to her?"

▶ "I am so sorry to hear this. I understand that this is a difficult time right now for your family. Is Buddy aware of it? What has his reaction been?"

▶ "I understand that this is a sensitive time for you and your family. I do have a resource here at the school with information that may help you talk with Lily about this in case they have questions at home. Would you like me to give you a copy?"

Talking with Children: Conversation Starters

Discussing miscarriage with a young child can be difficult; you can best manage the emotional charge of such conversations by being prepared. The examples of responses here offer some language you might use. Remember to let the child lead the conversation and ask questions.

> **Carlos, to another child:** "My mommy was going to have a baby, but it died."
>
> **Teacher, Ms. Selena (later):** "I heard you talking to Shawna about your mommy. I care a lot about you and your mommy. If you want to talk to me, I am here. Would you like a hug?"

The goal is to remind the child you are there to talk and to offer comfort. Note that Ms. Selena starts with acknowledging the conversation she overheard between the two children but does not offer additional details on miscarriage. She then makes sure Carlos knows that she cares about him and his mother. She reminds him of her presence and offers a physical comfort.

> **Gillian, to teacher:** "We're not having a baby now."
>
> **Ms. Selena:** "I did not know that. Thank you for telling me. How do you feel about that?"

The goal is to focus on Gillian's emotions. The teacher may not have any foreknowledge of the situation, so her response is to invite Gillian to share how she feels about it. Ms. Selena will then want to follow up with the family to express sympathy, let them know that Gillian shared the news, and ask how they would like her to support their daughter during this time.

> **Immanuel, to teacher (during circle time):** "Did you know my mom isn't going to have a new baby? Where did Mom's baby go?"
>
> **Ms. Selena:** "Thank you for telling me that, Immanuel. I want to talk to you and answer your question. Let's finish circle time and then we can talk."
>
> **Ms. Selena, to Immanuel (later):** "I understand that you have questions about Mom's baby. How are you feeling?"

The goal is to support Immanuel and keep circle time focused on group topics. This example showcases how important it is to be mindful of context. This is not a conversation that needs to take place in front of a class of children, and yet Immanuel needs affirmation that he has been heard and seen and will get his teacher's attention. Ms. Selena follows up with a question that doesn't assume knowledge but instead focuses solely on how the boy feels. This will help her meet his needs.

Following Up

Following any conversation with a child about a miscarriage, it is appropriate and strongly advised that you connect with the family or families of the children involved in the conversation. Share with the family what the child said or asked and how you responded. Ask the family how they would like the conversation handled if their child asks another question or further discussion takes place. This forges a partnership between school and home and also gives families appropriate notice to prepare for follow-up conversations the child may wish to have with them. (For examples, see "Framework for Parent Conversation Starters" in Part I, page 12.) Offer the family handout "Talking with Your Child About a Miscarriage" (page 87).

A child may also approach you for further discussion. If a child seeks you out again, allow them to lead the conversation and try to keep it focused on how they are feeling. For example:

> **Ms. Selena, to Gillian:** "You shared with me earlier that you were sad your mommy was not going to have a new baby right now. Would you like to talk more about this?" (pause) "Or maybe you'd like to paint a picture of how you are feeling?"

The goal is to reopen the conversation to allow Gillian to talk more if she would like to. Gillian may continue the conversation, perhaps ask additional questions, or artistically express what she may not be able to put into spoken words. The importance here is that Gillian knows the topic is acceptable to discuss and that her teacher is present and cares about what is happening her life.

Talking with Your Child About
a Miscarriage

The loss of an unborn child is painful. As difficult as this loss is for adults, it's important to recognize that children may feel the loss too. While young children have little to no concept of how a baby comes to be, they are likely to feel excited, curious, and joyful when a baby is expected. And, in the same way, they sense and feel the changed atmosphere when the baby is no longer coming.

Families do not always tell young children about the loss of an unborn child. If your child knows a baby was coming, it is important to explain directly and simply that the baby will no longer be arriving as expected. If children aren't told, they may overhear the news or notice hushed conversations. What was previously a joyous anticipation is now a mournful silence. If their questions about the baby are met with silence, they may conclude that they've done something wrong, yet have no clear idea of what that might be. Alternatively, if a child does not know a baby had been coming, they may witness emotional reactions in family adults with little understanding about what happened and why the grown-ups are now sad, leaving the child worried and confused.

This is why talking with children at a level they can understand is so important. When talking with your child about the loss of an unborn baby, it is always best to start with a simple statement about what has happened and how you feel. For example:

▶ "I think you saw Mommy crying. Mommy and I are sad because we are not going to have a new baby right now. We both love you very much."

▶ "Did you hear Mommy talking with Aunt Mia? We are sad, and so is Aunt Mia, because she is not going to have a baby right now. We all love you very much."

The goal is to share the important information and reassure your child. These simple statements acknowledge what the child saw or heard and provide an emotional label (sad) for the behavior. In each example, the parent gives the child a basic understanding of why the grown-ups are upset and affirms the family's love for the child. This helps maintain the child's sense of security and comfort while making it clear it's okay to talk about the situation.

Next, it's important to pause. The information is new, there are emotions to understand, and it may take your child a few moments to process what was said.

If your child's response is silence, that's okay. A simple follow-up question— "Are you okay? Do you have any questions for me? How are *you* feeling?"—allows them to respond if they wish.

Additional Questions and Answers to Consider

Your child may have questions, in the moment or later, that you will want to be prepared to answer.

> **Question:** "Why isn't Mommy having the baby?"
>
> **Answer:** "Mommy and I wanted to have the baby, but the baby did not grow. We hope a new baby will start to grow someday."

The goal is to answer your child in simple terms, clearly and reassuringly. Here the parent provides a basic explanation and expresses the family's hope for another baby. Avoid metaphors and abstract phrases such as "The baby is sleeping forever," "The baby passed away," "We lost the baby," or "It was not meant to be." These phrases are confusing for young children and may lead to unintentional anxiety. Explaining in simple, straightforward terms will make it easier for your child to process the information.

Some families may choose to offer faith-based responses, such as "The baby is in heaven" or "We need to pray for Mommy." Keep in mind the child's age, ability to understand, and familiarity with the faith concepts being offered.

> **Question:** "Why didn't the baby grow?"
>
> **Answer:** "We do not know why. You did grow when you were a baby, and you are growing healthy and strong. We are very happy for that."

The goal is to offer honest reassurance. It's okay to tell your child you don't have the answers. Reassure them that their health and well-being are not tied to the loss of the baby. Reiterate that your child is healthy and that you are happy to have them in your life.

> **Question:** "Why is Mama sad?"
>
> **Answer:** "Mama and I love you very much. We wanted to have a brother or sister for you, and we will have to wait. That makes us both feel sad. We are glad we have you."

Again, the goal is to answer honestly and to affirm your love for your child. A child may feel left out or resentful when parents' feelings are focused on the loss of the unborn baby. Your child may need reassurance about their worth and value in the family. Explain your feelings about the miscarriage, but couple this with a clear expression of the happiness your child brings to you.

Preparing for Unexpected Responses

Young children aren't always aware of what "should" and "should not" be said. This lack of life experience can lead them to make statements that are unexpected and may feel hurtful. Preparing for such remarks and considering why a young child might respond this way can help you support your child and buffer yourself from emotional reaction.

> **Child:** "At least no one else is going to die."
>
> **Adult:** "You are correct that we are all safe. Mommy and I are still very sad that we are not going to have another baby right now."

A young child responding this way may be trying to make sense of death. This statement may be your child's way of self-soothing and of reassuring themself that everyone else is safe. It's important for you to affirm the statement and to remind your child that you are still sad. Young children don't necessarily understand that others may feel different than they do. Saying directly how you feel can help your child begin to see this and grow in empathy.

> **Child:** "I don't want a baby."
>
> **Adult:** "Mommy and I are feeling sad because we did want a baby. But we are so happy that we have you, because we love you very much. Can you help me think of something we can do to show Mommy how much we love her?"

A child who says this may be trying to rationalize the loss by showing they accept the news. The statement might also reflect mixed feelings about the new baby. It's possible, too, that the child is trying to comfort the mourning parents by verbally dismissing the desire for the baby. If your child says something like this, it's critical not to deny the statement or scold them. The adult's response here reassures the child, reminds them of how the parents are feeling, and involves the child in an act of empathy.

> **Child:** "Aunt Mia can have another baby."
>
> **Adult:** "You are right. Aunt Mia might have another baby. Right now, we feel sad about the baby that died, and Aunt Mia feels sad about it too. You are very good at thinking of nice things to do for other people. Do you think Aunt Mia would like a special card you could make her?"
>
> *Or:*
>
> **Adult:** "You are trying very hard to think of something for Aunt Mia. She is sad that the baby died. What if we make her a card?"

With this statement a child may be trying to find an appropriate way to soothe the loss. It is important to acknowledge your child's attempt to offer sympathy, remind them of the adults' feelings, and then offer a more appropriate gesture. This helps your child focus their desire to help into an act of kindness that will be appreciated.

You know your child and your family's situation. As you continue talking with your child, use your own understanding of your child and take care not to jump to conclusions about how they are feeling. Talking together again at different times will help you better understand how your child feels and what support is needed.

Additional Resources for Families

My Sibling Still by Megan Lacourrege, illustrated by Joshua Wichterich. This book takes the form of a letter to surviving siblings from a deceased sibling lost to miscarriage, stillbirth, or infant death. It describes the emotions the family may experience and assures them of the deceased sibling's loving presence in their lives.

Return to Zero: H.O.P.E. A nonprofit organization for bereaved parents, supportive friends or family, and healthcare providers focused on providing support for the families after pregnancy or infant loss. (rtzhope.org)

Something Happened by Cathy Blanford, illustrated by Phyllis Childers. This children's book is a beautiful way for parents to help young children understand the pregnancy loss and to move through their own period of bereavement.

Death of a Pet

The death of a beloved animal can be just as devastating as the death of a human being. Animals hold a special place in the lives of their owners and often become a member of the family. Whatever the circumstances, it is nearly impossible to ever truly be prepared for death of a family pet. The loss of the animal's presence is felt in numerous ways and throughout different family routines.

For children, the loss of a family pet is frequently their first experience of death. Most children have a very difficult time making sense of the fact that their treasured cat, dog, parakeet, or bunny is gone forever. The age of the child and the amount of interaction they had with the family pet make the greatest impact on how a child responds to the death.

In talking about the death of a pet, young children need very concrete terminology. Speak gently, but be direct, using the words "dead" and "died." Children may need you to explain that the death of the pet is permanent and that they will not see the pet again. Tell children that everything that is alive will die one day. When something dies, its body does not work anymore. Explain that the pet's body did not work anymore and that the pet is dead. Young children may not be able to take all this in, so it's important to give them time to process and then revisit the topic again to see what questions they have.

Young children's feelings about the loss are likely to change over time. Open, honest conversations are important. Encourage children to share what they feel; offer comfort and provide them with ways to express those emotions.

Talking with Family Adults About the Death of a Pet

Pet death is frequently a topic that parents will readily share, though they may be emotional when they do. This is an opportunity for you to learn how the child has responded to the loss of the family pet and to determine what the parent expects from you in terms of supporting the child. Offer a simple, sensitive reply. Possible responses might include:

▶ "I'm really sorry to hear this. How is Willie doing?"

▶ "Oh, that's too bad. I am sorry. Has Carolina been talking about this or asking questions at home? If she talks to me about this, how would you like me to respond?"

▶ "I understand that this is a difficult time. I do have a take-home sheet with information that may help you talk with Nico about this in case he has questions at home. Would you like me to give you a copy?"

Talking with Children: Conversation Starters

In discussing the death of a pet with a child, the emotional charge of such conversations can be lessened by being prepared. The examples of responses here offer some language you might use. Remember to let the child lead the conversation and ask questions.

> **Robert, to another child:** "My cat Ringo died and is never coming back. He was old and sick, and his body died."
>
> **Teacher, Ms. Chantrelle (later):** "Robert, I heard you talking to Julian about your cat, Ringo, dying. I care a lot about you and your family, and I understand about having a pet you love die. How are you feeling about Ringo? If you want to talk to me, I am here. Would you like a hug?"

The goal is to reassure the child that it is acceptable to talk about the pet's death and that the teacher is a safe person who will listen. Ms. Chantrelle acknowledges objectively what she heard in the interaction between the two children. She knew and therefore used the pet's name, Ringo. Using the name signals to Robert that it's okay to discuss this topic and to express his emotions related to the death.

> **Tessa, to teacher:** "I don't want to read *Clifford the Big Red Dog*. It makes me sad because my doggie, Boomer, died. I don't like dog books anymore."
>
> **Ms. Chantrelle:** "I am sorry that your dog Boomer died, Tessa. Thank you for telling me that. I know you loved Boomer very much, and I understand how it might feel sad for you to read *Clifford the Big Red Dog* right now. We can read something different. Can you tell me what you loved best about Boomer?"

The goal is to let the child know she is heard and invite her to talk further or not, as she wishes. Tessa states directly that reading a book about a dog is sad for her, and Ms. Chantrelle appropriately acknowledges the feelings and offers a different book. She then asks an open-ended question about a positive memory of the dog. Considering this will allow Tessa an opportunity to further discuss the loss and label her feelings.

> **Ling, to teacher:** "I miss Bella. Why did Bella die?"
>
> **Ms. Chantrelle:** "That is a big question. It sounds like you are thinking about your dog, Bella, dying last week. Everything that is alive will die one day, and it does make us feel sad and miss our pets. Do you think you might feel better if you painted a picture of Bella? Maybe you could show what you miss most about her."

The goal is to answer the child's question and invite them to explore and express their feelings further. Note that Ms. Chantrelle uses very concrete language. She offers Ling a simple explanation of death and affirms the sadness Ling expressed. She then suggests a way for Ling to channel their feelings into something tangible by painting a picture.

Following Up

Following any conversation with a child about the death of a pet, it is appropriate and strongly advised that you connect with the family or families of the children involved in the conversation. Share with the family what the child said or asked and how you responded. Ask the family how they would like the conversation handled if their child asks another question or further discussion takes place. This forges a partnership between school and home and also gives families appropriate notice to prepare for follow-up conversations the child may wish to have with them. (For examples, see "Framework for Parent Conversation Starters" in Part I, page 12.) Check with the parent on the exact language they've used with the child so that any discussions at school use consistent vocabulary. Offer the family handout "Talking with Your Child About the Death of a Pet" (page 94).

A child may also approach you for further discussion. If a child seeks you out again, allow them to lead the conversation and try to keep it focused on how they are feeling. For example:

> **Ms. Chantrelle:** "Ling, I see you painted a picture. Can you tell me about it?"
>
> **Ling:** "This is me, and that's Bella. I drew her big ears with bows on them."
>
> **Ms. Chantrelle:** "Thank you for sharing your picture of you and Bella with me. I see her big ears with the pink bows. I also see the smile you drew on her face—it makes me feel happy."
>
> **Ling:** "I want a new puppy. Will my new puppy die like Bella died?"
>
> **Ms. Chantrelle:** "I understand you want to get a new dog, and you can talk to your mom and dad about that. I do not know if you will get a new dog soon, but yes—everything that is alive will die one day. Bella was an old dog, so she lived a long life. It still feels sad to say goodbye to a companion we loved. Can I give you a hug?"

Ms. Chantrelle asks Ling to tell her about the painting, thus giving the child an opportunity to talk and share emotions. This not only provides Ling a safe place to discuss what is happening in their life, but also builds a strong trusting relationship between the child and the teacher.

Talking with Your Child About
the Death of a Pet

The loss of a family pet is frequently a child's first experience of death. Most children have a very difficult time making sense of the fact that their beloved cat, dog, parakeet, or bunny is gone forever.

Young children generally lack a defined concept of death and often instead see death as a temporary absence. Adults frequently use words with young children that are seemingly softer than "dead" and "died," such as "went to sleep," "gone to a better place," "no longer in pain," or "crossed the rainbow bridge." While adults readily understand these terms, the ideas can be confusing for a child and may generate further anxiety.

Instead, young children need very concrete terminology. Speak gently, but be direct, using the words "dead" and "died." Often young children's concept of death comes from cartoons where characters may die and then come right back. Your child may need you to explain that the death is permanent and that they will not see their pet again.

Explain in simple but clear terms that everything that's alive will die one day. When something dies, its body does not work anymore. Explain that the pet's body did not work anymore and that the pet is dead.

Your child will need time to process the explanation, and their feelings about the loss are likely to change over time. Open, honest conversations are important. Encourage your child to share what they feel. Offer comfort and provide them with ways to express those emotions—through words, through play, with drawing or painting, by sharing memories.

Here are examples of ways to start a dialogue:

▶ "I think you heard me crying on the phone. Something very sad happened today to Rocky. Rocky always wanted to chase cars, and he got away and ran toward a car today. The driver was not able to stop in time. The car hit Rocky, and Rocky died, which means his body stopped working. He is not alive anymore because his body got hurt too badly." (pause) "How do you feel about Rocky dying?"

This example provides the child a very basic description of what happened to the pet and an understandable explanation of death. The adult labels the behavior (crying) and the associated emotion (sad). Doing this will help your child understand the emotional reactions they're seeing in you. Conclude by inviting your child to share how they feel about the pet's death.

▶ "I know you miss Snowball. I miss her too. Snowball was a very old cat, and her body stopped working. It is sad to me that Snowball died, and I wish she was still here. I remember how much you liked having Snowball sit on your lap and listening to her loud purr. How are you feeling about Snowball?"

The goal is to explain about the death and signal to the child that it is okay to discuss the topic. Here the adult provides some basic information about what death is and why Snowball died. It's important for your child to hear how you're feeling—this helps reassure them that their own feelings are acceptable. Talking about the death and special memories of the beloved pet lets the child think about and ask other questions about death and dying.

Next, it's important to pause. The words are new, there is a lot of emotion to understand, and it may take your child a few moments to process what was said.

If your child's response is silence, that's okay. A simple follow-up question— "Are you okay? Do you have any questions for me?"—allows them to respond if they wish.

Additional Questions and Answers to Consider

Your child may have questions, in the moment or later, that you will want to be prepared to answer.

> **Question:** "Now that Buzz died, is Slinky going to die too?"
>
> **Answer:** "Everything that is alive will die one day, but Slinky is not likely to die for a long time. Slinky is a puppy, and most dogs like him live for many years. We love Slinky, and we will take good care of him. We loved Buzz too, and we will miss him. How are you feeling about Buzz dying?"

This question likely reflects a child's anxiety and fear about the death of a beloved pet. Children may need reassurance that a surviving family pet is not immediately facing the same fate. Be honest and explain that all living things will die one day, but also quickly offer comforting words. Some children may feel guilty for continuing to love and enjoy a surviving pet while also missing and feeling sad about the loss of the other. Over time, conversations with you will help your child understand that both sets of feelings are okay and to be expected.

> **Question:** "Did it hurt Astro to die?"
>
> **Answer (if the pet died of old age or illness):** "Astro was a very old dog. His body got old and stopped working. That is what happens when something dies. You know he was hurting while he was living, but it did not hurt him to die. How are you feeling about Astro dying?"
>
> *Or:*

Answer (if the pet died accidentally): "Astro ran out in front of a car, and the car could not stop. The car hit Astro's body, and his body stopped working. That is what happens when something dies. It happened so fast Astro probably did not feel it. What else are you wondering and feeling about Astro dying?"

Answer questions about the physical process of death in simple terms. Young children cannot understand the physiology and too much explanation may generate greater anxiety. Even if the pet's death was traumatic, it is best to minimize any details and keep things very broad. Give a simple explanation and then prompt your child to share their emotions. Young children need to know that it is okay to be angry or sad or both, and to have other feelings as well.

Preparing for Unexpected Responses

Young children aren't always aware of what "should" and "should not" be said. This lack of life experience can lead them to make statements that are unexpected and may feel hurtful. Preparing for such remarks and considering why a young child might respond this way can help you support your child and buffer yourself from emotional reaction.

Child: "Daddy, I'm glad Mr. Whiskers died. He was so old."

Adult: "I know you loved Mr. Whiskers, Renée. And I also know that he was not as fun to play with as he got older and mostly slept all day. I am sad that he will not be our cat anymore, but I am happy that we had him for as long as we did."

A child who says this probably understands that her pet died of old age and is stating that, in the moment, she is able to accept it. This does not mean the child doesn't mourn the loss or that she won't experience other emotions with time. Appropriately, this father affirms his daughter's statement and then reminds her of how he feels about the pet's death. Young children often look to adults to model how to express feelings. It is perfectly acceptable and appropriate for you to share with your child your sorrow about a pet's death. It's also appropriate to help your child understand why they may not be feeling as much sadness as you do. When you use "feeling words," you help your child think about and express their own feelings, now or later.

It's also possible that your child may not fully comprehend what has happened. A similar comment a child might make is this:

> **Child:** "Okey dokey."
>
> **Adult:** "I'm sad that Bailey died. She was a very special dog to me, and I will miss her. Can we have a cuddle? That would make me feel better right now."

There is some comfort to be had in the naïveté of a young child's limited understanding. If it's not clear whether your child grasps the reality of the pet's death, you may want to explain the event again at some point. Regardless, it is appropriate and can be helpful for you to label how you are feeling. This does not negate what your child does or doesn't feel, but it offers them a different perspective of how the death impacts the adult. And regardless of how they feel about the pet, your child may welcome a hug or snuggle with you.

> **Child:** "It's okay, Mommy. Fluffs will come back."
>
> **Adult:** "Fluffs is not coming back. Fluffs is dead. That means his body is not working anymore. Fluffs died today."

This child's statement reflects that the child does not understand death and dying. The best response is to briefly explain it again. Your child may or may not be able to comprehend the explanation, and if they mention the pet coming back again, it may be a sign they're not developmentally or emotionally ready to understand and accept it. In that case, for the time being, let the child proceed with this limited understanding.

> **Child:** (silence)
>
> **Adult:** "Can I give you a hug?"

Silence can denote that your child does not understand and therefore is not reacting, or it can mean that they are still processing what they've been told and how they feel about the news. Respect this silence. Give your child a few moments to think and be still and then reassure them that you are here if they want to talk. Offer a hug or gentle squeeze. This will remind them that they're okay and will allow some space for your child to quietly feel whatever they are feeling. Even if a child does not understand what is happening, they sense the emotion in the family, and the extra dose of comforting will ease any anxiety they may feel.

> **Child:** "Can we get a new kitty cat now, Mommy?"
>
> **Adult:** "I understand why you want a new kitty cat, Landon. I am sad that Oreo died, and I miss him very much. We had Oreo for such a long time, and I need a little time to get over my sad feelings. When my sadness is not so big, we can talk about getting another kitty then. That would make me happy too."

This child's question likely expresses the child's sense of loss. It shows that Landon understands the cat will not be coming back and that he would like a new cat to fill the void. Often, though, adults need some time to cope with the loss of one family pet before adopting a new one. Here, in explaining this to a young child, the mother uses her words to describe her own emotions. This can also help the child understand and label his own feelings. This mother's response affirms the child's desire, labels how she herself is feeling, implies how her son *may* be feeling, and uses feeling words to help the child label his emotions.

You know your child and your family's situation. As you continue talking with your child, use your own understanding of your child and take care not to jump to conclusions about how your child is feeling. Talking together again at different times will help you better understand how your child feels and what support is needed.

Additional Resources for Families

The Goodbye Book by Todd Parr. This simple picture book provides toddlers and very young children an opportunity to connect with the many emotions felt when saying goodbye to something or someone they love.

The Tenth Good Thing About Barney by Judith Viorst, illustrated by Erik Blegvad. Geared toward children over the age of four, this picture book provides a child's firsthand story of grieving the death of his beloved dog and coming to find comfort in the memories of his pet.

When a Pet Dies by Fred Rogers. This children's book provides simple text, real photographs, and a child-appropriate explanation of death of a pet. Children will find comfort in knowing that it is acceptable to feel a range of emotions when a pet dies.

Death of a Family Member

Death is never easy. Whether a loved one has been battling a long-term illness, has reached a significant age, or dies suddenly, the human spirit can never be fully prepared to lose a close family member. Death is final, and this finality is difficult to process when the deceased person's impact and family members' connection to them lives on. The loss of an immediate family member is particularly difficult and has ripple effects on the full family. Not only is the loss profound and felt by all, but shock, grief, and exhaustion often impact how parents and children behave and interact.

The experience of death is different for children than for adults. Death is something abstract that somehow became a reality, and most children have a very difficult time making sense of the information. The age of the child and the deceased loved one's proximity and level of presence in the life of the child make the greatest impact on how the child responds to the loss of a family member. Young children do comprehend and sense the emotions and behavior of the adults around them.

In talking about the death of someone in their family, young children need to be spoken to in very concrete terminology. Speak gently, but be direct, using the words "dead" and "died." Most young children only have a concept of death from children's cartoons where characters may die and then come right back. Children may need you to explain that death is permanent and that they will not see the family member again. Explain in simple but direct terms to the young child that everything that's alive will die one day. When we die, our bodies do not work anymore. Young children may not be able to take all this in, so it's important to give them time to process and then revisit the topic again to see what questions they have.

Young children's feelings about the loss are likely to change over time. Open, honest conversations are important. Encourage children to share what they feel; offer comfort and provide them with ways to express those emotions.

Talking with Family Adults About the Death of a Family Member

It will likely be emotional for a parent to share the news of the death that has occurred in the family. A simple, sensitive response from you can help you appropriately acknowledge the topic and also provides a chance to determine what the parent expects from you in terms of supporting the child. Possible responses might include:

▶ "I am so sorry to hear that your father died. I am here to support Malachi and your family. Is Malachi aware of the death?"

▶ "I am sorry. What can I do to help support Suzy here at school?"

▶ "I understand that this is a very hard time. I do have a resource with information that may help you talk with Zach about this when he has questions at home. Would you like me to give you a copy?"

Talking with Children: Conversation Starters

When talking with a young child about the death of someone close to them, you can lessen the emotional charge by being prepared. The examples of responses here offer some language you might use. Remember to let the child lead the conversation and ask questions.

> **Orion, to another child:** "I don't want to play baby dolls. My baby brother died."
>
> **Teacher, Ms. Bethany (later):** "I heard you talking to Edith about your brother Joseph, who died. I care a lot about you and your family. If you want to talk to me, I am here. Would you like a hug?"

The goal is to reassure the child that it is acceptable to talk about his brother's death and that the teacher is a safe person who will listen. Ms. Bethany objectively acknowledges what she observed. In this case she knows and therefore uses the name of Orion's deceased baby brother, Joseph. The use of Joseph's name signals to Orion that it is okay to discuss this topic and that it is okay to express his emotions related to the death.

> **Luca, to teacher:** "My grandpa was really sick and then he died. I want him to come back."
>
> **Ms. Bethany:** "I am sorry that your grandpa died. Thank you for telling me. I know your grandpa was a special part of your family. Can you tell me more about how you're feeling?"

The goal is to affirm the child and help him further express his feelings. Ms. Bethany does not offer any additional information. She acknowledges what Luca has shared and responds with an open-ended question, allowing him to focus on his emotions.

> **Kiera, to teacher:** "My daddy died. I want him back. I want to have my daddy again."
>
> **Ms. Bethany:** "I am sorry that your daddy died, Kiera. I know this is hard for you and your family right now. I'd like to give you a hug—is that okay?" (child and teacher hug) "Can you tell me more about the feelings you are having now?"

Following Up

Following any conversation with a child about the death of a family member, it is appropriate and strongly advised that you connect with the family or families of the children involved in the conversation. Share with the family what the child said or asked and how you responded. Ask the family how they would like the conversation handled if their child asks another question or further discussion takes place. This forges a partnership between school and home and also gives families appropriate notice to prepare for follow-up conversations the child may wish to have with them. (For examples, see "Framework for Parent Conversation Starters" in Part I, page 12.) Check with the parent on the exact language they've used with the child so that any discussions at school use consistent vocabulary. Offer the family handout "Talking with Your Child About the Death of a Family Member" (page 102).

A child may also approach you for further discussion. If a child seeks you out again, allow them to lead the conversation and try to keep it focused on how they are feeling. For example:

> **Orion, to teacher:** "Are you going to die too?"
>
> **Ms. Bethany:** "That is a big question. It sounds like you are thinking about your brother dying. Everything that is alive will die someday, but I am healthy and safe, and I'm very happy to be here with you today. Would you like to draw a picture of Joseph?"

The goal is to answer honestly and reassuringly. Note that the teacher uses very concrete language. She focuses on giving Orion a very simple explanation of death and then reassures the child of her presence in his life. Ms. Bethany then suggests a developmentally appropriate way for Orion to channel his feelings into something tangible by drawing a picture. If he draws one, she can then ask him to tell her about the drawing in order to give him an opportunity to talk and share more about his brother and his emotions.

> **Kiera, to teacher:** "Do you want to see my picture?"
>
> **Ms. Bethany:** "I see that you drew a picture about you and your daddy. I notice your blue, red, and black colors here at the top of the page and here's you holding your daddy's hand at the bottom. Can you tell me about your picture? Tell me about what you are feeling in this picture with your daddy."

> **Luca, to teacher:** "This is my grandpa watching me from heaven."
>
> **Ms. Bethany:** "I see your grandpa is smiling in the picture. How does it feel for you to think of Grandpa smiling at you?"

The goal is to let the child think about and express their own emotions. Notice in each example how the teacher makes concrete observations about the drawings without assuming the emotions represented. This allows the child to lead the discussion about how they are feeling.

Talking with Your Child About
the Death of a Family Member

For children, the loss of a close family member can be sad, scary, and confusing. Most children have a very difficult time making sense of the fact that a beloved member of the family, maybe someone they have always lived with, is gone forever. The age of the child and the amount of interaction the child had with the person who has died make the greatest impact on how the child responds. Death in the family is painful for everyone and often creates changes in the family dynamic. Grieving parents may find it hard to speak thoughtfully with children about the death, yet it's important to do so.

Young children generally lack a defined concept of death and often instead see death as a temporary absence. Adults frequently use words with young children that are seemingly softer than "dead" and "died," such as "gone to a better place," "no longer in pain," "sleeping forever," or "crossed the rainbow bridge." While adults readily understand these terms, the ideas can be confusing for a child and may lead to further anxiety. Instead, young children need very concrete terminology. Speak gently, but be direct, using the words "dead" and "died." Often young children's concept of death comes from cartoons where characters may die and then come right back. Children may need you to explain that the death is permanent and that they will not see the family member again.

Explain in simple but direct terms that everything that is alive will die one day. When we die, our bodies do not work anymore. Explain that the loved one's body did not work anymore and that this person is dead.

Young children will need time to process the explanation, and their feelings about the loss are likely to change over time. Open, honest conversations are important. You can start a dialogue and signal to your child that you are there to talk about the death of the family member. For example:

▶ "I know you miss Uncle Teddy, and I miss him too. It is sad to me that Uncle Teddy died, and I wish he were still here. When you laugh, it reminds me of him and makes me think of him. How do you feel about Uncle Teddy dying?"

The goal is to let your child know it's okay to discuss the loved one. It is important to tell your child how you are feeling—this helps reassure them that their own feelings are acceptable. Talking about the deceased family member also gives your child the space and opportunity to ask other questions about death and dying.

▶ "I think you saw Daddy crying in the bedroom. Daddy is very sad that Paw-Paw died. Daddy loved Paw-Paw very much, and we did too. It's sad for Daddy that he won't be able to talk to Paw-Paw or hug Paw-Paw again. How are you feeling about Paw-Paw dying?"

The goal is to acknowledge and explain what your child saw and heard. Here the adult uses simple words to share what Daddy is feeling and why he feels sad. The adult makes a point of using the words "died" and "dying" and says clearly that Daddy won't be able to hug or talk to Paw-Paw again. Emphasizing the permanence of death with a statement like this may help your child understand that death is final.

Next, it's important to pause. The words are new, there is a lot of emotion to understand, and it may take the child a few moments to process what was said.

If your child's response is silence, that's okay. A simple follow-up question— "Are you okay? Do you have any questions for me?"—allows them to respond if they wish.

Additional Questions and Answers to Consider

Your child may have questions, in the moment or later, that you will want to be prepared to answer.

> **Question:** "Are you going to die too, Mommy?"
>
> **Answer:** "Everyone will die one day, but I'm not going to die right now. I am happy and healthy, and I am staying right here with you. I love you very much!"

This question likely reflects a child's anxiety and fear about the death of the loved one. A child who asks this needs reassurance that they are safe and that their family is safe. Be honest that everyone will die one day, but then quickly offer comforting words to ease your child's distress.

> **Question:** "Did it hurt Nana to die?"
>
> **Answer:** "Nana's body was very old. Her body stopped working and that is how she died. When her body stopped working, she did not feel anything. How are you feeling about Nana dying?"

The goal is to answer questions about the physical process of death in very simple terms. Young children cannot understand physiology, and attempting to explain bodily systems may generate greater anxiety. For example, saying that Nana's heart stopped beating may lead a child to keep trying to feel their heartbeat out of fear that their heart may stop. Even if a death was traumatic, it is best to minimize any details and keep things very broad. Give a simple explanation and then prompt your child to share their feelings with you. Young children need to know that it is okay to be angry or sad or both. They need affirmation that whatever they feel is okay and accepted.

> **Question:** "Why did God let Izzy die?"
>
> **Answer:** "That is a very hard question to answer. I think Izzy's body just could not live any more. I am very sad about it, and I am angry about it too. I did not want Izzy to die. Can you tell me how you are feeling about Izzy's death?"

Children may question religious teachings during emotional times, such as a death in the family. Rather than try to explain difficult religious concepts, it is usually better to first focus on the feelings behind a child's question. This can help the child regulate. Save conversations and teachings about religion for a time when your child is older or more emotionally ready.

Also important in relation to death and dying are religious beliefs in an afterlife or reincarnation. Very young children may not be able to grasp these concepts. A young child may ask to go visit the loved one or may feel that person is still available to talk or play together but being kept from them.

Some families may choose to offer comforting faith-based responses, such as "Izzy is with God now." Keep in mind the child's age, ability to understand, and familiarity with the faith concepts being offered.

Every family has a different spiritual and religious grounding, and of course you want to respond to your child in ways that fit your family's beliefs. At the same time, it's wise to look for the feeling behind the question and address that in a straightforward way. You may want to seek advice from a trusted priest, rabbi, minister, imam, or other spiritual advisor for ideas on how to answer your child's questions about the role of God or a higher power in a death in the family.

Preparing for Unexpected Responses

Young children aren't always aware of what "should" and "should not" be said. This lack of life experience can lead them to make statements that are unexpected and may feel hurtful. Preparing for such remarks and considering why a young child might respond this way can help you support your child and buffer yourself from emotional reaction.

> **Child:** "At least no one else is going to die."
>
> **Adult:** "Aunt Sarah did die, and I am very sad about that. Aunt Sarah was my sister, and I will miss her. You are correct that we still have the rest our family, and our family will remember Aunt Sarah."

A young child responding this way may be trying to contain the event or seek reassurance that others around them are not going to die soon. This does not necessarily mean the child doesn't comprehend and mourn the loss of the deceased family member. It's important to affirm the child's statement and then remind the child of the death that did occur and how the parents feel. Young children often look to adults to model how to express feelings. It is perfectly acceptable and appropriate to share with your child your sadness, anger, and loneliness about the loss of a family member. The "feeling words" you use can help your child better express their own feelings.

> **Child:** "It's okay that my cousin Rory died."
>
> **Adult:** "I am sad that Rory died. He was a very special person to me, and I will miss him very much."

There is some comfort to be had in the naiveté of a young child's limited understanding. If it's not clear whether your child grasps the reality of the death, you may want to wait and try to explain again at some later point. It's still appropriate for you to label how you're feeling. Doing this doesn't negate what your child feels or does not feel, but it offers your young child a different perspective on how the death impacts you.

> **Child (after the death of a great-grandfather):** "When is Great-Gran going to die?"
>
> **Adult:** "I am very sad that Great-G-pa died. I will miss him. We are so happy that Great-Gran is still alive. She will not live forever because none of us will. But she is still here, and we'll see her tomorrow. Great-Gran is also very sad that Great-G-pa died."

A child who says this is aware, to an extent, that all living things will eventually die. The child has drawn a connection that if one great-grandparent died, then it's likely the other great-grandparent will die soon too. In responding, the adult acknowledges the death, states their own feelings, affirms that Great-Gran is still alive and not dying now, and reminds the child of her feelings as well.

> **Child:** (silence)
>
> **Adult:** "I'm here if you want to talk to me. Would you like a hug?"

Death is a difficult concept for adults to handle, and it can be all the more complex for young children. Silence can denote that children do not understand and therefore are not reacting, or it can mean that they're still processing what they've been told and how they feel about the news. Respect this silence. Give your child a few moments to think and be still and then offer reassurance that you're here and willing to talk. Offer a hug or a gentle squeeze. This will remind your child that you love them and will allow some space for them to feel whatever they are feeling. Even if they do not understand what is happening, your child will sense the emotion in the family, and the extra dose of comfort will ease any anxiety they may feel.

You know your child and your family's situation. As you continue talking with your child, use your own understanding of your child and take care not to jump to conclusions about how they are feeling. Talking together again at different times will help you better understand how your child feels and what support is needed.

Additional Resources for families

The Goodbye Book by Todd Parr. This simple picture book provides toddlers and very young children an opportunity to connect with the many emotions felt when saying goodbye to something or someone loved.

I Miss You: A First Look at Death by Pat Thomas, illustrated by Leslie Harker. This illustrated children's book introduces the concept of death and explains, simply but realistically, how all living things will die one day. The book helps young children identify and label their emotions and come to terms with the big feelings of loss after someone they love dies.

Lifetimes: The Beautiful Way to Explain Death to Children by Bryan Mellonie and Robert Ingpen. This children's book provides a clear explanation of death, explaining how everything living has a beginning and will one day die—plants, animals, and people.

Something Very Sad Happened: A Toddler's Guide to Understanding Death by Bonnie Zucker, illustrated by Kim Fleming. This picture book is written to explain death simply to toddlers and preschool-age children while also providing appropriate emotional vocabulary. Color-coded words let you substitute the name and pronoun of the person who died as you read the book to your child.

Death of a Friend or Classmate

Death is never easy, but the loss of a child can be almost inconsolable. Whatever the circumstances that surround the loss, there is often intense grief when someone so young dies. Adults question why that child, why now, why so young. It is a break in the normative cycle of life, and the pain of the death touches everyone who was involved in the child's life.

The experience of death is notably different for children. Death is something abstract that somehow became a reality, and most children have a very difficult time making sense of the information. The death of a friend or a classmate is particularly hard for young children to process. A child who was here one day is gone the next, and the context in which the young child interacted with the deceased child is a constant reminder of the loss.

One important consideration when talking with a young child or a group of children about the death of a friend or classmate is how well the children knew their peer and how deeply they seem to be reacting to the loss. Consider the children's ages, the longevity of the friendship, and whether and how often they are inquiring about the deceased child. Examples of displays of grief may include crying, asking for the deceased friend, excessive clinginess, or direct conversations asking about what happened to the deceased classmate.

In talking about the death of another child, young children need to be spoken to in very concrete terminology. Speak gently, but be direct, using the words "dead" and "died." Most young children only have a concept of death from children's cartoons where characters may die and then come right back. Children may need you to explain that death is permanent and that they will not see the loved one again. Explain in simple but direct terms that everything that is alive will die one day. When we die, our bodies do not work anymore. Young children may not be able to process the explanation provided to them. It is important to give a child time to process and then to revisit the topic with them to see if the child has any questions.

With situations in which a child loses a friend or a classmate, fear and anxiety typically accompany sadness. Children need to be reassured that what happened to the friend or classmate is not something that is likely to happen to them as well.

Young children's feelings about the loss are likely to change over time. Open, honest conversations are important. Encourage children to share what they feel; offer comfort and provide them with ways to express those emotions.

Talking with Family Adults About the Death of a Friend or Classmate

In situations where a friend or classmate dies, the teacher may know before other families do. As quickly as possible, notify teachers directly affected by the death so they're prepared for any questions from families. If possible and appropriate, and if the family of the deceased child has granted permission, inform the parents of the other children in the classroom next. This provides families time to speak with their children before the subject is brought up in the classroom. If children do learn about the death before their parents do, notify families as soon thereafter as you can.

When talking with families, ask what information has been shared with their child, what the child's reaction to the news has been, and what support they want or need. Many families have little or no prior experience with the death of a child and so parents may be in shock. Offer information and support resources readily. In these early conversations, share information and ask questions with sensitivity, paying attention to what the family expects from you in terms of supporting the child. Possible conversation starters might include:

▸ "Thank you for letting me know that Dante's friend Kinjin died this weekend. This must be a very difficult time for Kinjin's family and for your own. How has Dante handled the news? Is there anything in particular you would like me to say to comfort him if he brings up Kinjin's death to me here at school?"

▸ "I'm not sure if you have heard that we've had very sad news. Some of the children already know that their classmate Magdelena died suddenly in a car accident Monday night. Has Winnie said anything about it to you? I need to share the news with the all the children today and I wanted to be sure you knew about it before I do that."

▸ "I am so sorry to hear how hard Siri is taking Olive's death. She told me she wanted to have her comfy in her cubby so she could snuggle with it sometimes, and I said she could do that. Are there other things you think might be helpful for Siri right now here at school?"

Talking with Children: Conversation Starters

If a classmate has died, you may need to share the news with the other children. When young children learn of a classmate's death, they are likely to feel anxious and worried. You can best manage the emotional charge of such conversations by being prepared. The examples here offer some language you might use. Your role is to share information simply and directly. In responding to children's concerns, remember to let the child cue the conversation.

> **Teacher, Mr. Joshua, to the class:** "I need to talk to you about something that happened. It is a very sad time for me because I learned that our friend Magdelena died Monday night. She was a special member of our classroom, and I feel sad that we will not get to see her again. Some of you may already know this from your family but I want you to know that you can talk to me. It is okay to share with me how you are feeling about Magdelena dying."

The goal is to share information with children honestly and in a way that allows them time and space to process the news and ask questions. The teacher tells the group about Magdelena's death and expresses his own sadness about it. He helps define what death means when he says that "we will not get to see her again." Mr. Joshua then opens the way for children to speak, now or later, about their feelings, letting them know he's there to talk.

> **Siri, at circle time:** "I want Olive to come back! I don't want Olive to be dead."
>
> **Mr. Joshua:** "We are all very sad about Olive's death. Olive was a good friend to many of us, and it makes me very sad that she died. I would like to read a book to you about how it feels to miss someone who has died, and then we can talk about how we are feeling."

The goal is to signal to children that it is okay to discuss this topic and okay for them to express their emotions related to the death. Here the teacher objectively acknowledges Siri's comment to the group. By using Olive's name, Mr. Joshua has solidified a message that it's acceptable to talk about her death. He offers to read a book about missing someone. This will provide a context for talking about death and the feelings that surround it. It also gives Mr. Joshua a tool to guide the discussion and an emotional buffer for his own feelings.

> **Vanessa, to teacher:** "My best friend Leah died of cancer. Mommy said I will never see her again."
>
> **Mr. Joshua:** "I am so sorry that your friend Leah died. Thank you for telling me. I know you and Leah were very good friends. How do you feel about Leah dying?"

The goal is to reassure the child that it is acceptable to talk about her friend's death and that the teacher is a safe person who will listen. Note that Mr. Joshua does not offer additional information to Vanessa's statement about cancer or about death. He acknowledges what she shared and responds with an open-ended question, encouraging Vanessa to focus on her emotions.

> **Dante, to teacher:** "Am I going to die too, like Kinjin did?"
>
> **Mr. Joshua:** "That is a big question. Everything that is alive will die one day, but Kinjin's death was an accident. You are healthy and safe, and I am very happy that you are here at school with me today. Would you like to make a story about your friend Kinjin and how you are feeling? You can draw a picture and tell me what you want it to say, and I can help you write the words."

The goal is to reassure the child and help him further express his feelings. The teacher uses very concrete language. He gives Dante a very simple explanation of death and then reassures him that he himself is healthy and safe. Mr. Joshua then provides a developmentally appropriate way for Dante to channel his feelings into something tangible by making a picture story. The offer to help write the words to go with the picture will allow for a discussion and give the teacher insight into what Dante understands about the death and how the boy feels about it.

Following Up

Following any conversation with a child about the death of a friend or classmate, it is appropriate and strongly advised that you connect with the family or families of the children involved in the conversation. Share with the family what the child said or asked and how you responded. Ask the family how they would like the conversation handled if their child asks another question or further discussion takes place. This forges a partnership between school and home and also gives families appropriate notice to prepare for follow-up conversations the child may wish to have with them. (For examples, see "Framework for Parent Conversation Starters" in Part I, page 12.) Check with the parent on the exact language they've used with the child so that any discussions at school use consistent vocabulary. Offer the family handout "Talking with Your Child About the Death of a Friend or Classmate" (page 111).

A child may also approach you for further discussion. If a child seeks you out again, allow them to lead the conversation and try to keep it focused on how they are feeling. For example:

> **Vanessa:** "Will Leah come back soon?"
>
> **Mr. Joshua:** "Leah has died. This means that she will not come back. You will not see her again. How do you feel about that? Would you like a hug?"

> **Dante:** "What if *I* have an accident too?"
>
> **Mr. Joshua:** "It sounds to me like you are worrying and thinking about what happened to Kinjin. What happened to him does not happen often at all. You are safe here in this classroom with me. Would you like to listen to a story in the beanbag chair?"

> **Winnie:** "Where did Magdelena go when she died?"
>
> **Mr. Joshua:** "When we die, our bodies stop working. This means Magdelena is not alive here with us any longer. Where do you think we go when we die?"

Always offer reassurance that the child is safe and you are there to talk and listen. Invite children to share their ideas and feelings and to feel free to come to you if they have questions or need physical comfort. Expect that many children will need time to process the death of their peer. And be sure to seek support for yourself as you grieve the loss of a child from your class.

Talking with Your Child About
the Death of a Friend or Classmate

Most children have a very difficult time making sense of the fact that another child—a friend or a playmate—is gone forever. A friend who was here one day is gone the next, and places and activities that the child and friend once shared are now a constant reminder of the loss. Young children react to death and exhibit grief differently from adults, and this needs to be considered when helping young children cope and accept the loss.

Young children generally lack a defined concept of death and often instead see death as a temporary absence. Grown-ups frequently use words with young children that seem softer than "dead" and "died," such as "gone to a better place," "no longer in pain," "sleeping forever," or "crossed the rainbow bridge." While adults readily understand these terms, the ideas can be confusing for a child and may generate further anxiety. Instead, young children need very concrete terminology. Speak gently, but be direct, using the words "dead" and "died." Often young children's concept of death comes from cartoons where characters may die and then come right back. Your child may need you to explain that the death is permanent and that they will not see their friend again.

Explain in simple but direct terms that everything that's alive will die one day. When we die, our bodies do not work anymore. Explain that the friend or classmate's body did not work anymore and so this person is dead.

Children need time to process this explanation, and their feelings about the loss are likely to change over time. Open, honest conversations are important. When a child loses a friend or classmate, fear and anxiety typically accompany sadness. Your child needs reassurance that what happened to the friend or classmate is not something that is likely to happen to them as well.

Start a dialogue with a simple explanation of death, making sure to signal to your child that it's okay to discuss the topic. For example:

▶ "Mason, I think you heard me talking and crying when I was on the phone with Mr. Patel tonight. I called to check on their family, and he told me that Rahul has died. I am very sad and angry that Rahul is dead. He was a good friend to you and to our family, and I will miss him." (pause) "How do you feel to hear that Rahul has died?"

The goal is to share the news with your child honestly and to open the door to talk more. It is also important to tell your child how you are feeling. This helps reassure your child that their own feelings are acceptable. By expressing the mixed emotions of sadness and anger, this parent lets Mason know that people feel more than one emotion at a time. The parent then prompts Mason to share his emotions now that he's heard about the death. What Mason says will indicate how well he comprehends death and what has happened to his friend.

▶ "I know it was very sad for us to learn today that Chanel died. She has been in your class for two years and she was a good friend of yours. Do you understand what happened to Chanel and what it means that she has died?"

The goal is to tell the child that it is okay to discuss the friend's death. Even if your child has experienced death before, it is a good idea to ask if they understand what has happened. This would be particularly appropriate in situations where their friend died suddenly or had an unknown illness that led to a quick passing. Talking about the deceased friend also gives your child the space and opportunity to ask other questions about death and dying.

Next, it's important to pause. The words are new, there is a lot of emotion to understand, and it may take the child a few moments to process what was said.

If your child's response is silence, that's okay. A simple follow-up question— "Are you okay? Do you have any questions for me?"—allows them to respond if they wish.

Additional Questions and Answers to Consider

Your child may have questions, in the moment or later, that you will want to be prepared to answer.

> **Question:** "Are you going to die too, Papa?"
>
> **Answer:** "Everyone will die one day, but I am not going to die right now. I am healthy and strong, and I am staying right here with you. I love you very much!"

A question like this most likely reflects a child's anxiety and fear about the death of someone close to them. The child needs reassurance that they are safe and that their family is safe. Be honest that everyone will die one day, but then quickly offer comforting words to ease your child's distress.

> **Question:** "Why couldn't the doctors make Trey better?"
>
> **Answer:** "The doctors are very smart, and they tried everything they could to make Trey better. Trey had a strong cancer, and the doctors used the best medicine they had to try to get rid of the cancer. But Trey's body stopped working and he died."

The goal is to answer honestly while affirming the healthcare providers' expertise and efforts. Young children may feel disappointed or panicked at the idea of doctors not being able to heal an illness. Here it is important to remind your child of the medical workers' ability and commitment to making people better. Emphasize the use of medicine, the commitment to care, and the effort. This is not a time to mention that some illnesses do not have a cure or are beyond the scope of modern medicine. These are abstract concepts that may elicit fear in a young child. Such a conversation can take place later and over time. Instead, for now, stress that all efforts were made. Follow with the simple explanation that the child's body stopped working and use the words "died," "dead," "death," or "dying" as opposed to vague terms like "passed" or "passed away."

Question: "Why did God let Mina die?"

Answer: "That is a very hard question to answer. Mina died because her body just could not live anymore, so it quit working. I am very sad about it, and I am very angry too. I did not want Mina to die. Can you tell me how you are feeling about Mina's death?"

Children may question religious teachings during emotional times, such as a death of someone close. Rather than try to explain difficult religious concepts, it is usually better to first focus on the feelings behind your child's question. This can help the child regulate. Save conversations and teachings about religion for a time when your child is older or more emotionally ready.

Also important in relation to death and dying are religious beliefs in an afterlife or reincarnation. Very young children may not be able to grasp these concepts. A young child may ask to go visit the friend or may feel that a classmate is still available to talk or play together but being kept from them.

Some families may choose to offer comforting faith-based responses, such as "Mina is with God now." Keep in mind your child's age, ability to understand, and familiarity with the faith concepts being offered.

Every family has a different spiritual and religious grounding, and of course you want to respond to your child in ways that fit your family's beliefs. At the same time, it's wise to look for the feeling behind the question and address that in a straightforward way. You may want to seek advice from a trusted priest, rabbi, minister, imam, or other spiritual advisor for ideas on how to answer your child's questions about the role of God or a higher power in the death of a friend or playmate.

Preparing for Unexpected Responses

Young children aren't always aware of what "should" and "should not" be said. This lack of life experience can lead them to make statements that are unexpected and may feel hurtful. Preparing for such remarks and considering why a young child might respond this way can help you support your child and buffer yourself from emotional reaction.

> **Child:** "At least I'm not going to die."
>
> **Adult:** "I am happy that you are safe and healthy. Jamal did die, and that makes me very unhappy. I will miss his smile and having him here for playdates. I feel sad and angry that Jamal died."

A young child responding this way may be trying to contain the event or seek reassurance that they are safe. If your child says this, it does not necessarily mean they do not comprehend and mourn the loss of the friend. It's important to affirm the statement, reassure your child that they're safe and healthy, and then remind them of the death that did occur and how you feel. Young children often look to adults to model how to express feelings. It is perfectly acceptable and appropriate to share with your child your sadness and anger about the loss of the friend or classmate. The "feeling words" you use can help your child better express their own feelings.

> **Child:** "It's okay that Skye died."
>
> **Adult:** "I'm sad that Skye died. She was a very special little girl and a nice friend to you. I will miss her very much."

There is some comfort to be had in the naiveté of a young child's limited understanding. If it's not clear whether your child grasps the reality of the death, you may want to wait and try to explain again at some later point. It's still appropriate for you to label how you're feeling. Doing this doesn't negate what your child feels or does not feel, but it offers your young child a different perspective on how the death impacts you.

> **Child:** (silence)
>
> **Adult:** "I am here if you want to talk to me. Do you need a hug?"

Death is a difficult concept for adults to handle, and it can be all the more complex for young children. Silence can denote that children do not understand and therefore are not reacting, or it can mean that they're still processing what they've been told and how they feel about the news. Respect this silence. Give your child a few moments to think and be still and then offer reassurance that you are here and willing to talk. Offer a hug or a gentle squeeze. This will remind your child that you love them, and it will allow some space for them to feel whatever they are feeling. Even if they do not understand what is happening, your child will sense your emotion, and the extra dose of comfort will ease any anxiety they may feel.

You know your child. Use that knowledge and take care not to jump to conclusions about how your child is feeling. Talking together again at different times will help you better understand how your child feels and what support is needed.

Additional Resources for Families

The Goodbye Book by Todd Parr. This simple picture book provides toddlers and very young children an opportunity to connect with the many emotions felt when saying goodbye to something or someone loved.

I Miss You: A First Look at Death by Pat Thomas, illustrated by Leslie Harker. This illustrated children's book introduces the concept of death and explains, simply but realistically, how all living things will die one day. The book and helps young children identify and label their emotions and come to terms with the big feelings of loss after someone they love dies.

Lifetimes: The Beautiful Way to Explain Death to Children by Bryan Mellonie and Robert Ingpen. This children's book provides a clear explanation of death, explaining how everything living has a beginning and will one day die—plants, animals, and people.

Something Very Sad Happened: A Toddler's Guide to Understanding Death by Bonnie Zucker, illustrated by Kim Fleming. This picture book is written to explain death simply to toddlers and preschool-age children while also providing appropriate emotional vocabulary. Color-coded words let you substitute the name and pronoun of the person who died as you read the book to your child.

Where Did My Friend Go? Helping Children Cope with a Traumatic Death by Azmaira H. Maker. This book, written for preschool- and early elementary–age children, carefully explains the sudden or traumatic loss of a friend. Through illustrations and simple text, the author answers common questions, labels emotions, and offers children suggestions on how to cope with the loss of a classmate or friend.

Death of a Teacher or Caregiver

Death in the school or other early childhood setting is painful for everyone and often creates changes in the day-to-day classroom dynamic. Grieving staff may find it hard to speak thoughtfully with children about the death, yet it's important to do so.

For young children, death is something abstract that somehow became a reality, and the death of a teacher, caregiver, or other staff member is particularly difficult for young children to process. The grown-up who was here one day is gone the next, and just being in the classroom may be a constant reminder of the loss. For a child, a teacher is much like a member of the family, and the death of a beloved teacher may be mourned in much the same way.

In talking with young children about the death of a teacher or another care provider, use very concrete terminology. Speak gently but be direct, using the words "dead" and "died." Young children generally lack a defined concept of death and often instead see death as a temporary absence. Children may need you to explain that death is permanent and that they will not see the adult again. Explain in simple, straightforward terms to children that everything that's alive will die one day. When we die, our bodies do not work anymore. Because children may not be able to take all this in, it's important to give them time to process and then to revisit the topic to answer any questions they may have. Be available to listen, offer comfort, and provide ways for young children to express their feelings.

Talking with Family Adults About the Death of a Teacher or Caregiver

When a teacher or caregiver dies, school leadership will generally send out a written notification to all families directly impacted by the death. In some situations, school leadership may also choose to tell parents via phone call or email, or in person. Guidance counselors in elementary school programs may also assist with informing families. Parents may have questions or want to discuss the death with other teachers, so it is important that all school staff are fully informed of what has happened and how the school leadership wishes the news to be shared and discussed.

It may be emotional for you to discuss with parents children's reactions to the death of your colleague. Being prepared with a simple, sensitive response can help you to both appropriately acknowledge the topic and determine what the parent expects from you in terms of supporting the child. For example:

- ▶ "I am sorry to hear that Anielle is worried about Ms. Kim. What has she asked you and how have you answered her?"

- ▶ "Thank you for letting me know that you've told Robin Ms. Kim is in heaven. Has that been comforting to him?"

Talking with Children: Conversation Starters

Some situations in which a child's teacher dies may lead to a planned discussion with the class or group of students. Remember, this needs to be discussed with parents first. Any family's request to exclude the child from a group conversation must be honored.

Here is an example of how the conversation might begin:

> **Teacher, Ms. Nichola, to the group:** "I want to talk about Ms. Shah. Some of you may already know that Ms. Shah died this weekend. This means we will not see her in the mornings or have her help in our classroom. Ms. Shah was a special teacher to me and to each of you. You may have some big feelings, and you can talk to me about these feelings. I have big feelings too, and I will miss her. You are allowed to talk about Ms. Shah. Do you have any questions?"

Difficult conversations are inevitable when working with young children, and this is especially true when a teacher who children were close to has died. The emotional charge of such conversations can be lessened by being prepared. The examples of responses here offer some language you might use. Remember to let the child lead the conversation and ask questions.

> **Emery, to another child:** "I don't want Ms. Shah to be dead. I want her to come back."
>
> **Ms. Nichola (later):** "Emery, I heard you talking to Chloe about Ms. Shah dying. I know Ms. Shah was a very special part of our school and was a teacher we all cared a lot about. I am sad that she is dead because I miss her too. While we know that she cannot come back, we can think about her and happy things we remember about her. Would you like to make a picture of something special you remember about Ms. Shah?"

The goal is to let the child know they are heard and to help them understand the death and their feelings about it. Here Ms. Nichola acknowledges objectively what she has overheard. She uses Ms. Shah's name, signaling that it's okay to discuss the teacher and her death. She also affirms Emery's and her own sad emotions, which tells Emery it's acceptable to express their feelings related to the death. Ms. Nichola guides Emery's understanding of death by reiterating that death is final and the deceased teacher is not coming back. She couples this with a suggested activity that offers a way to mourn by thinking of happy memories of Ms. Shah.

> **Meilani, to teacher:** "My mommy told me that Mr. Kenny died because of his heart. He isn't coming back to our school anymore."
>
> **Ms. Nichola:** "I am sad that Mr. Kenny died. He was a very kind man, and he did cook the best meals and snacks for all of us here at the school. You are right

that he is not coming back, but we can still think about him and talk about him. How do you feel about Mr. Kenny dying?"

Again, the goal is to make it safe for the child to talk about the death and to explore and express her feelings. The teacher leads by sharing her own emotions and does not assume how Meilani is feeling. Ms. Nichola reiterates the finality of death but then opens the dialogue for the child to feel comfortable talking about Mr. Kenny. The teacher acknowledges Meilani's statements and responds with an open-ended question, allowing the child to focus on her own emotions.

Colson, to teacher: "Are you going to die too?"

Ms. Nichola: "That is a big question. It sounds like you are thinking about Mr. Kenny dying. I am sad Mr. Kenny died, and I am even a little angry I did not get to say goodbye. Everything that is alive will die someday, but I am healthy and safe, and I am very glad to be here with you as your teacher today. Would you like to draw a picture of Mr. Kenny, or maybe a picture of you eating a lunch he made here at school? I would love for you to show it to me and tell me about what you draw."

The goal is to reassure the child. Note that the teacher uses very concrete language. She focuses on giving Colson a simple explanation of death but then reassures him of her presence in his life. The suggestion for Colson to draw and then talk about a picture sets the stage for him to channel his feelings into something tangible and then share them through words.

There are other activities to help children recognize, express, depict, or release feelings. Sharing and discussing stories helps the whole group, and children can return to books individually if they wish. Children might also play out interactions or feelings using puppets, dolls, or action figures. You might invite children to listen or move to music, sing or dance, or work with dough or fingerpaint.

Following Up

Following any conversation with children about the death of a teacher or care provider, it is appropriate and strongly advised that you connect with the family or families of the children involved in the conversation. Share with the family what the child said or asked and how you responded. Ask the family how they would like the conversation handled if their child asks another question or further discussion takes place. This forges a partnership between school and home and also gives families appropriate notice to prepare for follow-up conversations the child may wish to have with them. (For examples, see "Framework for Parent Conversation Starters" in Part I, page 12.) Check with the parent on the exact language they've used with the child so that any discussions at school use consistent vocabulary.

Offer the family handout "Talking with Your Child About the Death of a Teacher or Caregiver" (page 120).

A child may also approach you for further discussion. If a child seeks you out again, allow them to lead the conversation and try to keep it focused on how they are feeling. For example:

> **Emery:** "I don't understand why Ms. Shah can't come back! I want to see her."
>
> **Ms. Nichola:** "Death is hard to understand sometimes. Everything that is alive will die one day. You may have seen a flower or a tree die. Ms. Shah has died, and that means her body stopped working and that we will not see her again. While we will not see her face anymore, we still have lots of memories of her. What is the best thing you remember about Ms. Shah?"

> **Ms. Nichola, to the group:** "I have heard a lot of talk about Mr. Kenny dying and how sad we are. Mr. Kenny was a special part of our school community. It is sad that he was here last week and now will not be here anymore. Everything alive will die one day, and Mr. Kenny has died. This means we will not see him again. We can still talk about him though, and we can share memories of what we miss about him too. Would it help if we all made a card for Mr. Kenny's family letting them know how much we miss him and maybe sharing some of our favorite memories of him?"

Besides needing to understand the reality of death, children need to express and explore their feelings when they have lost someone important in their lives. Sharing memories and reaching out to the deceased person's family can help children through the grieving process and show them a way to cope with difficult or confusing emotions.

Talking with Your Child About
the Death of a Teacher or Caregiver

For children, the loss of a teacher or care provider can be sad, scary, and confusing. To a child, a teacher is much like a member of the family, and your child may mourn the death of a beloved teacher or another close adult in much the same way. Most children have a very difficult time making sense of the fact that someone who has been constant in their lives is gone forever. Places and activities where the teacher once was present are now a continuing reminder of the loss. Young children react to and exhibit grief differently from adults, and this needs to be considered when helping young children cope and accept the loss. Children's age and the amount of interaction they had with the person who has died make the greatest impact on how they respond. Family members may not feel the loss as acutely, so it's important to recognize how great it may be for your child. Speak thoughtfully about the death and stay open to ongoing conversations.

Young children generally lack a defined concept of death and often view it as a temporary absence. Grown-ups frequently use words with young children that seem softer than "dead" and "died," such as "gone to a better place," "no longer in pain," "sleeping forever," or "crossed the rainbow bridge." While adults readily understand these terms, the ideas can be confusing for a child and may arouse further anxiety. Instead, young children need very concrete terminology. Speak gently, but be direct, using the words "dead" and "died." Often young children's concept of death comes from cartoons where characters may die and then come right back. Your child may need you to explain that the death is permanent and that they will not see the teacher or caregiver again.

Explain in simple but direct terms that everything that is alive will die one day. When we die, our bodies do not work anymore. Explain that the teacher or caregiver's body did not work anymore and that they are dead.

Children need time to process the explanation, and their feelings about the loss are likely to change over time. Open, honest conversations are important. Encourage children to share what they feel. Offer comfort and provide them with ways to express those emotions.

In situations such as the death of a teacher or staff member at the school, your conversation may be the first time the child is hearing the news, so it is important to pick a time to talk when your child is well rested, calm, and comfortable. Start with a simple explanation of death and share the sad news, making sure to signal to your child that it's okay to discuss the topic. For example:

▶ "I need to talk with you about something. I know you know that people are alive, animals are alive, and even plants are alive. Everything that is alive will one day die. In people, when our bodies stop working, we die. When we die, we don't come back and that is the end of our life. I got a call from the director at your school, and she told me something that is very sad for me. Ms. Abdullah, your pre-K teacher, died today. That means her body stopped working, and we will not see her again. I know you loved Ms. Abdullah very much, and she was very special to Daddy and me too."

This example shows how death can be introduced to a young child. The goal is to give a straightforward explanation with enough, but not too much, information. Start by explaining what death is in very simple terms. Then share the news of the teacher's death and reiterate the finality of dying. Note that the adult in this example does not ask the child a question—the child needs time to absorb what they've been told. This is particularly important if it is a child's first exposure to or discussion of the death.

It is also important to explain to your child how you are feeling. This helps explain what children might observe and helps children understand that their own feelings are acceptable.

▶ "Alex, I think you saw your teacher Mr. Jenkins crying when we got to school this morning. Mr. Jenkins is very sad that Miss Claudia died. Miss Claudia was not your teacher, but she worked in your school for a long time, and she taught a lot of kindergarten students. It is sad for Mr. Jenkins that she is dead, and it is sad for me too. How do you feel about seeing Mr. Jenkins cry about Miss Claudia?"

This example acknowledges what the child saw and heard at school: his teacher exhibiting emotions. The parent explains simply what the teacher is feeling and why, using the words "died" and "dead." The parent also explains their own feelings. This is helpful, because children look to adults to guide behavior and emotional expression at times. Finally, the parent asks the child how he is feeling. Alex may be confused, worried, or upset or have another feeling about seeing Mr. Jenkins cry and about Miss Claudia's death. He may or may not be able to express what he feels.

Next, it's important to pause. The words are new, there is a lot of emotion to understand, and it may take the child a few moments to process what was said.

If your child's response is silence, that's okay. A simple follow-up question— "Are you okay? Do you have any questions for me?"—allows your child to respond if they wish.

Additional Questions and Answers to Consider

Your child may have questions, in the moment or later, that you will want to be prepared to answer.

Question: "Are you going to die too, Mommy?"

Answer: "Everyone will die one day, but I do not expect to die for a long time. I am healthy, and I am staying right here with you. I love you very much!"

This question likely reflects a child's anxiety and fear about the death of the adult at school. Children who ask this need reassurance that they are safe and that their family is safe. Be honest that everyone will die one day, but also offer comforting words to calm your child's distress.

Question: "Did it hurt Ms. Abdullah to die?"

Answer: "Ms. Abdullah's body stopped working and that is how she died. When her body stopped working, she did not feel anything. How are you feeling about Ms. Abdullah dying?"

The goal is to answer questions about the physical process of death in very simple terms. Young children cannot understand physiology, and attempting to explain bodily systems may generate greater anxiety. For example, saying that Ms. Abdullah was in a car accident may lead a young child to become fearful and anxious riding in a vehicle or having family members drive or ride. Note that the parent was careful in the words, "When her body stopped working, she did not feel anything." This is true. Even if a death was traumatic, it is best to minimize any details and keep things very broad. Give a simple explanation and then prompt your child to share their feelings with you. Young children need to know that it is okay to be angry or sad or both. They need affirmation that whatever they feel is okay and accepted.

Question: "Why did God let Mr. Paul die?"

Answer: "That is a very hard question to answer. Mr. Paul died because his body just could not live anymore, so it quit working. I am very sad about it, and I am angry about it too. I did not want Mr. Paul to die. Can you tell me how you are feeling about his death?"

Children may question religious teachings during emotional times, such as a death of someone close. Rather than try to explain difficult religious concepts, it is usually better to first focus on the feelings behind a child's question. This can help the child regulate. Save conversations and teachings about religion for a time when your child is older or more emotionally ready.

Also important in relation to death and dying are religious beliefs in an afterlife or reincarnation. Very young children may not be able to grasp these concepts. A young child may ask to go visit the teacher or may feel that person is still available to talk or play together but being kept from them.

Some families may choose to offer comforting faith-based responses, such as "Mr. Paul is with God now." Keep in mind the child's age, ability to understand, and familiarity with the faith concepts being offered.

Every family has a different spiritual and religious grounding, and of course you want to respond to your child in ways that fit your family's beliefs. At the same time, it's wise to look for the feeling behind the question and address that in a straightforward way. You may want to seek advice from a trusted priest, rabbi, minister, imam, or other spiritual advisor for ideas on how to answer your child's questions about the role of God or a higher power in a death in the family.

Preparing for Unexpected Responses

Young children aren't always aware of what "should" and "should not" be said. This lack of life experience can lead them to make statements that are unexpected and may feel hurtful. Preparing for such remarks and considering why a young child might respond this way can help you support your child and buffer yourself from emotional reaction.

Child: "At least no one else is going to die."

Adult: "You are correct that the rest of your teachers are safe and healthy. I am very sad that Mr. Perez died. I will miss him very much, and I know that you looked forward to his big high-five during morning drop-off."

A young child responding this way may be trying to contain the event or seek reassurance that others around them are not going to die soon. This does not necessarily mean the child doesn't comprehend and mourn the loss of the teacher or staff member. It's important to affirm the child's statement, reassure the child that other adults in the school are safe and healthy, and then remind the child of the death that did occur and how you yourself feel. Young children often look to adults to model how to express feelings. It is perfectly acceptable and appropriate to share with your child your sadness and anger about the loss of a valued teacher or staff member. The "feeling words" you use will help your child better express their own feelings.

Child: "It's okay that Miss Claudia died."

Adult: "I am sad that Miss Claudia died. She was your brother's teacher, and the other teachers at the school liked her a lot. Miss Claudia was a very special person to me, and I will miss her very much."

There is some comfort to be had in the naiveté of a young child's limited understanding. If it's not clear whether the child grasps the reality of the death, you may want to wait and try to explain again at some later point. It's still appropriate for you to label how you're feeling. Doing this doesn't negate what your child feels or does not feel, but it offers your young child a different perspective on how the death impacts you.

> **Child:** (silence)
>
> **Adult:** "I love you and you can talk to me. Would you like a hug?"

Death is a difficult concept for adults to handle, and it can be all the more complex for young children. Silence can denote that children do not understand and therefore are not reacting, or it can mean that they're still processing what they've been told and how they feel about the news. Respect this silence. Give your child a few moments to think and be still and then offer reassurance that you're here and willing to talk. Offer a hug or a gentle squeeze. This will remind your child that you love them and will allow some space for them to feel whatever they are feeling. Even if they do not understand what is happening, your child will sense the emotion in the family, and the extra dose of comfort will ease any anxiety they may feel.

You know your child. As you continue talking, use your own understanding of your child and take care not to jump to conclusions about how they're feeling. Talking together again at different times will help you better understand how your child feels and what support is needed.

....

Additional Resources for Families

The Goodbye Book by Todd Parr. This simple picture book provides toddlers and very young children an opportunity to connect with the many emotions felt when saying goodbye to something or someone loved.

I Miss You: A First Look at Death by Pat Thomas, illustrated by Leslie Harker. This illustrated children's book introduces the concept of death and explains, simply but realistically, how all living things will die one day. The book and helps young children identify and label their emotions and come to terms with the big feelings of loss after someone they love dies.

Lifetimes: The Beautiful Way to Explain Death to Children by Bryan Mellonie and Robert Ingpen. This children's book provides a clear explanation of death, explaining how everything living has a beginning and will one day die—plants, animals, and people.

Something Very Sad Happened: A Toddler's Guide to Understanding Death by Bonnie Zucker, illustrated by Kim Fleming. This picture book is written to explain death simply to toddlers and preschool-age children while also providing appropriate emotional vocabulary. Color-coded words let you substitute the name and pronoun of the person who died as you read the book to your child.

Big Conversations About Social Issues

"A school is a miniature society where children
learn to function in a real world."
—Marva Collins

Children live and must learn to adapt in a highly complex social world. Young children are learning who they are as individuals, who is there to care for them, and what it means to be a member of various social groups—their family, their culture, their ethnic community, their home community, their school community. They are learning how to accept others for who they are as individuals and becoming increasingly aware of the social intricacies of living in a diverse community and world. It's understandable that children will often question this complex world they are growing up in.

A classroom is a social setting, and thus a place where children's questions and observations about a range of social topics will arise. Children notice each other and have natural curiosity about things that are new or different to them. These observations might be about hair texture or skin color, cultural practices, gender, cognitive differences, or many other topics. Children also bring their observations from the outside world. While the situations and comments children present will vary, there are a few basic guiding principles that can help you prepare to talk with children about a range of social issues. The most important of these are to:

- ▶ stress respect, kindness, and a welcoming outlook toward all people

- ▶ affirm each child and each child's personal traits, family structure and circumstances, culture, and ethnicity

- ▶ emphasize that people are both similar and different and that differences are valued

Where possible, you'll want to speak with family adults before addressing an issue with their child, but many socially related topics may arise in your setting without this prior conversation. Whether families speak to you or not, when a conversation with a child comes up, allow the child to lead the conversation. In answering questions related to social dynamics, closely consider the child's developmental level. Within those parameters, answer children's questions directly and nonjudgmentally. Check back with parents when you and their child have spoken, and ask them how they want the topic approached.

As with all "big" conversation topics, children need simple, honest, respectful replies that are at a level they can understand. They need to be able to express their feelings and ideas and be affirmed and reassured. They need to know that what they seek to know is acceptable to discuss and that you are there to talk with them.

You, too, may want a safe place to reflect on your own responses to some topics; conversations around social issues may bring out intense personal feelings for you. Be sure to take time to examine and process these responses. Page 4 has information about forming a community of practice where, together, you and your colleagues can discuss and explore topics that affect you.

Race and Culture

Race is a social construct that we learn, implicitly and explicitly, starting early in life. When we talk about race, we focus on physical characteristics like skin color or hair texture. Culture is different from race: it's about how a group of people live—their interests, customs, and ways of interacting. The United States is a society composed of perhaps the most racially and culturally diverse population in the world, and oppression and prejudice are part of US history and present policies. Race and culture are part of everyone's identity, and talking about them with young children is important and does not have to be hard.

In a classroom, one of the roles of the teacher is to help children appreciate their own and others' uniqueness and see what they have in common; the differences make people special and make the world interesting and vibrant, while the similarities help us feel connected. Children are very apt to boldly state things they notice about others and to echo comments overheard from trusted adults. Therefore, it's important to always respond to the comments and questions of young children neutrally and calmly, recognizing that children are constantly seeking to understand and that the words they use, appropriate or not, are often repeated from something they've heard from someone else.

It's a misconception that young children do not see race. Young children are certainly able to visually discern differences among people's physical characteristics. Race, however, is a social idea that children learn about subtly and directly, starting in infancy. At home, young children are often encouraged (explicitly or implicitly) to identify with their own racial and cultural groups; yet, through overheard conversations and silenced questions, they also quickly learn that race and culture can be uncomfortable topics for adults. This dynamic leads children to have many questions.

How do young children develop a racial and cultural identity? Children as young as two begin to perceive and notice physical differences in others. By this point in development, children begin to absorb biases and stereotypes about themselves and others based on interactions with adults. Children this age may also begin to show preferences for playing with children of the same gender and skin tone. Children also show preference for familiar food, clothing, and cultural objects. By the time children are four years old, they seek labels for race and culture influenced by adult responses. A child may explicitly state that they are Jewish, that their mother wears a hijab, or that they are African-American or Ecuadoran or Vietnamese. By age five, children begin to take note of what it means to belong to one racial group versus another and may notice racial trends in terms of children's TV and movie characters, toys, and people in positions of authority (Derman-Sparks and Edwards 2019). Children this age may also repeat cultural and religious statements overheard by group leaders, such as telling another child that they are going to hell because they don't attend mass or telling another child that they should not eat meat because of their own family's dietary practices. By the time they reach elementary-school age, most children readily acknowledge their identity racially, culturally, and religiously and will repeat stereotypes and biases they've learned in their home and community.

When acts of blatant social injustice occur in society, adults naturally have strong emotional reactions. These reactions frequently lead them to explicitly coach their children to speak or behave in a certain way and to challenge or conform to what is happening socially. The young child, with an inherent curiosity to know why things are as they are, is apt to question the teachings and the reasoning behind why we do or do not say certain things or behave in certain ways toward others.

Less blatant but also hugely and continually impactful are microaggressions: subtle words and acts people use toward others, intentionally or not, that communicate racial or cultural bias. For example, someone may meet the parent of a Mexican-American child, assume the parent was not born in the US, and compliment them on their English-language skills. Or a White parent at the park may guide their child away from a game occurring among a group of Black children and encourage their child toward playing with other White children instead. People may not even recognize or understand that they are using microaggressions, but the effect on those receiving them can be very damaging. Children feel the hurt themselves and their confidence and self-esteem are eroded. They also observe adults' behaviors and responses.

Educators have a responsibility to uphold the value and self-esteem of all children in their care. Connecting with families and being open to understanding their perspectives and experiences is also important, as parents often teach young children specifically how to respond or not respond and encourage them to develop strong racial and cultural pride and identity.

And some aspects of culture are simply interesting to young children; a topic may not necessarily be touchy or uncomfortable to them but rather the subject of curiosity. For example, a child might ask a friend, "Why is your mom White and you're not?" or "Why does your daddy wear that little hat?" or "What's a pow-wow?" These questions inevitably turn back to race and culture and can lead to some very deep conversations.

Talking with Family Adults About Race and Culture

You may invite a cultural conversation with parents by sharing something from an exchange you've had with their child. A friendly inquiry or comment from you can show your interest and encourage the parent to help you know how you might support their child's cultural identity. For example:

▶ "Karlis was excited today about his Latvian music group and told me a little about Latvian Saturday School. Does he go to the school every week?"

- "I know you have shared that your family is Muslim. With Ramadan approaching, how can I best support Arif during this important time for all of you?"

- "Libby told us about her dragon kite she made with her daddy for the dragon festival. The children would love to see the kite and learn more about the festival. Would it be okay for Libby to bring her kite in to show us?"

When it comes to cultural or racial tensions, parents don't always share information, though they may do so at times. A simple, sensitive response from you can acknowledge the important topic and help you determine what the parent expects from you in terms of supporting their child. For example:

- "I am so sorry about the bullying and name calling that happened at the park this weekend. Thank you for telling me. I can understand that it was upsetting for Merrick. What has he said to you? Is there anything you've told him that I can reinforce here at the center?"

Talking with Children: Conversation Starters

Children will inevitably bring up race and culture, and the emotional charge of such conversations can be handled by being prepared. The examples of responses here offer some language you might use.

> **Sofia, at circle time:** "My cousin from Manila is coming to live here soon."
>
> **Brett:** "My mommy says too many people come here and they should stay in their own countries."
>
> **Teacher, Ms. Tameka:** "Many people come to live here from lots of different places. I wonder who else in our group has a family who moved here from a different country or has family in two places?"

The goal is to help children understand and appreciate that people come from different places and cultures. Because the topic was introduced in a large group, Ms. Tameka offers a simple and brief statement and then asks an open-ended question to involve children in the discussion in a developmentally appropriate way. Note that the teacher does not affirm or negate what children have learned at home. Instead, she turns the conversation to things children may have in common and adds context for them.

> **Josiah, to Oliver:** "You can't play with me because your skin is peachy colored and not brown like mine."
>
> **Ms. Tameka (in the presence of both children):** "Josiah, did you notice Oliver's face when you said that? In our classroom, we always treat each other with kindness and respect. I know you both love dinosaurs, and I think you'll have fun playing in the dinosaur cave. Shall I play with you?"

The goal is to help Josiah understand the impact of his words without shaming him, acknowledge Oliver's feelings, and help the children find common interests. Children who exclude others often do so on arbitrary terms ("I'm a girl and you're a boy," "It's my favorite toy"). Most children are not making racial or cultural exclusions pointedly, though they may if the movie or TV character they are role-playing is of a particular race. In all cases, you can remind children of the expectation of kindness, inclusion, and respect for all.

> **Mai-Lin, to teacher:** "My daddy said some White men killed a Black man just because he was Black."
>
> **Ms. Tameka:** "It sounds like you had a very serious conversation with your daddy. It is never okay to hurt other people. What happened makes me very sad and angry. It is important that we always treat each other kindly and respectfully. How do you feel about what your daddy told you?"

The goal is to acknowledge the serious topic and encourage the child to identify and express her feelings about what she's been told. Note that Ms. Tameka does not add any detail to Mai-Lin's statement. Instead, the teacher emphasizes the greater message of kindness, respect, and appreciation for others.

Following Up

Following any conversation with a child about culture or race, it is appropriate and strongly advised that you connect with the family or families of the children involved in the conversation. Share with the family what the child said or asked and how you responded. Ask the family how they would like the conversation handled if their child asks another question or further discussion takes place. This forges a partnership between school and home and also gives families appropriate notice to prepare for follow-up conversations the child may wish to have with them. Offer the family handout "Talking with Your Child About Race and Culture" (page 132).

Here are two examples; for more, see "Framework for Parent Conversation Starters" in Part I, page 12:

▶ "I wanted to make you aware of a conversation I had with Mai-Lin today. She talked to me about White men killing a Black man. She mentioned that her daddy told her the man was killed because he was Black. I don't know if you've discussed this with Mai-Lin in any more detail. She and I went on to talk about how important it is to always treat others with kindness and respect, and she told me she thought killing was scary and bad. How would you like me to respond if she brings this topic up again at school?"

▶ "During circle time, two of the children brought up the topic of immigration. I explained that many people want to come live in our country and we had a class discussion about people in our families who live in other places or who moved here from somewhere else. I wanted you to be aware of this in case the topic comes up or you want to talk more at home about it. I do have a resource on talking with children about race and culture, and I'm happy to give you a copy if you think it would be helpful."

A child may also approach you for further discussion. If a child seeks you out again, allow them to lead the conversation and try to keep it focused on how they are feeling. For example:

> **Josiah, to teacher:** "Oliver said I have dirty skin. That's not true!"
>
> **Oliver, to teacher:** "It looks dirty to me!"
>
> **Ms. Tameka (to Josiah):** "You're right, Josiah—you do not have dirty skin. People have lots of skin colors, and Oliver's skin and your skin are different colors."
>
> **(to Oliver):** "It's nice that people are different in some ways. It's fine to notice a difference, but we always need to remember to show respect and kindness when we talk about differences."
>
> **(to both):** "Skin color comes from something called *melanin*. Melanin is tiny bits of color we have in our skin. Everybody's skin has melanin. Oliver, your skin has a little bit of melanin and, Josiah, yours has more melanin. That is why your skin colors look different."

As always, the goal is to answer honestly and reassuringly without shaming either of the children, and in this case to provide very basic, accurate information about skin colors. Here, the teacher affirms Josiah while reminding Oliver to be kind. In simple terms she helps both boys understand that the difference in skin color is due to melanin levels—she provides factual information to help the children know why they have different skin tones.

Talking with Your Child About
Race and Culture

It is a common misconception that young children do not see race. Race can be seen in our appearance—our skin color, hair texture, face shape, and other physical features. Young children are certainly able to see differences in people's physical characteristics. Race, however, is a social idea that children learn about, subtly and directly, starting in infancy. Culture is different from race: it's about how a group of people live—their interests, customs, and ways of interacting.

Many aspects of race and culture are interesting to young children. For example, a child might ask a friend, "How come your hair is straight if your dad is Black?" or "What's that dot on your grandma's forehead?" or "What's a powwow?" Children are curious, and so they ask.

Children as young as two begin to sense and see physical differences in others and to absorb views about themselves and other people based on interactions with adults. By the age of four, a child may label their diet as kosher, say their mother wears a hijab, or share that they speak French at home. Soon after, they may start to make judgments about other people's ways of doing things. A child whose family is vegetarian may tell another child it's mean to eat meat. A child whose family is Christian may tell another child they're going to hell because they don't go to church.

Young children also learn early on that race and culture can be uncomfortable topics for grown-ups. They overhear our conversations. We may shush them when they ask questions about other people's skin tone, way of speaking, or beliefs. At the same time, many families encourage children to identify with their own racial and cultural group. This dynamic is not unusual, but it's confusing for children. Adults also coach children to speak or act in certain ways or to conform to, or challenge, some widely discussed social incidents, actions, and movements.

All these aspects inevitably turn back to race and culture and can open some very deep conversations. Young children don't necessarily mean to be unkind or inappropriate with their remarks or questions, and it's wise to respond calmly and without scolding. Children need to feel free to bring up things they wonder about. In talking with your child about race and culture, it can be helpful to focus on how people are different and how they're alike—the differences make us special and the similarities help us feel connected. Stress the importance of kindness and respect.

To talk with your child, start with a simple statement to let them know it's okay to discuss the topic. For example:

▶ "Kendra, I loved meeting your friends in your classroom today. You have friends who are boys and friends who are girls, friends who are tall and friends who are smaller, friends with different skin colors, friends with different kinds of hair, friends with different clothes, and friends with different names. Can you tell me more about some of your friends?"

The goal is to emphasize that differences are nice and to be expected. Here the parent acknowledges the child's diverse classroom, describes a variety of ways the children are different, and then asks Kendra to share more about her classmates. Kendra may talk about any number of differences—or likenesses. This parent might also ask what Kendra likes to do with her friends as a way to help her think about things they have in common. The prevailing message is about appreciating everyone and being kind and welcoming.

In explaining a specific cultural difference, use a respectful, matter-of-fact approach:

▸ "Robbie's mom told me today that Robbie can't come to your Halloween party. I know you wanted him to be here. Robbie's family does not celebrate Halloween like we do. Robbie is still your good friend, and you and he can play together when Halloween is over."

The goal is to be straightforward about a cultural difference and to reassure the child that the friendship remains. The parent breaks the potentially disappointing news in a way that shows respect for Robbie and his family. Reassuring her child and affirming that the children will be able to play together later also sends the message that differences don't need to keep people apart.

▸ "Jackson, I know you overheard me use a word you may not have heard before: *racism*. Racism is when people treat other people unkindly and unfairly just because of the color of their skin. This is never okay. You can be proud to be Black just like Daddy and me. We are kind and fair to other people—Black people, brown people, White people."

The goal is to be honest while affirming your child's identity and emphasizing kindness and acceptance. In this example, the mother acknowledges the word Jackson heard—racism—and then defines it in clear and simple terms. She uses the situation as an opportunity to support her son's positive racial identity and to stress that it's right to be kind and fair to people of all races.

After any exchange like this, it's important to pause. The words are new, there is a lot of emotion to understand, and it may take your child a few moments to process what you've said.

If your child's response is silence, that's okay. A simple follow-up question— "Are you okay? Do you have any questions for me?"—allows them to respond if they wish.

Additional Questions and Answers to Consider

Your child may have questions, in the moment or later, that you will want to be prepared to answer.

> **Question:** "At lunch, my friends all ate barbecue pork. I told them we don't eat pork and Amy wanted to know why. Why can't I eat pork like my friends do?"
>
> **Answer:** "We are Jewish. That is our religion, and part of our religion is keeping kosher. Pork is never kosher. We keep kosher to honor our beliefs, and that means we do not eat pork. Some of your friends have different beliefs, which is okay too. Our diet, what we eat, is an important part of our family and our religion."

The goal is to answer honestly and emphasize your family's cultural identity and beliefs. Long before young children can truly comprehend the complexities of faith and religion, they may question or challenge cultural practices. Explaining your family's beliefs and customs is important to helping your child develop a sense of cultural identity. When faith and religion play a part, spiritual leaders may be able to provide additional answers that can help your child better understand.

> **Question:** "Today, my friends said I couldn't be Princess Elsa because my skin is black. Why can't I be Princess Elsa?"
>
> **Answer:** "You can be; you would be a great Princess Elsa. Your friends might have said you couldn't be Princess Elsa because in the Elsa movie the cartoon character Elsa has white skin. Next time, you can tell your friends that you can be whoever you want to be. Remind them that we need to treat all people kindly and fairly."

The goal is to help your child challenge a stereotype while respecting herself and others. When children play together, racism can occur intentionally and unintentionally. It is important that parents help their children learn how to challenge the stereotypes they encounter. Children need reminders of kindness and fairness, too, both of which are concepts even young children understand well.

> **Question:** "Junie wanted to be Princess Elsa today, but I told her she can't because she's Black. Elsa's not Black, so Junie can't be her, right?"
>
> **Answer:** "It's true that Princess Elsa in the movie looks White, but Junie *can* be Princess Elsa. Anybody can be Elsa—Junie, or you, or another girl, or one of the boys. Next time, you can ask Junie to be Princess Elsa. How do you think she felt when you said she couldn't be?"

The goal is to help your child understand that stereotypes and exclusion are wrong and do not help people have fun and get along. The parent does not shame the daughter, but makes it clear that it was wrong to tell Junie she could not be Elsa because of her skin color. By explaining all the different children who might be Elsa, the parent also expands her daughter's understanding of how limiting stereotypes can be. Importantly, this parent also asks the child how Junie might have felt. This question opens the door for the daughter to grow in empathy and perhaps apologize.

> **Question:** "Why is my skin called white? It doesn't look white to me. It looks pink."
>
> **Answer:** "*White*, *black*, and *brown* are words we use to describe skin color, but they really are not the right words. Every one of us has different skin colors, and it is wonderful that we are all different and special. There are lots of other special things about people—the things they like, the things they do, the way they treat other people . . . Can you tell me some things that make you special?"

Children will frequently question the use of *black* and *white* to describe skin tone. A child who has learned colors in school is likely to point out that the color terms generally used to describe skin tones are inaccurate. Affirm a child for this observation. Ask your child to describe their skin to you. (Some children may offer their favorite color, such as blue or purple, rather than a color that is closer to the actual skin tone.) Then consider continuing your conversation by asking your child to describe other features of themself with a reminder that our skin tone is only one quality we have. We are all people with different personalities, likes, dislikes, quirks, character traits, and many other attributes.

Preparing for Unexpected Responses

Young children aren't always aware of what "should" and "should not" be said. This lack of life experience can lead them to make statements that are unexpected and may feel hurtful. Preparing for such remarks and considering why a young child might respond this way can help you support your child and buffer yourself from emotional reaction.

> **Child:** "Mom, I don't want to eat at Burhaan's house. The food is smelly and they talk loud and funny to his grandma."
>
> **Adult:** "Burhaan's family is from Somalia, Micah, and the language his grandma knows best is called Somali. Our language and food may seem very different to him too. Food we're not used to might smell or taste unusual to us, at least at first. It's not kind to call it smelly, though. That could hurt Burhaan and

his family's feelings. We are invited to Burhaan's for dinner next week, and I told his mother I would bring a salad. I'll make the one with pears and raisins so you'll have something you specially like to eat. Okay? And maybe you and Burhaan can sing your song for the family—his grandma might enjoy that."

A statement like this is most likely a child's honest expression of discomfort about being in an unfamiliar home environment. Young children who are comfortable in their own home are often uncomfortable in a home setting that feels different. This parent acknowledges her child's difficulty with the situation and uses respectful words to explain a little about Burhaan's family and grandmother. She also lets Micah know that the words he used could be hurtful, and offers a way to help make the next visit to Burhaan's house a little more comfortable. The mother helps support the children's friendship and, over time, Micah may begin the feel more at home with Burhaan's family.

Child: "I wish my skin could be white/black."

Adult: "You are made exactly the way you are supposed to be. I love you exactly like you are. Everyone is made differently, and that is what makes us so special. What do you like best about you? What makes you special?"

For young children, statements such as this might truly be a wish for what they don't have, or they could show some recognition of injustice experienced by one racial group from another. Affirm your child about their own physical appearance. An important follow-up question could be, "Why would you want your skin to be a different color?"

Child: "I hate White/Black people."

Adult: "*Hate* is a big word. You don't like what happened. I feel angry about it too. We do not hate people, though. We do not hate anyone because of the color of their skin. Even though bad things happen, people are mainly good and kind. It's important for us to always be kind to others. Most of the time they'll be kind back to us."

A child expressing a statement of hate needs to be guided to label and manage feelings. When children see racial or social injustice, anger and sadness are expected and appropriate. But young children need to be drawn away from broadening their response to everyone in a particular group. Generalizing like this leads to stereotyping, and true feelings of hatred lead to more hatred. Instead, help your child recognize and express emotions, such as fear and anger, and offer ways to manage or release those feelings.

Emphasize messages of mutual kindness and respect to help your child remain optimistic and open to accepting and looking for acceptance from others.

Additional Resources for Families

All the Colors We Are / Todos los colores de nuestra piel, by Katie Kissinger. This bilingual (English-Spanish) children's book explains in simple terms why people have variations in skin tone. Children will be drawn to the photographs and will work toward building a positive racial identity and appreciation for others.

Culture and Diversity by Marie Murray, illustrated by Hanane Kai. This picture book explains what culture is and how culture affects people's lives. With simple explanations and examples, children can learn to respect the cultural similarities and differences of others.

I'm Like You, You're Like Me: A Book About Understanding and Appreciating Each Other by Cindy Gainer, illustrated by Miki Sakamoto. A children's book that provides an introduction to diversity with colorful illustrations and fun text. Children will learn to appreciate and accept differences in themselves and others as the book explores hair color, hair texture, eye color, skin tone, homes, likes, dislikes, and more.

What If We Were All The Same! by C.M. Harris, illustrated by Eric Everett. This children's book is aimed at early elementary–age children and challenges the reader to think of what the world would be like if there were no diversity. By showing an alternate reality, the book then helps children understand why they should be proud of the defining features that make each of us special.

A World Together by Sonia Manzano. This picture book, written by Sesame Street's "Maria," offers a real-life photographic look into cultures and cultural practices around the world. The photographs are all accompanied with simple explanations to expose children to worldwide multiculturalism and help each child learn to appreciate their own cultural heritage and the cultural heritages of others.

Hunger and Food Insecurity

The United States Census Bureau reports that approximately 14 million children in the US directly experience food insecurity (Bauer 2020). The number of food insecure households, where parents may buffer children from feeling the effects of hunger, is greater still. In Canada, 1.2 million children live in households that are food insecure (Tarasuk and Mitchell 2020). Unemployment rates and low wages are directly related to the rates of food insecurity, because expenses like rent or a surprise repair bill can leave families with little money for food. Beyond the physical impact of hunger, there is added emotional stress on the household and family members. Families in this situation often feel shame or face judgment, but many families face food insecurity at some point. All families need healthy food, and the demands of food insecurity challenge the ability to provide this.

It's very likely that in your school or program there are children who are stressed by living in a family where there is not enough food each month as well as children who are hungry or undernourished. The combined effects of food insecurity and chronic stress in the home can seriously impact young children's health, physical and emotional development, school readiness, school performance, and behavior.

You may have situations in the classroom that require conversation around food scarcity or food insecurity. You might overhear discussions about faraway relatives starving in a drought-ridden area or about a family close to home who is using a local food bank. Or you may notice a new behavior change in a child, which could be tied to hunger or food insecurity. Some behavioral changes include aggression or bullying not usually observed, sudden significant weight gain or loss, asking to take some food home, ravenous ingestion of food beyond what would generally be expected, or attempting to hide food.

Talking with Family Adults About Food Insecurity

Given the attempt to buffer children from the effects of food insecurity and the associated shame felt by some families unable to sufficiently feed the household, food insecurity can be a difficult subject to broach. Often family adults will avoid sharing information about a lack of food at home. If a parent does approach you, a simple, sensitive response can help you respectfully acknowledge the situation and open a dialogue on how you can support the child at school. Possible responses might include:

▶ "I'm sorry your family is dealing with this. As you know, we do offer meals and snacks here at school, so I'll keep an eye out to make sure Brendan is eating throughout the day."

▶ "This must be very difficult for you. I'm glad you told me. Mabel usually leaves before our afternoon snack, and now I'll know to send a snack home with her."

Hunger and Food Insecurity: How Educators Can Help

While most public preschool and school-age programs have elements of food and snack provisions for children, that is not a consistent offering in private child care or private school settings. To find additional ways to fight childhood hunger in your school or program, please explore the following websites:

★ Resilient Educator has an article, "Hunger Pains: Teaching Hungry Students" by Jennifer Gunn (resilienteducator.com/classroom-resources/hunger-pains -teaching-hungry-students/)

★ National School Lunch Program (fns.usda.gov/nslp)

★ No Kid Hungry (nokidhungry.org)

Talking with Children: Conversation Starters

When dealing with the issue of food insecurity and hunger, it's important to make sure a hungry child gets something to eat and equally important not to single a child out in front of the group. As with any difficult conversation, being prepared is the key.

Your observations might lead you to suspect a child is not getting sufficient food at home. In that case, you might ask the child something like this:

▶ "Ariana, I see that you are trying to hide some of your snack in your pockets. Were you wanting to take some of the snack home with you?" (pause) "It's okay to take it home. I'd just like you to tell me more about why you want to save snacks for home."

Children may also let you know about issues with hunger or food insecurity. The examples of responses here offer some language you might use.

Jeanie: "I don't get breakfast at home anymore because Daddy isn't working. Do you eat breakfast at home?"

Teacher, Ms. Celeste: "I did not know you were not eating breakfast at home. Thank you for telling me. I do eat breakfast at home. Breakfast is important, and I can get you something to eat this morning. I will see what we can do to get you some food each day while you are here at school with us. Can you tell me more about mealtimes at home right now with Daddy not working?"

The goal is to respect and support the child and learn more about their food situation. Note that this teacher focuses on the statement behind the child's question. She acknowledges what Jeanie has shared and thanks her for trusting her with the information. This is particularly important in situations of potential food insecurity, as feelings of shame, embarrassment, or anxiety often occur. Ms. Celeste lets Jeanie know there are resources at school, and asks her to elaborate on the home conditions.

> **Pavel:** "When school got closed, I didn't have food at home. What do I do if school gets closed again?"
>
> **Ms. Celeste:** "I am sorry that you did not have enough food at home when school was closed. Now that I know that, I will do what I can to help you. Any time you have a worry like this you can talk to me about it."

The goal is to answer the child's question and offer both practical and emotional support. It is important to reassure Pavel of any available attempts to provide assistance and to follow through. Many schools and communities provide meal assistance for children during school breaks. A child like Pavel needs reassurance that the adults around him will do what they can to help. This will give him confidence and build trust. Secondarily, note how Ms. Celeste circles back to invite Pavel to talk more, now or in the future. Pavel may be scared, angry, or sad, or may even feel shame. Connecting to him emotionally can help her learn how best to support him. Ms. Celeste can then also offer a reassuring hug.

> **Yusef:** "The man on the radio said a lot of people are starving because they don't have enough food. Are we going to run out of food too?"
>
> **Ms. Celeste:** "That is a big question. There are people in our world who do not have enough food. We have food for you and all of our classmates here at school, and we will not run out of food here."

The goal is to answer the child's question honestly, at a level that is developmentally appropriate. Here, the teacher does not add any additional detail to what the child overheard. When children acknowledge having seen a news story or heard a radio broadcast or podcast, it is best not to assume specifics or add any additional depth. Yusef could have heard a local news story about community food insecurity, a national news story on food scarcity in other parts of the country or world, or a feature about an aid organization. To avoid providing details he may not know, Ms. Celeste answered the question simply with information relevant to him. This is a respectful way to acknowledge the question and affirm the child's security in the present environment. It's also possible that Yusef is thinking and talking about "other people" because his own family is experiencing food insecurity, so Ms. Celeste will need to circle back to learn more about the impetus for the boy's concerns.

Following Up

Following any conversation with a child about hunger or food insecurity, it is appropriate and strongly advised that you connect with the family or families of the children involved in the conversation. Share with the family what the child said or asked and how you responded. Encourage them to talk with their child and ask parents how they would like the conversation handled if their child asks another question or further discussion takes place. This forges a partnership between school and home and also gives families appropriate notice to prepare for follow-up conversations the child may wish to have with them. (For examples, see "Framework for Parent Conversation Starters" in Part I, page 12.) Depending on the situation, offer whatever resources or assistance you can, or provide the family handout "Talking with Your Child About Hunger and Food Insecurity" (page 142). For example:

▶ "I had a conversation with Yusef today where he shared with me that he'd heard a news story about people not having enough food. He asked if we were going to run out of food too. I wasn't sure what story he was referring to, and I was careful not to prod. I did assure him that he has food here at school. Has Yusef mentioned the news story or had any other concerns about food at home?"

▶ "I wanted to let you know that today, in a private conversation, Nora shared with me that there was not as much food at home as there used to be. She said she gets to eat but you sometimes do not. Nora also told me she feels sad about this and wants to help. Our family resource center has information about food pantries and meal programs here in our town. The family resource coordinator would be glad to speak with you and give you more information about this. Would you like to talk to her? Please let me know if there is anything I can do to help here at school. Is there something you'd like me to say or do if Nora talks to me about this again?"

Note: If you see continued indications that a child is routinely hungry or if you suspect a child's hunger indicates neglect, be sure to follow all mandatory reporting measures required by your state or province and those stipulated by your organization or school to protect the child.

Talking with Your Child About
Hunger and Food Insecurity

Conversations about hunger and food insecurity may surface after a child overhears a news story, interacts with a classmate, or sees adjustments being made around food in a friend's home or their own. Maybe your child tells you they want to save food to bring to school to give to a classmate. Or perhaps your child asks why you aren't offering some favorite meals or snacks right now. Your child may speak to you directly about a topic like this, or you may notice something and invite the conversation. For example:

▸ "I know you were listening when Daddy and I were watching the news this evening. The news was talking about how many people do not have jobs right now and this means it may be harder for some families to buy enough food."

▸ "You're right that we don't have some of your favorite foods in the cupboard. I do not have a job right now so I am not spending as much money on food as I used to. I am still doing all I can to make sure you get plenty to eat."

Many families face food insecurity at one time or another. The idea of not having enough food can cause anxiety both for young children experiencing food insecurity and for those who learn of other people' food shortages. When you talk about this with your child matter-of-factly and with understanding, you can help ease that anxiety.

When children ask questions, it is important to remember that they are seeking information. Simple answers and straightforward explanations are almost always all a child needs in the moment. Your family can decide the depth of information to share and the timing based upon developmental readiness and the situation.

▸ "I saw you looking in the refrigerator. I know we don't have a lot of food in there right now, but we have enough. Things are hard right now, but Daddy and I are doing all we can to keep you safe and healthy. Can I give you a hug?"

The goal is to help your child feel cared for and secure, even during a challenging time. You want to reassure your child and ease their anxiety without going on the defensive. This example provides an explanation that is simple and age-appropriate. It lets your child know that you will make sure they remain safe and healthy.

▸ "I heard you were asking about people who may not have enough food to eat. This is a struggle for some people in our community and in our world. Lots of organizations are working to help the people get the food that they need to feed their families. We're fortunate to have plenty of food, and we can help other people. Would you like to do something to help people who may not have enough food to eat?"

This example explains food insecurity in a simple and not-too-frightening manner. Affirming the child's safety and security is an important step to easing anxiety. Giving your child a way to help can empower them all the more and can make a difference for people in need. You might donate food from your own cupboards or volunteer to help sort cans at a food bank. Or you could start a donation jar at home where your child and other family members can collect coins for chores they complete in order to make a contribution to a food organization.

Next, it's important to pause. The words and the concept are new, there is a lot of emotion to understand, and it may take the child a few moments to process what was said.

If your child's response is silence, that's okay. A simple follow-up question— "Are you okay? Do you have any questions for me?"—allows your child to respond if they wish.

Additional Questions and Answers to Consider

Your child may have questions, in the moment or later, that you will want to be prepared to answer.

Question: "Do people die when they don't have enough food to eat?"

Answer: "We all need food to eat to keep our bodies healthy and strong. If people do not have enough food to eat, their bodies can become weak and unhealthy. Sometimes people can die from not getting enough good food to eat. There are lots of people who are working to stop hunger."

A child who inquires whether hunger might lead to death has likely already heard that it can. Answer the question honestly, and pair this with affirmations of community helpers and aid organizations to show your child that there are people trying to stop this from happening.

Question: "Why can't some people get the food they need?"

Answer: "Food costs money. Sometimes people do not have enough money to buy the food they need. There are places where people can go to get food for free when they need it."

Do not elaborate on what situations can lead to food insecurity unless your child asks. Volunteering that this may be related to job loss, for example, may unintentionally cause young children to fear such a thing happening to them. Instead, answer the question and reiterate the care organizations and services that are attempting to remedy this problem.

Preparing for Unexpected Responses

Young children are not always aware of what "should" and "should not" be said. This lack of life experience can lead them to make statements that are unexpected and may be off-putting. Preparing for such remarks and considering why a young child might respond this way can help you support your child and buffer yourself from emotional reaction.

> **Child:** "I'm glad we have all the food we want!"
>
> **Adult:** "I am happy about this too. We do have the food that we need to keep our family healthy and strong. We should still think about how we can help other people. It's important to care and to always try to help when we can."

A child saying this probably doesn't intend to be insensitive about other people's difficulties. Rather, the child is expressing pleasure, and possibly relief, about their own good fortune Affirm this and then remind your child to be empathetic and helpful toward others.

> **Child:** "I want to give our food away, so nobody is hungry."
>
> **Adult:** "You have a very kind heart. You are thinking of how to help other people, and that makes me very happy and proud of you. We can donate some food, and I think we can help in other ways too. How about if I find out more about how we can help people who don't have enough food?"

This child's show of empathy reflects emotional maturity. When your child expresses a selfless desire to help others, affirm that impulse and help them find ways to channel it into a mindset of service and social responsibility.

> **Child (in regard to another person's food insecurity):** "I don't care."
>
> **Adult:** "It is important that we do care. You can be very glad that we have plenty of food to eat in our family, but other people do not, and that makes me sad. We want to always be happy for what we have. We need to also try to think of how we can be kind and helpful to other people. People will help us if we ever need help, and we need to help others when we can."

Young children are naturally egocentric, and it's important not to scold or scoff in response to a comment like this. Instead, gently guide your child to take a broader perspective and see where the needs of others may differ from their own needs. Kindness and helpfulness are two concepts that young children can grasp well, so these are good concepts to start from in helping young children learn to have empathy toward other people.

> **Child (in regard to their own family's food insecurity):** "I don't care."
>
> **Adult:** "I want us to be able to buy whatever we want and eat all the things we love most. I know you miss your special treats—I miss some too. But right now we need to be more careful about which foods we choose so we can stay healthy. We are all right, though, and we love you very much. How about a hug?"

In this situation, a child's "I don't care" may mean the child wants special foods and snacks despite the family's troubles. Alternatively, the child could be trying to show support by stating that they accept the situation. To the extent possible, always reassure your child about their own security. Showing empathy and love will comfort your child and increase that sense of security.

....

Additional Resources for Families

Lulu and the Hunger Monster™ by Erik Talkin, illustrated by Sheryl Murray. This compelling book is written from the perspective of a young girl and her personal experience with hunger. This book introduces some of the effects of hunger and focuses on the resilience of Lulu and the helpfulness of others.

Maddi's Fridge by Lois Brandt, illustrated by Vin Vogel. This children's book written for early elementary–age children tells the fictional story of two friends when one learns the other is facing food scarcity. Through an engaging but simple storyline, children are guided through how to be supportive, understanding, and empathetic when others face adversity.

Uncle Willie and the Soup Kitchen by DyAnne DiSalvo-Ryan. This beautifully illustrated book explains both hunger and homelessness in a child-appropriate manner. This book is a great introduction to service learning as the story explains soup kitchens and volunteerism.

Physical and Cognitive Differences

Adults who do not have disabilities, or do not know people who do, often wonder how to talk about a person with a disability, or even how to interact with someone who has a physical or cognitive challenge. Potential feelings of awkwardness stem from not knowing how the person regards their condition, not being sure what's acceptable to talk about, and not being confident in the words to use. Certain disabilities have marked physical distinguishing characteristics, while others can be more difficult to discern. This may lead an adult to further question what to say, how to act, how to accommodate the person's needs, and how the person may respond.

Young children tend to be far less hesitant. Young children can recognize that people have unique features that make each person an individual. They notice what is different from their own experience or from what they know. This natural curiosity leads to questions such as why another person is in a wheelchair, has a hearing aid, doesn't speak clearly, or doesn't join in. How we respond to a child's questions about these personal differences is important. The child is truly seeking to understand and should be answered respectfully.

First, acknowledge the curiosity and answer questions very matter-of-factly. Stress to children the *person* separate from the disability. When explaining why a person behaves or speaks a certain way or uses assistive devices, do not refer to people who do *not* have such exceptionalities as "normal"; this implies that people with disabilities are "abnormal." Remind young children to always treat others kindly and respectfully. Also emphasize ways in which people are the same, so children perceive and seek unity and inclusion as opposed to exclusion.

Talking with Family Adults About Physical and Cognitive Differences

When children with diagnosed differences or medically supported accommodations enroll in an early childhood or elementary program, the school will work closely with the family to ensure the right accommodations are in place in the classroom. While it's always important for all teachers involved with any child to collaborate closely, it's especially critical in the case of a child with special needs. Equally important is communication between families and teachers. Teachers need to not only fully understand the accommodations for the child but also have time to openly talk with the family. The conversation should be built around learning about the child's interests, learning style, and preferences, not the cognitive or physical difference. The conversation will naturally go that way eventually, but, if possible, allow the family to volunteer it. Parents of a child with a disability are often strong advocates for their child and can offer many insights along with critical information. To open up a first conversation, you might say something like this:

▶ "I am so pleased to welcome Mischa into our classroom. Can you tell me about her and what her interests are? I want to be sure I can provide a warm transition for her into our classroom, so I appreciate anything you can tell me about her."

Talking with Children: Conversation Starters

Difficult conversations are inevitable when working with young children, but the emotional charge of such conversations can be lessened by being prepared. Some parents may request a group conversation with the other children about their child and their child's exceptionality. Other times group conversations may lead naturally from books about inclusion or about children with physical or cognitive differences. The examples here offer some language you might use. Remember to let the child lead the conversation and ask questions.

> **Teacher, Mx. [miks] Darnel, to class:** "I am very excited to share with you that someone new is joining our class today. His name is Lincoln, and he is five years old, just like most of you. Lincoln has one sister and a pet dog, and his favorite thing to do is play with his toy cars. Lincoln and his family also want you to know that he has something called autism. Because of his autism, Lincoln does not like loud sounds and he does not speak much. When Lincoln is in our classroom, he is going to have a special helper who comes and helps him communicate. I'm happy Lincoln is going to be in our group. Let's all welcome him and be kind and helpful while he learns about our classroom and about our routine here in kindergarten. Do you have any questions?"

The goal is to prepare children to welcome a new classmate who has some physical and cognitive differences. The teacher first emphasizes the similarities between Lincoln and the other children. As the family requested, Mx. Darnel introduces the term *autism*, briefly describes some of Lincoln's traits and behaviors related to his autism, and explains that an aide will come support him in the classroom. Then the teacher sets expectations for children to welcome and help the newcomer. Finally, Mx. Darnel invites questions, letting children know it's okay to be curious and setting the stage to clear up any confusion and make the new child's transition to the classroom as smooth as possible.

> **Franco, to teacher (during storytime):** "Why does that girl have those things on her legs?" (points to book illustration)
>
> **Mx. Darnel:** "That is a good question. This picture shows a child who has a difference from the other children in the story. What Franco noticed is these metal braces on the bottom of this girl's legs. Some of us wear glasses to help us

see better, and the girl in our book wears braces on her legs to help her stand up stronger. I don't know why she has the braces, but I do know they will help her legs be stronger and help her walk and play. We're all made differently, and we're also alike in many ways." (points to illustration) "This girl likes to play and ride a scooter. I am happy there are things like leg braces and eyeglasses to help children who need them. What are some things about you that make you special and unique?"

The goal is to give a straightforward answer and emphasize the similarities among all children. The teacher uses the child's question about a character in a book to lead into a conversation about physical differences. Mx. Darnel emphasizes the child first and the physical support equipment second. They make a comparison of the child's leg braces to eyeglasses, which young children are likely to be more familiar with.

Sandrita: "Will Dionne ever get better from her Downs syndrome?"

Mx. Darnel: "Dionne is made the way she is, and she will always have Downs syndrome. She is six years old just like you, and she is here to learn and to make friends just like you. How can we make sure that we include Dionne?"

The goal is to answer the child's question honestly and encourage her to be accepting and welcoming. Mx. Darnel acknowledges the permanency of Dionne's physical and cognitive difference while also emphasizing that she is like other children in the classroom in many ways. The teacher provides a direct but gentle reminder of inclusivity and invites Sandrita to think of ways to make Dionne be welcome and take part with others.

Child: "Why does Aarush talk like that?"

Mx. Darnel: "We are all made differently. Aarush was born with ears that are not able to hear sounds the same way your ears do. He learned to talk without hearing other people's words very clearly, and so the words he says sound different. The doctors put a special hearing implant in his ear, and this now helps Aarush hear sounds more like you and I do. He still speaks in his own way, though. I can understand Aarush very well, and I think you can too. I'm glad we can all talk and understand each other. We are all different and that is what makes us interesting and special."

Again, the goal is to answer the question and encourage inclusiveness. If the teacher knows the cause of the speech or behavioral difference, it is acceptable to explain this in very simple terms to the child. Children asking such questions are being curious, not critical. After explaining the cause for the speech or behavioral difference, again emphasize that we all have differences and ways we're alike.

> **Gee-Gee:** "Can I try out Ty's wheelchair?"
>
> **Mx. Darnel:** "No. Ty uses his wheelchair to be able to move about our classroom. His wheelchair works like legs to help him get around. We need to treat Ty's wheelchair as part of his body and remember that it's something that helps him. You can ask Ty to show you how it works. I think he'll be happy to show you."

The goal is to make it clear the wheelchair is not a toy and is for Ty only, while fostering curiosity and friendliness between the two children. The teacher gives a kind but direct "no" and guides Gee-Gee to understand that the wheelchair is a personal item that has an important purpose just for Ty. In suggesting Gee-Gee ask Ty to show her how the wheelchair works, Mx. Darnel sets a tone to break down possible discomfort or awkwardness and encourages her to talk directly to Ty about his assistive equipment.

Following Up

Following any conversation with a child about physical or cognitive differences, it is appropriate and strongly advised that you connect with the family or families of the children involved in the conversation. Share with the family what the child said or asked and how you responded. Ask the family how they would like the conversation handled if their child asks another question or further discussion takes place. This forges a partnership between school and home and also gives families appropriate notice to prepare for follow-up conversations the child may wish to have with them. Offer the family handout "Talking with Your Child About Physical and Cognitive Differences" (page 151).

Here are two examples; for more, see "Framework for Parent Conversation Starters" in Part I, page 12:

▶ "I wanted you to know that today during morning meeting, a classmate asked about why Madison has a hearing device. Madison didn't seem bothered by the question and she explained her implant to her classmates herself. I was proud of how she handled it, and I'm happy to talk more about this with the class if you would like that or if you think Madison would."

▶ "I thought you'd like to know about a conversation I had with Demetrius today. He asked me why one of his classmates talks differently. The classmate that he wondered about has a speech impediment. I explained a little bit to him about it, and I think he might bring it up at home. I have an information sheet on talking with children about differences like this, and would be happy to give you a copy if you like."

A child may also approach you for further discussion. If a child seeks you out again, allow them to lead the conversation and try to keep it focused on how they are feeling and how to support each child involved. For example:

Sandrita: "I don't want to play with Dionne. She can't kick the ball and it's not fun to play then."

Mx. Darnel: "I understand it may be different playing with Dionne, but we need to treat everyone kindly. Dionne is your classmate just like everyone else, and she likes having friends to play with too. Maybe instead of soccer you could ask her to draw with you. Yesterday, I noticed that she drew a picture of a rainbow using all different crayons. I know you like to draw too, so you might have fun doing that together. Would you like me to help you invite Dionne to draw with you during free time?"

Mx. Darnel does not scold Sandrita for her hesitancy to interact with Dionne. Instead of scolding, acknowledge a child's feelings and then focus on kindness and fairness, which are concepts young children understand well. Gently guide the child to seek alternate ways of interacting with the classmate in a way that may be more enjoyable for all.

Talking with Your Child About
Physical and Cognitive Differences

Young children understand that we all have unique features that make each of us an individual. They notice what is different from their own experience or from what they know. This natural curiosity leads to questions such as why another person uses leg braces to walk, has a hearing aid, doesn't speak clearly, or doesn't join in. Children might ask these questions about a classmate or family friend or when they encounter a stranger. How you respond to a child's questions about these personal differences is important. Your child is truly seeking to understand and needs thoughtful, respectful answers.

First, acknowledge the curiosity and answer questions very matter-of-factly. Stress to your child the *person* separate from the disability. When explaining why a person behaves or speaks a certain way or uses assistive devices, do not refer to people who do *not* have such exceptionalities as "normal." This implies that people with disabilities are "abnormal." Remind your child to always treat others kindly and respectfully. Importantly, be sure to also emphasize how people are the same, so your child recognizes what we all have in common and seeks to include and learn about others rather than exclude them.

▶ "I noticed you looking at the woman who was in a wheelchair. Her wheelchair makes her unique in one way, but in many ways she is like you and me. She is shopping for groceries just like us. The lady's wheelchair works as her legs to help her move. It's okay to notice that she has a wheelchair, and it's good to be respectful and give her room to get by. But we don't want to stare—staring isn't respectful."

▶ "Your teacher said you have a new friend in your class named David. David is four years old, just like you. He loves to run and play. David has Downs syndrome, so you might notice that he looks a little bit different from you and sometimes it might take him a little longer to learn something. Otherwise David is a happy, healthy little boy just like you."

Next, it's important to pause. The words are new, there is a lot of new information to understand, and it may take your child a few moments to process what you've said.

If your child's response is silence, that's okay. A simple follow-up question—"Are you okay? Do you have any questions for me?"—allows them to respond if they wish.

Additional Questions and Answers to Consider

Your child may have questions, in the moment or later, that you will want to be prepared to answer.

Question: "Do I have to play with Simon? He cries and yells when it's not his turn. Sometimes he gets really bad—he hit himself one day!"

Answer: "Simon has autism and sometimes has a hard time handling his big feelings. He is six years old just like you, and he likes a lot of the same things you do. I understand that he gets very upset sometimes, but he wants friends just like you do. Maybe there is another way you could play with Simon. Does he like trains? You could play together with your train set. I would like you to think of ways you could play with Simon because we all need kind friends."

Question: "A girl in my class talks with her hands because she can't hear. She has a helper in the class who talks for her. How can I be her friend if I can't talk with her?"

Answer: "If your new classmate talks with her hands because she can't hear, she is using sign language. Sign language is her way of talking. I bet her helper can teach you some signs to be able to say hi and introduce yourself. You could also play with her while she has her helper to talk for her. It will be different than playing with some other classmates, but I think it could be fun and you'll have a chance to learn her language."

The goal is to encourage children to be open to differences and to find ways to under-stand each other and get along. In these examples, the parents acknowledge the difficulty their children face in befriending other children with special needs and then offer ideas for activities that might help them enjoy time together. Let your child know you want them to be open and welcoming, and help them think of ways to overcome barriers. Remind them of what they have in common—shared interests, a wish for friendship. While new problems may still arise, all the children involved will benefit from learning ways to be kind and include others who are different from themselves in some ways.

Preparing for Unexpected Responses

Young children are not always aware of what "should" and "should not" be said. This lack of life experience can lead them to make statements that are unexpected and may feel hurtful. Preparing for such remarks and considering why a young child might respond this way can help you support your child and buffer yourself from emotional reaction.

> **Child:** "That lady putting our groceries in the bag asked me funny questions. Is she retarded?"
>
> **Adult:** "The lady who helped with our groceries has a brain that works a little differently than ours. She is a helper and was being friendly to you—that is why she asked you so many questions. *Retarded* is not a kind word. Remember that we're always kind to other people and we speak kindly about them. Next time, you can smile and talk with her. Maybe you can ask her name and tell her yours. That will show her that you're friendly too."

Words matter. Children hear words in conversations, through media exposure, and from other children, and it is important to help children understand that some words are degrading or hurtful and to discourage the use of those words. Experts who, years ago, used the term "mental retardation" now refer to *intellectual disabilities* or *intellectual developmental disorder*. In this situation, do not scold your child for the using the term, but gently guide them toward seeing the positive attributes in others and toward appropriate behavior responses and language.

> **Child:** "I'm glad I don't have Downs syndrome."
>
> **Adult:** "I am happy that you are happy and healthy. David is a happy, healthy boy too. We all have special things that make us who we are—how we look, how we talk, who our friends are, and even what we like. No one is the same, and I like that. What is something that makes you special?"

A child responding this way may be expressing self-pride as well as showing empathy for the challenges faced by someone with a physical or cognitive disability. Affirm how much you like your child exactly the way they are, and then affirm the other individual's value and self-worth as well. This shifts your child's mindset away from noticing disabilities to seeing positive traits and commonalities. Use feeling words and ask your child to share what they like best about themself, to help them practice this view focused on attributes.

> **Child:** "I don't want to be friends with Andrew because he talks funny and moves his hands like this." (mimics Andrew's actions)
>
> **Adult:** "It's important that we are kind and friendly to everyone. Andrew has autism. He may talk and act in a different way than you at times, but everyone needs a friend. Can you think of a game you can play or a toy that Andrew might like too? Do you think he likes playing with race cars as much as you do? I would be very proud if you could find a way to include him, and I think you might feel happy if you do that."

For a child encountering a peer with a special need for the first time, there can be discomfort in knowing how to interact, what to say, and what questions to ask or not ask. This may lead some children to shy away. Remind your child how important it is to include others and to be open to making and being a friend. Affirm your belief that your child is able to do this and assure them of how proud they will feel in doing so. If possible, you may want to help facilitate the interaction to help show your child what they have in common with the other child.

Additional Resources for Families

Accept and Value Each Person by Cheri Meiners, illustrated by Meredith Johnson. This picture book depicts a wide variety of children and discusses how to respect differences in others, be inclusive, and learn to value other people for exactly who they are. This book is clear and straightforward, with real-life illustrations, and includes discussion prompts and activities that will help further conversations with children.

Different Just Like Me by Lori Mitchell. This book celebrates diversity in ability, age, and support equipment usage as a young girl explores her community around her. Through this character's interactions in her community, she learns that she has more in common with people than differences with a resounding message of inclusion.

Ian's Walk: A Story about Autism by Laurie Lears, illustrated by Karen Ritz. This award-winning children's book tells the story of Ian, who has autism, from the viewpoint of his sister. Through childlike text and images, children are introduced to autism and some more common behaviors of children on the autism spectrum.

You Are Enough: A Book About Inclusion by Margaret O'Hair and Sofia Sanchez, illustrated by Sofia Cardoso. An upbeat, colorful picture book inspired by a young actress with Downs syndrome, this book highlights all kinds of disabilities and differences—physical, cognitive, cultural—and emphasizes how children can enjoy, help, and learn from one another.

Family Structure

Families are formed in a variety of ways, and children in your setting are likely to come from a range of differing family compositions. Children may live in one-parent families, two-parent families, stepfamilies, or foster families. They may have parents or caregivers of different genders or the same gender. The adults who care for children may be their parents, grandparents, or other people.

With the divorce rate in the United States somewhere in the range of 40–50 percent of marriages, many children have divorced parents and thus have varied living arrangements (APA 2021). Some children split time evenly between two parents, while other children reside primarily or solely with one parent. Many live in one or more stepfamilies. Multigenerational households are on the rise as well, with estimates showing 1 in 4 families in the US to be multigenerational (Generations United 2021). And while exact statistics vary, in the US approximately 2 million to 3.7 million children under the age of 18 may have a parent who is gay, lesbian, bisexual, or transgender (Gates 2015).

The families you serve and the people who work beside you in caring for and teaching young children all have their own distinct idea of what *family* means. Family helps inform the basis of a child's own identity and is thus an essential concept to young children. Children learn that family are the people present in their life at home; they learn how people in families relate to each other based on the interactions they have with these people. Because family is an important central concept to young children, they will naturally talk to one another about their own families. Children also watch TV, videos, movies, and apps, and family structures in media portrayals are continually shifting, allowing children to see depictions of themselves and their families and also introducing children to family structures that are different from their own.

When children first learn about family structures that are new or unfamiliar to them, it is natural and expected that they may have questions. At the same time, every family loves their children and all children should feel validated in loving their families. Just as individuals are unique, so too are families. Children can understand and accept this when it's explained in simple terms.

Talking with Family Adults About Family Structure

Many families share about their family structure and their child's family members when joining a school or classroom. Some programs may have forms that specifically ask about who is present in the child's home. Beyond this, some families may readily share with teachers about their specific family structure. A simple, sensitive response from you can help families feel accepted and support a strong school-home relationship. For example:

Shea's grandfather: "I see on the calendar that there's a Muffins for Mom event at the school next week. My wife and I raise Shea—we're her grandparents. Shea's mom and dad are both out of the picture, so we raise her as our own. Shea sometimes gets upset when special things about moms come up. We're worried what she'll think about Muffins for Mom."

Teacher, Ms. Conner: "I'll be sure to let Shea and all the children know that they may have whoever they wish come to school for Muffins for Mom. You, her grandmother, or any other family member or friend are invited to attend with Shea. I'm so glad you talked with me about this. We want all our school events to be for all families, and I'm sure there are others who are wondering about this as well. I will share this with the staff here so we can think about different themes for events like this so children and families will be sure to feel as welcome as we want them to feel. Thank you for bringing this up."

Ozzie's mom: "I wanted you to know that Ozzie is not just an only child but I am a single parent. His dad and I were never together, and he is not in the picture at all. It is just Ozzie and me. Sometimes he'll talk about wanting a dad, so I wanted you to know."

Ms. Conner: "Thank you for sharing that with me. If Ozzie does mention anything about wanting a dad, how would you like me to respond to him?"

Talking with Children: Conversation Starters

Some children may readily volunteer information about their family arrangements. Other times conversations may lead naturally from observations about books during storytime or from children's questions. You can manage the emotional charge of such conversations by being prepared. The examples of responses here offer some language you might use. Remember to let the child lead the conversation and ask questions.

Matias, to Keshawn: "I saw your daddy this morning. I have *two* daddies!"

Keshawn: "No, you don't! You can't have two daddies! I'm going to ask Ms. Connor."

Keshawn, to teacher: "Matias said he has two daddies. I told him he does not but he said he does. He can't have two daddies, can he?"

Ms. Conner, in the presence of both children: "Yes, Keshawn, Matias does have two daddies. Every family is different. Some families have a dad and a mom, some families like Matias's have two dads, some families have two moms, some have just a mom, some have just a dad. There are many kinds of families. Matias's daddies love him just like your mommy and daddy love you."

The goal is to answer the child's question respectfully and affirm both children's family arrangements. Ms. Conner explains that families can have a variety of structures and that everyone's family is accepted. She draws attention to similarities between the children by emphasizing their parents' love for each of them.

> **Nora, to Adele:** "Is that your stepmom? Is she mean like Cinderella's stepmom?"
>
> **Adele:** "No—she's not mean. Her name is Trish and she's nice."
>
> **Nora:** "My sister said a stepmom can't love you like a real mom."
>
> **Adele:** "That's not true. Trish loves me."
>
> **Ms. Conner, stepping in:** "I hear you two talking about stepmothers. Adele, you're right that your stepmom Trish is nice, and I know she loves you. Nora, *Cinderella* is a make-believe story. That stepmother isn't real. Most stepmothers are kind people who love every child in their family. Some families have a mom and dad, and some have a stepmom and a dad or a stepdad and a mom. There are lots of different kinds of families, and people in families love each other."

The goal is to reassure Adele and make sure both children understand that a stepparent loves and cares for the children in their care. Nora is not necessarily trying to be mean; she is stating what she knows from her own exposure to the idea of having a stepmother. Adele seems confident about her stepmother's love, but the teacher takes advantage of this moment to help expand Nora's understanding of family love while at the same time affirming Adele.

> **Jocko, during storytime:** "That girl doesn't have a daddy. I don't have a daddy either. I have my mom!"
>
> **Ms. Conner:** "Yes, the girl in our story is like you—she doesn't have a daddy. Some people don't have a daddy and some people do. Can anyone tell me something else they notice about the girl's family?"

The goal is to affirm the child's observation, and his family situation, and then refocus the group on the story. By asking what children notice about the character's family, Ms. Conner can open up the discussion to other ways families are alike and different.

Following Up

Following any conversation with a child about family structures, it is appropriate and strongly advised that you connect with the family or families of the children involved in the conversation. Share with the family what the child said or asked and how you responded. Ask the family how they would like the conversation handled if their child asks another question or further discussion takes place. This forges a partnership between school and home and also gives families appropriate notice to prepare for follow-up conversations the child may wish to have with them. (For examples, see "Framework for Parent Conversation Starters" in Part I, page 12.) Check with the parent on the exact language they use with the child so that any discussions at school use with consistent vocabulary. Offer the family handout "Talking with Your Child About Differing Family Structures" (page 159).

A child may also approach you for further discussion. If a child seeks you out again, allow them to lead the conversation and try to keep it focused on how they are feeling. For example:

> **Keshawn:** "I asked my mommy, and she said it's better to have a mom and a dad than to have two dads. I'm glad I have a mommy and a daddy."
>
> **Ms. Conner:** "You love your mommy and daddy, and they love you. There are many kinds of families who love each other: families with a dad and mom, families with just a mom or just a dad, families with two moms or two dads, and other kinds. I'm glad you're happy in your family."

The goal is to affirm the child's family and emphasize the value of all families. Ms. Conner does not question what Keshawn's mother has told him. Instead, she emphasizes his family's love and the love all families have for each other.

> **Shea:** "I don't like Mother's Day because I don't have a mommy. I have Grandma and Grandpa."
>
> **Matias:** "I have Papa and Daddy, and we have Papa's Day instead of Mother's Day. And we have Daddy's Day instead of Father's Day."
>
> **Nora:** "I like Mother's Day! We give Mommy breakfast in bed, and I help make it. She says it's her favorite day of all."
>
> **Ms. Conner:** "Families are all different and that's something that makes each of our own families so very special to us. Mother's Day is one way to celebrate a family and Father's Day is another. Did you know there is also a Grandparents Day? There are lots of ways to have special times for people in our families, aren't there?"

The goal is to affirm each child and their family traditions, and to support a child who is feeling left out. Here the teacher acknowledges the ideas the children shared and finds a logical and helpful way to point Shea to a way to celebrate her grandparents. This might lead to planning various inclusive events for children and families or to helping Shea learn more about Grandparents Day. The teacher might also follow up this conversation by sharing a book such as *Stella Brings the Family* (about a girl who brings her two daddies to a school Mother's Day celebration) or *The Family Book* by Todd Parr (about love in families of all varieties). Find other book ideas on the subject of family on page 163.

Talking with Your Child About
Differing Family Structures

Family is an important concept for a child, the basis of a child's identity. Children first understand the concept of family as the people in their own home. Grounded in this, they will be curious when other children's family structures, living arrangements, practices, and traditions are different from their own. Whether from watching children's programming and other TV, videos, and movies or from making day-to-day discoveries about other children's families, your child is bound to come to know about differing family structures. It's natural that this will lead to questions.

Young children know that individuals are different and have unique qualities that make them special. You can draw this same parallel when speaking with your child about the concept of family: every family is different and has unique qualities that make it special. Children will understand and accept this when it's explained in simple terms.

You can start a discussion about differing family structures with a simple prompt, signaling to the child that it's okay to talk about the topic. For example:

▶ "I enjoyed watching that TV show with you. I think you noticed that the boy named Gerald had a family that was a little different from our family. What did you notice about Gerald's family that's different from ours?"

The goal is to open a conversation about different types of families. If your child identifies how the family structure differs from yours (for example, having both a mom and a dad rather than a single parent or having two dads rather than a dad and a mom), use this as an opportunity to talk about different family structures. Explain that every family loves their children and has things that make it special and unique. Talk together about what makes your family special.

Perhaps instead of noticing the makeup of the family, your child may notice that Gerald's family lived on a farm while your family lives in a city, or that Gerald's family had a dog and yours does not. Affirm these differences and that every family has things in common and things that are different. Or perhaps your child did not perceive anything to be different. In either of these cases, you may wish to point out the different family structure or you may decide to bypass that detail until the child brings up the topic at some future time.

Here's another example:

▶ "Gillian, I think you heard Daddy and me talking about going to visit your classmate Sally's family this weekend for a cookout. You know Sally from school, but this will be the first time we go to her home. Sally's family has different family members than ours. In our family, we live in our apartment with a mom, a dad, you, and your brother. In Sally's family, she lives in her house with her mother, her two little sisters, and a man named Dave who is Sally's new stepdaddy. Sally's family is very special to her, just like ours is special to us. We are going to have a lot of fun at the cookout!"

The goal is to prepare your child for meeting a family different from their own. In this example the mother explains that the family will be going to visit a friend's home for the first time. She provides important information about how Sally's family is different from theirs. She uses clear, objective language to explain their own family structure and compares it to Sally's simply, matter-of-factly, and without any judgment. The parent then shifts the conversation back to the happy anticipation of the upcoming get-together.

Next, it's important to pause. The words are new, there is a lot to understand, and it may take the child a few moments to process what was said.

If your child's response is silence, that's okay. A simple follow-up question— "Are you okay? Do you have any questions for me?"—allows them to respond if they wish.

Additional Questions and Answers to Consider

Your child may have questions, in the moment or later, that you will want to be prepared to answer.

> **Question:** "Quinn has two daddies, two mommies, and two houses. Why does he have so much family?"
>
> **Answer:** "Quinn's mommy and daddy had Quinn. Then they each married someone new and went to live in different houses. This means Quinn has a mommy and a stepdad, *and* he has a daddy and a stepmom. It is a lot of family, and that is special for him. Every family is different, and every family loves their children."

The goal is to answer the question simply and honestly. Avoid going into any detail on divorce, remarriage, or intricacies of blended families. This question is about the structure of one child's family relative to another's. You want to ensure that your answer addresses the question your child has asked and does not push further into questions they haven't asked. Acknowledge or state who you know to be in Quinn's family, affirm the unique qualities that every family has, and assure your child that differing types of families are expected and accepted.

> **Question:** "I thought you had to have a mommy and a daddy to have a baby. How did Malik's family have a baby with two mommies?"
>
> **Answer:** "That is a good question. I don't know how Malik's family had a baby because that is private to them. I do know that Malik's mommies both love him very much, and he has a special family just like we do."

While it may be tempting to try to explain various ways to bring a child into the world, a simple answer will likely suffice. Avoid bringing up prior relationships, sperm donation, surrogates, or other adult explanations, which will be confusing to a young child. Let the child know that the question is private and not one you have an answer to. Follow this by acknowledging that every family is special and affirming the acceptance of all families.

> **Question:** "How can Jordan have a new brother that's not a baby? I thought new brothers had to be babies."
>
> **Answer:** "That is a big question. Sometimes parents have a baby together. Sometimes, instead, they *adopt* a child who doesn't have a mommy or daddy to take care of them. That's what Jordan's parents did: they adopted a little boy, one who's not a baby, to be part of their family and to be a brother for Jordan. Jordan now has a brother, and that makes me very happy for him and his family. Every family is special."

As always, the goal is to answer simply and honestly. Young children often ask questions that delve into complex social dynamics. This child has the typical concrete understanding that new siblings are babies. The parent's very basic explanation of adoption introduces a new word and gives a simple description of how Jordan's parents brought an older child into their family. In conversations like this, always show acceptance and point out that every family is unique and special.

Preparing for Unexpected Responses

Young children are not always aware of what "should" and "should not" be said. This lack of life experience can lead them to make statements that are unexpected and may feel hurtful. Preparing for such remarks and considering why a young child might respond this way can help you support your child and buffer yourself from emotional reaction.

Child: "I want to marry Chastain when I'm a grown-up!"

Adult: "You have a long time before you decide who to marry. That is a grown-up decision. I know that Chastain is a good friend to you."

A young child might make this comment about a peer of any sex, and may be trying to make sense of the idea that families and marriages can take many forms. The child might also simply really like the friend and be expressing that they want to be with that friend always. The appropriate response is to affirm that your child can marry whoever they wish when they are grown. Remind them that marriage is for grown-ups and that the child has a long time before they might marry anyone.

Child: "I don't think someone should have two mommies or two daddies."

Adult: "Every family is special just the way it is. Our family is special, and other families are special too. I love being in our family with you and Daddy and Tasha."

This child is reacting to the concept of family being different and is probably trying to understand something distinct from their own personal experience. Respond kindly, never harshly, when your child expresses an opinion. Remind your child that every family is different and special just the way it is. Emphasize that no one type of family is better than another and that we love and support our friends and their families no matter what the structure of the family may be. Reassure your child of how important your own family is and how much your child is valued in the family.

Child: "I like Janelle's family. I wish Grandma lived with us like her Mimi lives with her."

Adult: "Janelle does have a nice family and I know you love spending time with your grandma. Grandma doesn't live with us, but our family is special too. One special thing is that we get to go on an airplane together to visit Grandma. Everyone's family is different and that is okay."

This child has noticed and accepted a family structure that's different from their own. You can agree that it's nice for Janelle to have her grandmother live with her and also affirm for your child their own family arrangement, pointing out something that makes it special. After acknowledging your child's desire to have more time with Grandma, you might next suggest a phone call, email, or video visit to respond to that wish to see her.

Additional Resources for Families

All Kinds of Families by Suzanne Lang, illustrated by Max Lang. This board book is written for toddlers and very young preschoolers. It celebrates a wide variety of family structures through colorful, fun illustrations and simple text. For older children, check out the similar picture book *Families, Families, Families!* also created by Suzanne Lang and Max Lang.

Families by Shelley Rotner and Sheila M. Kelly. This book of authentic family photos captures family fun and family traditions across a wide range of families of varying structures and sizes, including multigenerational families.

The Family Book by Todd Parr. This is a fun and colorful book about the love people have for their families and the many varieties of families. Other related books by Todd Parr include *The Mommy Book, The Daddy Book, The Grandma Book,* and *The Grandpa Book*.

My Family, Your Family by Lisa Bullard, illustrated by Renée Kurilla. This children's book, told by a child narrator, explores diversity in family structures and family members within the child's neighborhood.

Stella Brings the Family by Miriam B. Schiffer, illustrated by Holly Clifton-Brown. Stella's class is having a Mother's Day celebration; Stella has Papa, Daddy, and lots of other loved ones, none of them a mother. An engaging book with Stella finding a fun solution to her problem.

Sex and Sexuality

Like many adults, children often have a sense of wonder about pregnancy and childbirth. The announcement of a new baby or seeing an infant will frequently spark young children's questions. "Where do babies come from?" "How did the baby get in there?" "How will the baby get out?" "Do I have a baby in my tummy?" Children often have other questions as well, such as why they do or don't have a penis or vulva, and they may simply want to discuss the interesting differences between their own and other children's bodies.

Questions about babies, birth, sex, and sexuality can make adults uncomfortable. Often adults want to quickly quiet and divert the questions out of fear of saying too much or encouraging further questions. The reality is that young children are naturally curious about their bodies, and conversations about sex and pregnancies at an early age can help young children better understand their own body parts and differences among people.

Commonly, parents and teachers struggle with not only what to share and how much to share but also the language to use with young children. The American Academy of Pediatrics encourages the use of accurate terminology with children from a young age, including *vagina*, *penis*, *breast*, *buttocks*, and *private parts* (AAP 2019). Regarding sex and the creation of a baby, simple explanations and direct answers to questions are always advised.

Any time children pose questions about their bodies, the bodies of others, sex, or babies, this is also an appropriate moment to remind children about modesty, privacy, and respect for other people's privacy and personal space.

Note: If there is ever suspicion of abuse or neglect based upon the child's verbal sharing, heightened attention and focus on sexual behaviors, or observed behaviors, be sure to follow all mandatory reporting measures required by your state or province and those stipulated by your organization or school to protect the child.

Talking with Family Adults About Sex and Sexuality

Parents may share with you the news of a pregnancy or a child's comments about sex or sexuality. While it's preferable that these topics be discussed with parents before a child brings up the subject, it's also likely that a child will initiate a conversation with you. Being ready with a simple, sensitive response can help you appropriately acknowledge the topic and also provide a chance to determine what the parent expects from you in support of the child. Possible responses might include:

▶ "This is such an exciting time, and I am very happy to hear that you are expecting a new baby. Is Raven aware, and has she asked any questions about the baby or where babies come from that I should be aware of?"

▶ "I appreciate your telling me Makiko has been curious about children's private body parts. If she brings this up to me, our practice is to use proper names for body parts. Is that okay with you?"

▶ "I understand that it's tricky to answer all of Florian's questions. I do have some pages of information I can provide to you that may help you talk with him when he has questions at home. Would you like a copy?"

Talking with Children: Conversation Starters

You are also likely to have situations in the classroom that require some conversation related to sex and sexuality, body privacy, or personal space. For example, "Samuel, I see that Annabelle is already in the bathroom. We need to make sure we always give each other privacy and personal space in the bathroom."

Learn More About Discussing Sex and Sexuality with Children

The American Academy of Pediatrics and its family portal, HealthyChildren.org, offers basic guidance to help you understand and respond to young children's sexual questions and behaviors. The following organizations and resources offer additional, more practical and in-depth information:

★ amaze jr. Geared to parents, amaze jr. is a web-based source of podcasts and videos with age-appropriate information and content for young children. (amaze.org/jr/)

★ "Sexual Development and Behavior in Children." This downloadable information sheet for parents and caregivers of young children is jointly created by the National Center on the Sexual Behavior of Youth (NCSBY) and the National Child Traumatic Stress Network (NCTSN). Find it at nctsn.org.

Difficult conversations are inevitable when working with young children, but the discomfort of such conversations can be handled by being prepared. The examples of responses here offer some language you might use.

Ebony, to teacher: "I have a *gina* and my brother has a wee-wee. Do you have a gina, Ms. Angie?"

Teacher, Ms. Angie: "You do have a vagina, and yes, I have a vagina too. Our vagina is a private body part. Your brother has a penis, which is also a private body part. Since we are in the classroom now learning about trains, let's talk about what we are finding out about trains this week. Can you tell me one new thing you learned?"

The goal is to answer the question matter-of-factly, using accurate language, and move the conversation back to something more appropriate for the moment in the classroom. While it is common for young children to call their private parts by unique or baby language terms, using the correct terms as well can prevent them from assuming that accurate terminology is wrong or taboo. Here, Ms. Angie does not question Ebony's words but uses correct terminology and addresses only the question that she raised. Importantly, she doesn't silence or shame the child for asking an innocent question out of curiosity. She then turns to the current learning topic to focus the conversation on a classroom-related subject.

This approach would also work well if Ebony had made this comment in a group setting. It is important to answer and address the question, but it is then equally appropriate to refocus all the children on the learning at hand.

> **Francine:** "My mommy has a baby in her tummy. It's a boy baby. How is he going to get out?"
>
> **Ms. Angie:** "I am happy for your mommy and your family that you will have a brother soon. Your brother is growing in your mommy's *uterus* until he is big and strong enough to be born. When he is ready, your mommy will go to the doctor or special medical worker, and this person will help get the baby out. Then you will have a brother. How do you feel about having a baby brother?"

The goal is to directly answer the question the child posed without going into great detail. The teacher does not give in-depth birthing information. Most children understand that doctors are able to do specialized tasks, and so the simple statement that a medical professional will assist is likely to ease the child's curiosity. This response is equally appropriate for vaginal or caesarean section birth. The teacher also defines the *boy baby* as Francine's brother and asks how she is feeling about the new baby on the way. The introduction of a new sibling can evoke many emotions in children, and it is also therefore important to also reiterate support and emotional availability for any future conversations that may arise.

> **Joshua:** (touches his own genitals during storytime)
>
> **Ms. Angie, to Joshua (later, privately):** "I saw that you were touching your penis during storytime today. Your penis is your private body part and you can touch your own body parts when you are at home or in the bathroom. Here at school around other people is not the right time to touch your private parts. What was your favorite part of the story today?"

The goal is to guide Joshua about what's appropriate in a group setting without shaming him. It may also be wise to handle this situation when it occurs, especially with very young children. Many children self-touch without realizing it—sometimes as a way to soothe themselves (similar to thumb-sucking). If it's addressed later, some children won't be able to connect the conversation to something they didn't realize they were doing. Ms. Angie or another teacher in the room could quietly say something to Joshua in the moment without drawing others' attention: "Remember, your penis is private and you can touch it when you're alone, not during storytime."

Following Up

Following any conversation with a child about sex or sexuality, it is appropriate and strongly advised that you connect with the family or families of the children involved in the conversation. Share with the family what the child said or asked and how you responded. Ask the family how they would like the conversation handled if their child asks another question or further discussion takes place. This forges a partnership between school and home and also gives families appropriate notice to prepare for follow-up conversations the child may wish to have with them. Offer the family handout "Talking with Your Child About Sex and Sexuality" (page 168).

Here are two examples; for more, see "Framework for Parent Conversation Starters" in Part I, page 12:

▶ "I wanted to make you aware of a conversation I had with Ebony today. Privately, she shared with me that she has a vagina and her brother has a penis. She asked if I had a vagina, and I told her that I do. Then I switched the conversation to a different topic."

▶ "Francine told me that your family is expecting a new baby. I am very excited to hear this news! She wanted to know how the baby was going to get out of Mommy's "tummy." I explained very simply that the baby would continue to grow in your uterus until he was ready and that then the doctor or other healthcare provider would help get the baby out. I didn't go into any further detail, but I expect she may ask. I do have a resource including a list of good children's books to explain pregnancy and childbirth, if you would like a copy."

A child may also approach you for further discussion. If a child seeks you out again, allow them to lead the conversation and try to keep it focused on simple responses and how they are feeling. For example:

> **Lulu:** "I want to have a baby in my tummy like my Aunt Daria!"
>
> **Ms. Angie:** "I didn't know your Aunt Daria is going to have a baby. That is very exciting! People can decide to have babies when they're adults. You still have a long time before you are a grown-up."

Note that this teacher does not chastise or minimize the child's statement. Instead, Ms. Angie captures Lulu's interest by expressing excitement about the baby. She then simply explains that having babies is an adult event.

Talking with Your Child About
Sex and Sexuality

Young children are naturally curious and are drawn to ask questions about things they don't understand—and this includes sex and sexuality. A pregnant parent and a newborn baby are both readily recognized by young children, and many children may ask questions about how the pregnancy came to be, how the baby got inside the parent, and how the baby will get out. Children often have other questions as well, such as why they do or don't have a penis or vagina, and they may simply want to discuss the interesting differences between people's private parts.

This chart summarizes information from the American Academy of Pediatrics (AAP) about what young children are generally able to understand and should have explained to them at different ages. You may choose to withhold certain information or share additional information at your own discretion and depending on the readiness of your child.

At this age:	Children can generally understand:*
1–2 years	Names of body parts, including genitals
	Our bodies are private
3–4 years	Babies grow when a sperm meets an egg
	Babies grow in a uterus
	When it is and is not appropriate to be naked
	Safe versus unsafe touches
5–8 years	Touching one's own body is acceptable but should be done in private
	Basics of puberty such as body hair, pubic hair, breast development, and penile erections
	Importance of personal hygiene
	Possibly the basics of sexual intercourse

* Compiled and adapted from publications of the American Academy of Pediatrics and HealthyChildren.org.

Commonly, parents struggle with not only what to share and how much to share but also the language to use with young children. The AAP encourages the use of accurate terminology with children from a young age, including *vagina*, *penis*, *breast*, *buttocks*, and *private parts*. Regarding sex and the creation of a baby, simple explanations and direct answers to questions are always advised.

When young children ask questions, it's important to remember that they are curious or seeking information. Simple answers and matter-of-fact explanations are almost always all a child needs in the moment. It's up to you to decide the depth of information you will share and the timing based on your child's developmental readiness and your family's preferred approach. For example:

> **Family adult:** "I saw you looking when I was changing your cousin Zara's diaper today."
>
> **Gino:** "She looks different than me."
>
> **Family adult:** "Zara has a vulva as her private part. This is different from your penis. Some people have a penis and some people have a vulva. We are all made differently."

The goal is to acknowledge and respond to your child's observation respectfully. The adult does not shame or scold Gino for being curious, but matter-of-factly provides the correct words for the boy to understand why his cousin's genitals look different from his own.

▶ "I heard you were asking at school today about where babies come from. That is a good question. Every baby starts with two tiny things: a sperm and an egg. The egg is not like a chicken egg! It's so tiny you can't even see it. Some bodies have sperm and some bodies have eggs. The baby then begins to grow inside a special place called a uterus. You grew from Daddy's sperm and Mommy's egg."

This example explains reproduction in a simple, scientific, accurate way. The child is also introduced to some new words, such as *uterus*. This supports the focus on using accurate language with children.

▶ (speaking quietly) "I see you are touching your penis under your underwear and shorts. Your penis is your private body part, and you can touch your own body parts. When we are around other people, like now in the grocery store, it is not the right time to touch your private parts."

Here again, even in public, the adult doesn't scold the child. Briefly and directly, the parent explains that touching private parts is okay, but not when others are around.

Next, it's important to pause. The words are new, there is a lot of information to understand, and it may take the child a few moments to process what was said.

If your child's response is silence, that's okay. A simple follow-up question— "Are you okay? Do you have any questions for me?"—allows them to respond if they wish.

Additional Questions and Answers to Consider

Your child may have questions, in the moment or later, that you will want to be prepared to answer.

> **Question:** "Did Mommy eat the baby in her tummy?"
>
> **Answer:** "No. It looks on the outside like Mommy has a baby in her tummy, but the baby is actually in a place inside Mommy called a uterus. This keeps the baby safe and lets it grow until it is ready to come out."

This example emphasizes the importance of helping young children better understand body systems. The idea of a baby being in a stomach is scary to some children, particularly once they have learned that food we eat goes into our stomachs. When a child asks a question like this, be sure to clarify where the baby actually is, using correct terminology (*uterus* rather than *tummy*).

> **Question:** "Tomás told me a man puts his penis in a girl's vagina to make a baby. Is that true?"
>
> **Answer:** "A baby can be made that way. One grown-up's penis goes inside the other grown-up's vagina. The sperm from the penis goes inside and meets up with the egg. There are some other ways that babies are made, but no matter how, making a baby is for grown-ups. It should always be done when both grown-ups want to do it together."

The goal is to answer honestly and begin to teach basic boundaries. Young children may be exposed to sex through media, through older siblings or friends, or through overhearing family discussion. While it may feel uncomfortable, it is best to always answer openly and honestly. This is also an opportunity to talk about consent in a child-appropriate way. Children need to understand that sex is how babies are made, that sex is an adult behavior, and that sex should only occur when both adults want to do it.

Preparing for Unexpected Responses

Young children are not always aware of what "should" and "should not" be said. This lack of life experience can lead them to make statements that are unexpected and may be off-putting. Preparing for such remarks and considering why a young child might respond this way can help you support your child and buffer yourself from emotional reaction.

> **Child:** "I want to make a baby."
>
> **Adult:** "One day when you're a grown-up, you can decide if you want to make a baby. Right now, I am happy you are my daughter and get to be a little girl."

A child wishing to have a baby is not likely thinking about sexual behavior. This statement likely reflects a very innocent desire to be a parent or to experience something you are experiencing. Acknowledge your child's desire in the same way you would if they wished to be an astronaut one day.

> **Child:** "I wish I had a penis like Saul."
> **Adult:** "People are made with different body parts. You were born with a vulva. Saul was born with a penis. We are made differently, and that's what makes each of us special. What are some other things that make you special?"

Often when a child says they want to have a penis, or a vagina, or a vulva, the child is simply remarking on a difference that is interesting or imagining what it would be like to have that body part. Explain simply the biological differences and then allow your child to share what they find special about themself.

> **Child:** "Can I see sex?"
> **Adult:** "No. Our private parts are private, and sex is private."

It's hard to know exactly what a child has in mind with this question—it may be about seeing other people's genitals or about having sex or about curiosity regarding what *sex* actually means. The adult here makes a brief, honest reply. Children understand about privacy early and this simple explanation does not shame the child. It's important not to scold your child but to view the question as yet another attempt to seek information.

Additional Resources for Families

It's Not the Stork! A Book About Girls, Boys, Babies, Bodies, Families, and Friends by Robie Harris, illustrated by Michael Emberley. This informative children's book is written to answer children's questions about sex, sexuality, and different genitals in a simple yet accurate manner appropriate for children in preschool and early elementary school.

My Body Belongs to Me by Jill Starishevsky, illustrated by Angela Padrón. A picture book that focuses on helping young children understand that private parts are ours alone. In simple rhyming language, children are reminded to let an adult know if someone ever touches their private parts.

My Body! What I Say Goes! A book to empower and teach children about personal body safety, feelings, safe and unsafe touch, private parts, secrets and surprises, consent, and respectful relationships by Janeen Sanders, illustrated by Anna Hancock. The book emphasizes privacy and the differences between safe touches and unsafe touches in a child-appropriate way.

Sex Positive Families. At this website you can request a "Sexual Behaviors in Childhood Guide" and a book, *Sex Positive Talks to Have with Kids* by Melissa Carnagey, LBSW, which includes conversation starters and activities for every age and stage on topics that include bodies, sex, safe and unsafe touch, consent, gender, and many more. (sexpositivefamilies.com)

"Sexual Behaviors in Young Children: What's Normal, What's Not?" This web page from HealthyChildren.org has helpful information about children ages two to six: common behaviors, red flag behaviors, body safety teaching tips, and other suggested resources. To find the link, go to healthychildren.org and type in "Sexual behaviors of young children" in the search box.

What Makes a Baby by Cory Silverberg, illustrated by Fiona Smyth. This brightly colored book explains the process of fertilization and embryonic growth in vibrant illustrations and with straightforward text to help young children understand what happens inside the body that leads to a baby.

Gender

Gender and sex are not synonymous. Sex refers to the biological aspects of maleness or femaleness, whereas gender implies the psychological, behavioral, social, and cultural aspects of being male or female (that is, masculinity or femininity) (APA 2020). Simply put, sex is about biology, anatomy, and attributes while gender is about identity and concept of self. Gender refers to the attitudes, feelings, and behaviors that a given person or culture associates with a person's biological sex. There has been increasing public discussion of gender fluidity and of issues related to gender-neutral restrooms, athletic qualifications, and pronoun usage with people who are transgender and/or nonbinary. With a wide range of opinions on the topic, conversations with adults about gender can sometimes be difficult and uncomfortable.

For their part, young children are naturally curious and openly ask questions about gender, just as they do with other topics they are trying to understand. Children develop a gender identity across the early childhood years. Around age two, children become conscious of and may point out physical differences in males and females. Prior to their third birthday, many children will readily label themselves as a "boy" or a "girl." By age four, most children have a well-defined gender identity and may label behaviors, play, preferences, and cultural practices as "boy things" or "girl things" (Rafferty 2018).

All young children need opportunities to explore gender roles and to be exposed to gender in a variety of contexts. When children show preferences and interests not traditionally aligned to gender roles, they may be subject to teasing, discrimination, or disapproval from other children and from adults as well. Even when they are not explicitly expressed, children are still aware of assumptions made about gender. When children encounter gender expressions that are not strictly binary or that challenge traditional gender stereotypes, young children will question what they've observed.

Talking with Family Adults About Gender

Adults may approach a teacher or school leadership team member to discuss gender or their child's desired gender expression. This would likely be centered around the child's choice of clothing, pronouns, or self-expression of being a boy, a girl, or nonbinary. This conversation should be held privately, be approached with an attitude that seeks to understand, and aim for a collaborative agreement on the best way to support the child.

Family adult: "I wanted to talk with you about John-Michael. John-Michael has been saying at home for a while now that he feels he is really a girl on the inside. We have been open and have listened closely to his words. Now he's asked for us to let him dress in clothes more like what his sister wears. It's uncomfortable for us, but we do let him wear her clothes. I don't know how this will be received by the other children in the class so I wanted to talk with you about it."

Teacher: "Thank you for letting me know this. It sounds like your biggest concern is how classmates will react to the clothes John-Michael wants to wear. Is there a certain way you'd like me to explain it to them? Are there other concerns you have or things that you would like me to do to make sure John-Michael is comfortable here at school?"

Talking with Children: Conversation Starters

Conversations about gender are going to come up when working with young children, and you can lessen the emotional charge of these discussions by being prepared. The examples of responses here offer some language you might use. Remember to let the child lead the conversation and ask questions.

Natalia, to Hugh: "Baby dolls are just for girls! You can't play with these!"

Teacher, Mr. Donovan, to Natalia (later): "I heard how you were speaking to Hugh. Baby dolls in our classroom are for anyone who wants to play with them. There are no toys here that are just for girls or just for boys. I wonder if you were angry because you wanted to play with the baby dolls by yourself?" (Natalia nods) "In our class we want to be kind and respectful to everyone. What is a nice thing you could say to Hugh next time?"

The goal is to set a tone of mutual respect. The teacher gently informs Natalia that nothing in the classroom is gender defined, and he helps her label the emotion she may have been feeling. He then invites Natalia to think of a more kind and inclusive response. Some ideas might include telling Hugh, "I know you like the baby dolls, but I want to play by myself now. You can have them in a little while" or "How about I play with this doll and you play with that one?" Mr. Donovan can also talk with the class as a group to make clear that all the toys are for all the children and to emphasize that everyone in the classroom is to be treated with kindness and respect.

Dawn, to Mr. Donovan: "Is Jayden a boy or a girl? She looks like a girl but she wears boy clothes and plays boy games."

Mr. Donovan: "Jayden is Jayden. The nice thing about each person in our classroom is that we all get to be exactly who we are. Jayden dresses, acts, and plays games that Jayden likes, just like you dress, act, and play games that you like. I like Jayden exactly the way Jayden is, and I like each of you exactly the way you are. It is important to me that we are all kind and respectful to each other."

The goal is to acknowledge, not silence, the child's question, and to model respect. The teacher kindly and informatively shares with the child that each person is unique and free to express themselves however they choose. Mr. Donovan does not label Jayden's gender or use gender pronouns, because the gender Jayden identifies with may not be known. By not labeling Jayden as a girl or a boy, the teacher models a respectful appreciation for others. He then turns the conversation back to the expected social behavior of showing kindness and respect to all.

Following Up

Following any conversation with a child about gender, it is appropriate and strongly advised that you connect with the family or families of the children involved in the conversation. Share with the family what the child said or asked and how you responded. Ask the family how they would like the conversation handled if their child asks another question or further discussion takes place. This forges a partnership between school and home and also gives families appropriate notice to prepare for follow-up conversations the child may wish to have with them. (For examples, see "Framework for Parent Conversation Starters" in Part I, page 12.) Check with the parent on the exact language they've used with the child so that any discussions at school use consistent vocabulary. Offer the family handout "Talking with Your Child About Gender" (page 177).

A child may also approach you for further discussion. If a child seeks you out again, allow them to lead the conversation and try to keep it focused on how they are feeling. For example:

> **Natalia:** "My daddy says boys shouldn't play with baby dolls."
>
> **Mr. Donovan:** "In our classroom, all of the toys and materials are for everyone. That includes the baby dolls."

The goal is to explain classroom expectations. Notice that this teacher does not scold the child or counter the teaching from home. Instead, he references what is expected and permitted in the school setting.

> **Jeffrey:** "I like being a boy and playing with trucks."
>
> **Mr. Donovan:** "I like that you like being a boy and playing with trucks. You can play with any toys you wish, and I like you exactly the way you are."

The goal is to affirm the child without affirming a gender stereotype. Mr. Donovan simply echoes Jeffrey's preference and endorses it with a universal statement of acceptance.

Learn More About Gender and How to Talk About It

Gender Justice in Early Childhood. This organization composed of educators, researchers, and others offer a helpful web page with many downloadable resources useful to teachers, including a classroom audit tool, suggestions for working with persona dolls, and recommendations of children's picture books that offer an expansive view of gender. Helpful for talking with young children and their families is the PDF "Loaded Language: Changing How We Talk About Gender," with phrases to avoid and ideas for what to say instead. To find the tools, choose the Resources tab from the top menu at genderjusticeinearlychildhood.com.

Talking with Your Child About
Gender

It's important to bear in mind that gender and sex are not the same thing. *Sex* is about biology and anatomy—physical attributes—while *gender* is about identity and concept of self. Young children are naturally curious and openly ask questions about gender, just as they do with other topics they are trying to understand. Children develop a gender identity across the early childhood years. Around age two, children become conscious and may point out physical differences in males and females. By the age of three, many children will readily label themselves as a "boy" or a "girl." By age four, most have a well-defined gender identity and may label behaviors, play, preferences, and cultural practices as "boy things" or "girl things."

Ideas about traditional gender roles have long been established and reinforced through social norms. Culture and religion also play in an important part in a family's perspective on gender. When children show preferences and interests not aligned to traditional gender roles, other children or adults may tease or criticize. When children encounter gender expressions that are not strictly binary or that challenge traditional gender stereotypes, it's natural for them to question what they've observed.

All young children need opportunities to explore gender roles and to be exposed to a balanced view of gender through books, toys, and activities. This means balanced depictions of males and females in roles, occupations, and settings. Children need to be free to choose to play with dolls and with trucks, to learn music or sports or dancing, and to imagine themselves as firefighters, doctors, fairies, pirates, mothers, fathers, and more. You know your child and your family's situation. As you continue talking together, use your own understanding of your child and take care not to jump to conclusions about how they're feeling. Talking together again at different times will help you better understand what your child understands about gender, how they feel about it, and what support they may need.

If your child brings up the topic of gender, you can respond in a way that shows the topic is okay to be discussed. For example:

▶ "You asked me if the cashier in the checkout line was a boy or a girl. I know you're curious. I don't know the answer, but it doesn't matter. That cashier is exactly who they are, just like you are who you are and I am who I am. You are just right, exactly as you are, and so is the cashier."

The goal is to answer honestly and reassuringly. This example is typical of a question that might come up in a public place. You can begin by making it clear the question was okay to ask. You can then explain why a gender label is not important. Be sure to reassure your child that they are acceptable exactly as they are and make that connection to the cashier as well.

Another possibility in a situation such as this is to model a respectful interaction in the moment. For example, if you see the cashier has a nametag that says "Max," you might give a friendly greeting: "Hi, Max. How are you today?" Your child will observe that you did not silence the question and, at the same time, you showed courtesy to the cashier. You can follow up later to answer your child and explain that you don't know the person's gender but that we are all to be respected and valued just as we are.

▶ "I wanted to let you know that your teacher this year is going to be Mx. *[miks]* Anderson. I know that sounds different from what we have called teachers before, but Mx. Anderson prefers to be called Mx. instead of Mr. or Ms. Mx. Anderson does not want to be seen as just a man or just a woman. I am happy that you have Mx. Anderson as your teacher, and I am sure you are going to learn many things from Mx. Anderson. What are you most looking forward to learning this year?"

The goal is to prepare your child for a teacher who is nonbinary. Offer a simple explanation of what the teacher prefers to be called and give a broad explanation of why. Assure your child that you're comfortable with this teacher assignment and emphasize what they will learn from the teacher in the coming year.

Next, it's important to pause. The words are new, there is a lot to understand, and it may take the child a few moments to process what was said.

If your child's response is silence, that's okay. A simple follow-up question— "Do you have any questions for me?"—allows them to respond if they wish.

Additional Questions and Answers to Consider

Your child may have questions, in the moment or later, that you will want to be prepared to answer.

Question: "I thought all boys have a penis. So if he has a penis, he's a boy, right?"

Answer: "Most boys have a penis. When they are born, children have different private parts. Some have a penis and some have a vulva. When a baby is born, the doctor or nurse might see a penis and say, "It's a boy." Or if there is a vulva, they may say, "It's a girl." But those body parts do not decide who somebody really is. Sometimes people who have a penis may know they are not a boy. And sometimes people who have a vulva may know they are not a girl. Or they may not be either one. No matter what body parts we have, we are all special and can be who we want to be."

This child is questioning the concept of gender (identity) in contrast to sex (physical body parts). At birth, physical body parts do define humans as male and female—or as boy and girl, which is more readily understood by a young child. Explain this to your child as simply as possible. Use the appropriate terminology (or the words you use in your home for private parts), and answer very matter-of-factly. Avoid going into a discussion of sex versus gender, gender-affirming surgery, or any other adult topic—these are far too complex for a child to process.

> **Question:** "Am I a boy or a girl?"
>
> **Answer:** "Why do you wonder if you are a boy or a girl?" (pause)
>
> **Question:** "I mostly like boy stuff, but I like ballet, and that's for girls, isn't it?"
>
> **Answer:** "Ballet is for girls *and* for boys—it's for anyone. You decide every day what activities you do and what you wear and what you like to play with. Daddy and I let you make those choices."

A child asking this is likely wondering about their self-identity. Try to learn more about why the child has asked. Then address the question about gender by clearly stating that they're free to choose which activities, clothing, or playthings they are interested in.

Preparing for Unexpected Responses

Young children are not always aware of what "should" and "should not" be said. This lack of life experience can lead them to make statements that are unexpected and may feel hurtful. Preparing for such remarks and considering why a young child might respond this way can help you support your child and buffer yourself from emotional reaction.

> **Child:** "I want to be a boy, not a girl!"
>
> **Adult:** "You were born with a vulva, but you get to be whoever you are. You can dress how you like and play with whatever toys you choose. I want you to be exactly who you want to be."

A child who says this is probably trying to make sense of the idea of gender conformity or nonconformity. The child may or may not be trying to express a specific gender identity. The appropriate response is to note that your child is physically female or male as determined by body parts and that they can express themself however they feel is best. Remind your child that boys and girls can be and do anything that they wish to be or do.

Child: (silence)

Adult: "If you have any questions, you can always talk to me." (Offer a hug.)

Silence can denote that the child does not understand and therefore is not reacting, or silence can mean that the child is still processing what they've seen or been told. Respect this silence. Give your child a few moments to think and be still and then reassure them that you are there if they want to talk. Remind your child that they are loved and can always talk to you about things that they're curious or worried about.

Additional Resources for Families

Jamie Is Jamie by Afsaneh Moradian, illustrated by Maria Bogade. This children's book challenges gender stereotypes and reinforces how important it is to appreciate and respect each other without social limits. The book is also a good reminder about being kind, gentle, and accepting. A second book, *Jamie & Bubbie*, by the same author and illustrator, continues a story line about Jamie and explains the importance of not assuming people's pronouns based solely on appearance.

Julián Is a Mermaid by Jessica Love. This picture book tells the tale of a young boy experimenting with dressing up as the beautiful mermaids he has seen, irrespective of gender stereotypes. His abuela demonstrates acceptance for his imagination and individuality.

Sparkle Boy by Lesléa Newman, illustrated by Maria Mola. A picture book that challenges gender stereotypes with the main character, a boy, who engages and shows interest in activities that are stereotypically for girls. The story emphasizes the importance of acceptance and respect for all.

When Aidan Became a Brother by Kyle Lukoff, illustrated by Kaylani Juanita. This is a heartwarming story about a child whose family thought he was a girl and then grew to understand and help him live his life as the trans boy he really was. A good book for families with a transgender child that addresses becoming an older sibling along with other transitions families face.

Big Conversations About Upheaval and Violence

"When little people are overwhelmed by big emotions, it's our job to share our calm."

—L. R. Knost

Our world is full of crisis. Much as we want to protect children from knowing about upheaval and violence or experiencing it themselves, the reality is that young children do experience and learn about crises at school, in the community, and in the wider world. A school or neighborhood shooting, a protest or an uprising, a natural disaster, a terror event, a pandemic—all such occurrences happen frequently enough that many children will be touched by at least some of them at an early age. While one might assume children will be more deeply affected by direct personal experiences, simply knowing about a mass shooting or a destructive hurricane, however far away, can be terrifying for a young child.

To the extent that we can, it's important to shield children from learning about traumatic events that do not directly affect them. Nonetheless, since many events do affect children, and since many others come into their awareness, adults need to be prepared to answer children's questions about them sensitively and in ways that are appropriate to the specific circumstance. Broadly, conversations with children will come about from two types of situations:

▶ a crisis that the child has experienced or witnessed directly or is likely to experience

▶ a crisis that the child has seen or heard about that is not likely or is far less likely to directly affect the child

In both situations, the key points to emphasize are:

▶ There are many helpers involved in helping people and making things better.

▶ Adults will always work to keep children safe.

It's best if you are able to talk with parents before addressing an issue with the child, but many topics may arise in your setting without this prior conversation. Whether families speak to you or not, when a conversation with a child comes up, always allow the child to lead the conversation. This means answering only what the child has asked, without offering more information, or giving only those details necessary to calm children or prepare them for a future happening. Check back with parents when you and their child have spoken, and ask them how they want the topic approached. And as with other "big" topics, children need simple, honest, respectful replies that are appropriate to their developmental stage. They need to express their feelings about what's happening and to be reassured and comforted. They need to know you are always there to talk with them and will do all you can to keep them safe.

Adults, too, are affected by crisis. Schools and communities may directly experience upheaval from violence, social unrest, a pandemic, or other pressures, and adults must grapple with the same kinds of pressures that children do. Crises around the globe are also continually brought home to adults, with a constant feed of news that can generate immense levels of stress, making the task of supporting children all the more challenging. Pay attention to your own feelings as you converse with children and families about violence and upheaval, and take time to examine and process your emotions and responses. See page 4 for information about forming a community of practice where you and other adults in your setting can support each other to do this.

Natural Disaster

Nature is a thing of wonder, but it can also be a source of fear and anxiety when natural disasters strike. For adults, the idea of a natural disaster generates a feeling of unpredictability and apprehension about the possibility of such an event happening close to home. With the earth's changing climate, some kinds of disasters—fires, droughts, heat waves, torrential rains—are occurring with greater frequency, causing additional stress and worry. Even with foreknowledge of an impending event (such as a tornado or hurricane), and even with preparation for it (such as stocking up on batteries, water, dry goods, and flashlights), there is still uncertainty about the severity, the duration, and the impact it might have.

The magnitude and impact of natural disasters are difficult for a young child to understand or to truly conceptualize. The vocabulary used to talk about these disasters—words like *hurricane, twister, flooding, Richter scale, FEMA*—are mysterious to a young child, adding to the level of anxiety. Children feel the tension and concern when adults prepare for an anticipated storm or talk about its aftermath. Children often may hear snippets about what occurred or is projected to occur, see an image of wreckage without context, observe grown-ups scurrying to stock goods at home or to board windows, and witness emotional reactions among adults directly or indirectly affected. All of this adds to the mystery and fear about the unknown.

When young children do experience or learn about natural disasters, it is highly likely that they will exhibit physiological and psychological symptoms. Children may report new fears, show increased emotional reactions such as crying, or have unsettling dreams or night terrors. Exposure to any element related to the natural disaster (such as a building vibrating when a truck goes by after a child has heard of or experienced an earthquake) may elicit a fear response. Children need to be reassured that they are safe and reminded that it is okay to talk about anything that scares them.

Talking with Family Adults About a Natural Disaster

If the community or a family has been directly affected by a natural disaster, adults are likely to bring a lot of emotion to the topic. Be sure to provide families with information and referral resources your school or program has available as well as a copy of "Talking with Your Child About a Natural Disaster" (page 187). Additionally, you will want to speak with parents about how the natural disaster has affected the family personally and about any conversations they have had with their child. Even if there has been no disaster locally, adults may share if a child has learned about one elsewhere or has seen images or heard stories that have frightened the child. When talking with families, it is important to learn what information has been shared with their child and what the child's reaction to the news has been so far, and to ask the family what support they want or need. Possible conversation starters might include:

▶ "There has been a lot of news coverage about the hurricane. Has your family felt the effects of this storm? And how has Aliyah responded to all of this?"

▶ "I wanted to touch base with you briefly about the flooding. I understand how disruptive it's been and am wondering how Liam responded to our school closure last week and to the community flooding."

Talking with Children: Conversation Starters

Despite efforts to shield young children from news coverage, conversations, and visual images related to the natural disaster, if a child is exposed, it's important to talk with the child directly about what happened, emphasizing the helpers involved and offering reassurance about the child's safety. Difficult conversations are inevitable when working with young children but the emotional charge of such conversations can be lessened by being prepared. In the classroom or group setting, the conversation and questions should be led by the child; the text that follows gives examples of how this may be approached.

> **Silas, to Braden (during play):** "You build the houses, and then I'm gonna be the big hurricane and I'm gonna blow them all down and flood them all up just like in Texas!"
>
> **Teacher, Mr. Phan, to Silas (later):** "I heard you talking to Braden about a hurricane. That was a scary thing that happened in Texas. I am very glad there are so many helpers working to get it all cleaned up and to keep the people there safe. If you want to talk to me, I am here. Would you like a hug?"

The goal is to check in with the child and let him know it's okay to talk about the hurricane he heard about. Mr. Phan acknowledges what he overheard in the interaction between the two children. He also uses the name of the location of the hurricane because the child used the name—this is not a new detail offered. The teacher then turns the conversation to the helpers who were assisting and offers himself as a safe person to talk to; he pairs this with the offer of physical comfort, a hug. Through playing, Silas may have emotionally navigated anxiety he might have had and he may decline further conversation or the hug. He still knows he can talk and get a hug when he does want to.

> **Coral, to teacher:** "Did you know there was a big fire in Montana burning down all the trees and houses? I saw it on the TV and the fire is getting bigger and bigger and bigger."

Mr. Phan: "I do know about that fire in Montana. I want you to know that even when bad things happen in the world, there are always people there to help. Firefighters, safety officers, nurses, doctors, teachers, moms, and dads are helpers—there are lots of people who are helping to put out that big fire and make things better. How are you feeling about what you saw and heard?"

The goal is to acknowledge what the child has said and to calm and reassure her. Here the teacher affirms what Coral saw and heard, including the location of the fire, which she had mentioned. Mr. Phan then turns Coral's focus away from the natural disaster and toward the community helpers. It's important to emphasize safety: children need to know that when scary or destructive things happen in the world, there are always people who are there to intervene, help, and keep people safe. The teacher then asks an open-ended question, allowing Coral an opportunity to further discuss and label her emotions.

Isla, to teacher: "Is the tornado going to happen again? I don't want it to come back. I don't want it to come back!"

Mr. Phan: "You are talking about the tornado that came through our area two weeks ago. That was scary for all of us, but I want you to know that you are safe. There are lots of helpers in our community who work to keep us safe every day—TV and radio announcers, emergency workers, builders, electrical workers, teachers, and our families too. We heard the sirens and got messages on our phones to follow the safety rules, so we stayed safe. You are safe here at school and safe here in our classroom. Sometimes big things happen in nature, like that tornado, and that is why we practice our safety drills here at school. And the community helpers have been cleaning up and rebuilding since the tornado happened. Can you tell me more about how you feel when you think about the tornado?"

The goal is to emphasize safety and helpers and to encourage the child to explore and express her feelings further. Isla's distress is obvious, and Mr. Phan uses very concrete language and labels the fear she's expressed. He does not silence the question, but he does help shift Isla's focus away from the tornado and toward the community helpers and the community safety practices. He connects safety to the school with the reminder about safety drills and then asks to know more about Isla's feelings, allowing her an opportunity to further share about her emotions.

Following Up

Following any conversation with a child about a natural disaster, it is appropriate and strongly advised that you connect with the family or families of the children involved in the conversation. Share with the family what the child said or asked and how you responded. Ask the family how they would like the conversation handled if their child asks another question or further discussion takes place. This forges a partnership between school and home and also gives families appropriate notice to prepare for follow-up conversations the child may wish to have with them. (For examples, see "Framework for Parent Conversation Starters" in Part I, page 12.) Offer the family handout "Talking with Your Child About a Natural Disaster" (page 187).

A child may also approach you for further discussion. If a child seeks you out again, allow them to lead the conversation and try to keep it focused on how they are feeling. For example:

> **Coral:** "I want the fire to stop in Montana! My uncle has a special job and he jumps out of planes where there are big fires. I don't want him to get hurt!"
>
> **Mr. Phan:** "I did not know your uncle was a firefighter. Some firefighters do help fight big fires from planes. That is a big job, and I am sure your uncle had a lot of special training to be that kind of helper. Would it make you feel better to draw him a picture to let him know you are thinking about him and want him to be safe?"

Affirm the helpers. Notice how Mr. Phan responds to Coral's distress by stressing the uncle's training in his role as a community helper. The teacher then helps the girl channel her anxiety into something tangible to express her love and concern for her uncle.

> **Isla:** "My neighbor, Mr. Barnes, had to move away. His roof got torn off by the tornado and he can't live there until they fix it. I want him to come back home."
>
> **Mr. Phan:** "I am sorry Mr. Barnes's home was damaged in the tornado. The tornado is gone now, and I am sure there are helpers who will do what they can to fix Mr. Barnes's home. Would you like to make him a card to let him know you want him to come back soon?"

Offer tangible ways to express empathy. Here the teacher says clearly that the tornado is gone. Even for children who readily understand that the storm is no longer an imminent threat, this statement reaffirms their safety. Mr. Phan helps Isla find a concrete way to express how she is feeling and connect with her neighbor.

Talking with Your Child About a Natural Disaster

We all want to protect children from knowing about a major natural disaster or experiencing it themselves. Yet the reality is that young children do experience and learn about such events occuring near home and far away. Simply knowing about a destructive hurricane in another place can be terrifying for a young child, and it's important to shield children from this knowledge to the extent that we can. Still, no amount of vigilance can completely insulate children from overhearing conversations, catching a brief TV or radio segment, or seeing a photograph on a phone screen or in a newspaper or magazine. And because no parent can prevent a wildfire, a tornado, or another unexpected disaster, it's also possible children will experience a traumatic incident firsthand.

The magnitude and impact of natural disasters are difficult for a young child to understand or to truly conceptualize. The words used to talk about these disasters—*hurricane, twister, flooding, Richter scale, FEMA*—are mysterious to a young child, adding to the level of anxiety. Children feel the tension and concern when adults prepare for an anticipated storm or talk about its aftermath. Children often may hear snippets about what occurred or is projected to occur. They may see an image of wreckage out of context. They may observe grown-ups scurrying to stock goods or board windows. They may witness emotional reactions among adults. All of this adds to the mystery and fear of the unknown.

When young children do experience or learn about natural disasters, it is highly likely that they will exhibit physiological and psychological symptoms. Your child may talk about new fears or show increased emotional reactions such as crying, unsettling dreams, or night terrors. Exposure to anything related to the disaster (such as a flame-up on the barbecue grill after hearing of or seeing a wildfire) may arouse a fear response. It's critical for you to reassure your child that they are safe and to remind them that it is okay to talk about anything that scares them.

Your child may ask a question, or you may need to start with a simple prompt, signaling that it's okay to talk about the topic. It's especially important to do this in situations where you think your child may be aware of a natural disaster in the news, or of an impending event, and you don't know how much they've seen or heard about it. For example:

▶ "I saw you looking at the magazine cover in the grocery store line. That was a picture of something very sad that happened in a place far away called (name of place). What happened there is called a *tsunami*. I don't think you've ever seen a picture like that one before. How did it feel to see that?"

This remark lets your child know that you observed what they saw and that it is okay to talk about it. It provides a chance for your child to share how it felt to see the picture as well as a safe place to turn with other questions. Notice that the adult uses the word *sad*. That's important because hearing how grown-ups feel can help reassure children that their own feelings are acceptable. Also note that the parent explains only basic facts—the name of the faraway place and the name of the storm—and does not immediately provide any additional details. This approach avoids creating anxiety or fear by bringing up information the child may not need to know. Labeling the tsunami, a new term for the child, lets the parent direct the conversation to the type of natural disaster and away from the destruction the child saw.

▶ "Kimberlee, I didn't know you were watching the TV behind Papa and me. We were watching the news to learn about a hurricane. A hurricane is a storm with a lot of rain and strong wind. It has already gone through an island called Puerto Rico. I'm not sure what you saw or heard. Can you tell me what you heard and how you're feeling?"

The goal is to ascertain how much your child saw and heard and to learn how they are feeling about it. In this example, the parent first acknowledges that the adults were watching the news and then opens dialogue to encourage the child to share what she saw. Kimberlee may not have observed or heard anything, or she may have taken in the entire story of the hurricane and the damage it caused. Rather than volunteer too much information, ask your child what they saw. Then, by asking about how they are feeling, you can gain insight into how your child interpreted what they saw or heard.

Next, it's important to pause. The words are new, there may be a lot of emotion to understand, and it may take your child a few moments to process what was said.

If your child's response is silence, that's okay. A simple follow-up question— "Are you okay? Do you have any questions for me?"—allows them to respond if they wish.

Additional Questions and Answers to Consider

Your child may have questions, in the moment or later, that you will want to be prepared to answer.

Question: "Did people die when that tsunami happened?"
Answer: "Yes, but a lot of people were saved. There were lots of helpers there like Coast Guard, rescue workers, doctors, and nurses. I'm very sad that some people died, but I am thankful that people were there to help save so many. How do you feel?"

A question like this may reflect your child's anxiety and fear about what they saw. Your child needs an honest response paired with reassurance that adults were present to intervene and help. Be honest about the event; a child who questions this likely already knows the answer. Share your sorrow or fear over what happened, but pair that with an expression of gratitude for the people who helped. Conversations like this will help your child understand that both sets of feelings are accepted and expected. Focusing on the helpers is reassuring and positive, and may ease your child's anxiety.

Question: "Why did that tsunami happen?"

Answer: "That is a big question. Sometimes things like this happen in nature. The earth beneath the ocean can change and make a very big wave happen. Sometimes the wave makes storms. I don't really understand all about it, but I do know that it does not happen very often. There are special scientists who study this type of nature event, and they help warn people if it is going to happen again. Do you think we should make a picture for the weather scientists in *our* community, who keep *us* safe every day?"

Young children will commonly want to know why something occurred. A natural disaster can be very difficult to explain. Keep the account simple and scientific, and emphasize that these events do not occur often. Even in an area that is more commonly struck by particular natural disasters, it is best to ease anxiety in the moment. Focus on those who are there to help predict and address such a natural disaster. This will reassure your child that they are safe and that there are people to assist. Offering a way your child can show appreciation to disaster helpers shifts the focus toward the helpers and away from the fear or anxiety about the event itself.

Question: "Is that hurricane going to come and wreck our house?"

Answer: "It's true that the hurricane may bring a lot of rain and wind to our town. We have done what we are supposed to do to prepare. We have shutters on our windows to protect the glass. We have extra food and water to drink, and we have lots of flashlights with batteries in case the power goes out. We are ready and will do all we know to do to be safe through the storm. Would you like to keep a flashlight by your bed tonight?"

Give your child simple explanations and a sense of calm. Children notice changes around them and can sense anxiety. Ease your child's concerns by explaining simply why certain steps are being taken and by reassuring them of their safety and security. Find a way to involve your child in safety steps.

Preparing for Unexpected Responses

Young children are not always aware of what "should" and "should not" be said. This lack of life experience can lead them to make statements that are unexpected and may feel hurtful. Preparing for such remarks and considering why a young child might respond this way can help you support your child and buffer yourself from emotional reaction.

> **Child:** "I want to see a tornado!"
>
> **Adult:** "Tornados are amazing things that happen in nature, and they are very powerful. We can get a book about tornados from the library to see more about them. A tornado can do a lot of damage, and I am glad we are safe here in our home and have a safe place to go in the basement if a tornado does come."

A child saying this may be curious or excited by the idea of a tornado. Children are naturally curious and naïve, so don't scold your child for such a remark. The most appropriate response is to acknowledge that tornados are fascinating and incredible things in nature and to explain that what your child saw or heard about was serious and not something to wish for. You may also want to explain that you are sad about what happened in the picture or conversation your child witnessed. Young children often look to adults to model how to express emotion. However, this is not a time to tell more about the event or to elicit sadness from your child. Focusing on helpers or on how to be safe during a tornado can ease anxiety.

> **Child:** "I want to see what happened."
>
> **Adult:** "I know you are very curious, and it is good to be curious and want to know more. Looking at photos of that earthquake makes me feel sad because a lot of people lost their homes and a lot of buildings were damaged. I would much rather think about something happy that we both like, such as getting ready for Bubbe to visit tomorrow."

This statement probably indicates that a child has natural curiosity and does not fully understand what has occurred. You can explain to your child that seeing pictures of sad things makes us sad. Instead, have the child think of something they feel happy about and talk about that together.

> **Child:** (silence)
>
> **Adult:** "Would you like a hug?"

Silence may denote that your child does not understand and therefore is not reacting, or it might mean that they are still processing what they've been told and how they feel about it. Respect this silence. Any exposure to natural disasters is difficult for adults to handle and can be overwhelming for young children. Give your child a few moments to think and be still and then reassure them that you are there if they want to talk. Offer a hug, a cuddle, or some cozy time together. This will remind them that they are loved and will allow some space for your child to feel whatever they are feeling. Even if your child does not understand what is happening, they will sense your emotion, and the extra dose of comforting will ease any anxiety they may be feeling.

In discussing natural disasters, your most critical goals are to understand what your child is feeling and to help them feel safe and secure. You know your child. Use that understanding, always taking care to listen and observe and not jump to conclusions about how they may feel or what they may know or not know. Talking together is the key to understanding and supporting your child.

Additional Resources for families

Earthquake! (Natural Disasters) by Marion Dane Bauer, illustrated by John Wallace. This easy-reader, nonfiction book explains in simple terms what an earthquake is and what causes it. The book will serve to answer many of the scientific questions a child may have in a developmentally appropriate way for preschool and early elementary–age children. Other books in the same series include *Flood!* and *Volcano!*

I Am the Storm by Jane Yolen and Heidi E.Y. Stemple, illustrated by Kristen and Kevin Howdeshell. This book is a wonderful telling of multiple families' preparedness and resilience through a variety of storms: tornado, blizzard, forest fire, and hurricane. The book beautifully presents the power both of storms and of the families who come through them.

Yesterday We Had a Hurricane by Deirdre McLaughlin Mercier. This book, written by a primary-school teacher, tells of a hurricane experience from the perspective of a young child. With simple text and illustrations, the book helps young children learn more about hurricanes, why they occur, and what the effects of these storms are.

Social Upheaval

Incidents of social upheaval have ripple effects across communities and the world. Wars, displacement, migration, civil unrest, and health crises affect many of us, directly or indirectly. Glimpses of videos or photos of death, devastation, and turmoil imprint images that are difficult to remove from one's memory, as do protest marches with angry exchanges, police or military presence, sirens, and curfews. A pandemic, such as the COVID-19 outbreak that began in 2020, affects individuals everywhere. We live in a time when the constant presence or reminders of turmoil can lead to chronic anxiety, stress, and trauma for adults and consequently for children as well.

Young children are very perceptive to the emotionality and stress level of those around them. A quick-tempered response, a grown-up fighting back tears, a TV or radio quickly silenced, or hushed conversations put children on alert. More noticable and pronounced measures such as a change to online school at home, collecting money or goods for struggling communities, or hearing heated disagreements about ways to address social issues can elevate the agitation. Children are egotistical by nature and so they may tend to take any crisis as a personal threat, whether it directly affects them or not. This can lead some children to intense levels of worry and panic.

Talking with Family Adults About Children's Responses to Social Upheaval

Parents may share with teachers that their child has been impacted by or exposed to media coverage of crisis and how the child has reacted. Teachers may notice children's responses to social tensions in the community or will want to share with families issues that arise among children at school. A simple, sensitive response or query from you can help you acknowledge the concern and also provide a chance to determine what the parent expects from you in terms of supporting the child. For example:

▶ "Today during circle time, Nikki asked about the uprisings that have been occurring in response to the recent shooting. I was able to speak with her about her feelings and she shared that she is scared about what she has seen and heard on the news. We talked about the community helpers who've been helping the situation and I reassured her that she's safe here at school. If Nikki brings this up to me again, how would you like me to respond to her? "

▶ "I think you should know that there has been talk among the children about families being separated at the border. I haven't heard Tyden say anything, but I wonder if he has brought this up at home?"

Talking with Children: Conversation Starters

In talking with young children about any kind of social upheaval, you can lessen the emotional charge of such conversations by being prepared. In the classroom or group setting, the conversation and questions should be led by the child. The text that follows gives examples of how this may be approached.

> **Katja, to Cee-Cee:** "You have to wear a mask and not breathe on me or we are all going to get sick."
>
> **Teacher, Ms. Acorn:** "I heard you talking together about wearing a mask. This is something we do to keep ourselves and our friends safe and healthy. Can you tell me how it feels to wear a mask and to see other people wear masks?"

The goal is to respond to the child's words while easing the fear and anxiety-provoking elements. The teacher's explanation of why people wear masks demystifies the behavior and keeps the conversation objective and factual. Ms. Acorn then prompts Katja and Cee-Cee to share how they are feeling about the health precautions.

> **Kayen, to Geraldine (on the playground):** "Let's play war together like those countries shooting missiles. I'm going to shoot you dead!"
>
> **Ms. Acorn, to Kayen (later):** "You and Geraldine like to play together. I heard you talk about countries shooting missiles. What do you know about countries at war with missiles?"

The goal is to understand what the child knows about the topic and any feelings related to it. Notice how this teacher does not scold Kayen for this attempt at pretend weapon play. Instead she asks him to elaborate on what he knows about the war he referenced. By asking what he knows, Ms. Acorn ensures that she does not share information that Kayen is not aware of. Following his response, she may remind Kayen and Geraldine not to pretend to shoot at people who aren't part of their play, or guide their play in a different direction to avoid involving other children.

> **Manuel:** "I am so sad. My cousins live in Cuba and they want to come live here. Why can't they come here? I want to see my cousins!"
>
> **Ms. Acorn:** "I can see why you feel sad about that, Manuel. Family is important to all of us, and I understand why you want your cousins to come live here. Would you like to draw a picture or write them a letter to let them know you are thinking about them?"

The goal is to acknowledge the emotion. Note that Ms. Acorn does not offer additional information, nor does she allude to the politics of immigration. The role of the teacher here is to acknowledge the child's comment, empathize with his emotion, and attempt to guide him toward a way to express his feelings in an age-appropriate and comforting way.

Following Up

Following any conversation with a child about crisis or social upheaval, it is appropriate and strongly advised that you connect with the family. Share with the family what the child said or asked and how you responded. Ask the family how they would like the conversation handled if their child asks another question or further discussion takes place. This forges a partnership between school and home and also gives families appropriate notice to prepare for follow-up conversations the child may wish to have with them. (For examples, see "Framework for Parent Conversation Starters" in Part I, page 12.) Check with the parent on the exact language they've used with the child so that any discussions at school use consistent vocabulary. Offer the family handout "Talking with Your Child About Social Upheaval" (page 196).

A child may also approach you for further discussion. If a child seeks you out again, allow them to lead the conversation and try to keep it focused on how they are feeling. For example:

> **Kayen, to Ms. Acorn:** "Did that country shoot more missiles? Are there going to be missiles here?"
>
> **Ms. Acorn:** "You are asking big questions. I do not know if there have been any more missiles in that country." (Name the country if the child identified it earlier.) "I do know that we are very safe here at our school. My job is to keep you safe and to help you learn. How are you feeling?"

The goal is to reassure the child and help him explore and identify his feelings. The teacher does not add any additional detail to Kayen's question, and she admits to not having insight into further details. She then reinforces the child's safety and turns the focus to his emotions.

> **Nikki:** "Monica said there was a protest and windows got broken and people were throwing rocks. What's a protest?"
>
> **Ms. Acorn:** "A protest is when people are unhappy or angry about something and they want change to happen, so they gather to speak up about what they want and make their feelings and wishes heard. It is okay for people to protest. Sometimes during a protest there are people who throw or break things. I hope they can find peaceful ways to show what they want so everyone can stay safe.

It is okay to be unhappy or angry, and there are many ways to show how we feel. In our classroom, we practice using our words and calming our bodies so we can say how we feel."

The goal is to answer the question directly and objectively without sharing any political elements. The teacher keeps the conversation focused on the behaviors and the emotions that young children easily understand.

Talking with Your Child About
Social Upheaval

The world is full of unrest and upheaval. A war, a refugee crisis, a protest, a pandemic—all such occurrences are common enough that children are bound to be touched by at least some of them at an early age. Much as we want to protect children from knowing about a major social crisis or experiencing it themselves, the reality is that young children do experience and learn about such events occuring near home and far away. Simply knowing about an explosion or a missile launching in another place can be terrifying for a young child, and it's important to shield children from this knowledge to the extent that we can. Still, no amount of vigilance can completely insulate a child from overhearing conversations, catching a brief TV or radio segment, or seeing a photograph on a phone or in a newspaper or magazine.

Young children naturally have a very narrow worldview and approach the world from an egocentric perspective. Even as children move into the later preschool years and begin to understand that the world is bigger than themselves, it is inconceivable to many children to think of a world where their life, their freedom, or their health is at risk. This protective buffer that children have is one we want to carefully monitor and maintain. Even when crisis and upheaval occur close to home—as in the case of a pandemic or a social uprising—it's still important to vigilantly work to reassure children that they are safe and that it is okay to talk about anything that scares them. Emphasizing children's own safety and the presence of helpers in crisis situations is key to easing children's anxiety.

If your child shows interest in, makes observations of, or asks questions about social crises, it is best to lead into the conversation with a gentle prompt that lets them know that it's okay to talk about the topic. For example:

▸ "I did not know you were there watching the screen behind Daddy and me. We were watching the news to learn about what is happening in the world. I don't know what you saw or heard. Can you tell me what you heard and how you are feeling?"

The goal is to learn what your child saw and heard. When you realize your child has viewed or overheard news you didn't intend for them to know, acknowledge that you were watching the news and unaware of their presence. Then open a dialogue for your child to share what they saw. This is important because you don't want to volunteer more than is necessary: a child may not have seen or heard anything, or they may have taken in an entire story of displaced refugees, a missile attack, or local violent unrest. Then ask how your child is feeling. This can give you insight into how your child interpreted what they saw or heard.

Next, it's important to pause. The words are new, there is a lot of emotion to understand, and it may take the child a few moments to process what was said.

If your child's response is silence, that's okay. A simple follow-up question—"Are you okay? Do you have any questions for me?"—allows your child to respond if they wish.

Additional Questions and Answers to Consider

Your child may have questions, in the moment or later, that you will want to be prepared to answer.

> **Question:** "Did people die during that riot?"
>
> **Answer:** "Yes, some people did die during that riot. People were angry and there was violence. There were lots of big feelings. I am sad and upset that it happened, but we are safe here at our house."

The goal is to give a truthful response paired with reassurance that the child is safe. Be honest about the event; a child who asks a question like this may already know the answer. To the extent possible, emphasize the safety of where your child lives. Try to stay objective and express your own feelings without raising your voice or visibly showing fear or anger. This will help your child better understand the behavior that occurred, and your child will see that big feelings can be expressed calmly rather than violently.

> **Question:** "Is the virus making people die?"
>
> **Answer:** "Yes. It makes me very sad but some people have died from the virus which is why we are (getting vaccines/wearing our masks) and being very safe and careful. I want people everywhere to be able to keep safe from the virus. I am happy that you are here with me and that we are safe together."

Again, the goal is to answer honestly and reassuringly in order to ease any anxiety the child may have. Your child may also wonder why you, or they themself, don't have a vaccine, or when they can get one, or if it will hurt. Answer all such questions as simply as possible and remind your child that you are keeping them safe.

Preparing for Unexpected Responses

Young children are not always aware of what "should" and "should not" be said. This lack of life experience can lead them to make statements that are unexpected and may feel hurtful. Preparing for such remarks and considering why a young child might respond this way can help you support your child and buffer yourself from emotional reaction.

Child: "At least we aren't going to die."

Adult: "It's true that we are safe here and that makes me very happy. I'm also sad, though, that other people have died."

A young child who says this may be expressing relief about their own safety or trying to make sense of death. It's important to affirm that your child is right. When you express your own happiness about the family's safety and sadness for the greater loss of life, your child can begin to learn that it is possible and acceptable to feel more than one emotion at the same time.

Child: "Wars are stupid!"

Adult: "You are right that there are much better ways to solve problems than fighting. We use our words to talk things out. We can think of ways to solve problems that make everyone happier. Sometimes with big problems in the world, people get angry and stop being willing to talk them over. That is when wars happen. Wars make me sad. The world would be a much happier place if people would always talk to each other kindly and work together."

This child's remark may mean the child wishes there were not wars, or it may show a beginning understanding that war does not solve problems the way the child has been taught to solve them. Support this. Use your own words to affirm your child's wisdom and the problem-solving skills they've been taught: using words, being kind, and compromising.

Child: "Why are there so many bad things?"

Adult: "There are bad things that happen, and I wonder if you are talking about the news story we saw of the children in refugee camps." (Pause to confirm this.) "While there are bad things that happen in this world, I want you to also remember all of the people that they showed who are there helping—health workers, people who brought food, teachers, and guards to make sure the children were safe. Whenever bad things happen, there are always helpers."

A proactive focus upon safety and help can ease your child's anxiety. Children have a hard time conceptualizing not being safe or cared for. This is a scary thought and seeing bad things happen to themselves, to others, and in the broader world can be quite unsettling. While you cannot always shield your child from this exposure, you can help them focus on the positive change that people and organizations seek to make by aiding, assisting, and preventing many "bad things."

> **Child:** (silence)
>
> **Adult:** "Would you like a hug?"

Silence can denote that children do not understand and therefore are not reacting, or it can mean that they're still processing what they've been told or seen and how they feel about it. Respect this silence. War, displacement, pandemics, and social uprisings are difficult concepts for adults to handle and can be overwhelming for young children too. Give your child a few moments to think and be still and then offer reassurance that you are here and willing to talk. Offer a hug or a gentle squeeze. This will remind your child that you love them and will allow some space for them to feel whatever they are feeling. Even if they do not understand what is happening, your child will sense your emotion, and the extra dose of comfort will ease any anxiety they may feel.

In helping your child cope with concerns about any kind of troubling or frightening events, keep in mind the famous saying from Mr. Rogers, who told children: "When I was a boy and I would see scary things in the news, my mother would say to me, 'Look for the helpers. You will always find people who are helping.'" This is true, and knowing there are adult helpers can go a long way toward helping young children feel safe and hopeful.

Additional Resources for Families

Global Conflict by Louise Spilsbury, illustrated by Hanane Kai. This book, part of a larger picture book series, helps young children understand about war and conflict in simple terms and with appealing illustrations. The book is ideal for young children who need a very simplified explanation of war and a reiteration of their own safety. Other titles in the series include *Refugees and Migrants* and *Racism and Intolerance*.

Pete and the Pandemic by Lindsay McDanel and Christina Reichart, illustrated by Lisa Wee. This children's book, written during the peak of the 2020 COVID-19 pandemic in the US, helps young children understand how to label feelings and make sense of the world when the community is changing radically around the child.

Something Happened in Our Town: A Child's Story About Racial Injustice by Marianne Celano, Marietta Collins, and Ann Hazzard, illustrated by Jennifer Zivoin. This book for kindergarten and early-elementary students follows two families, one Black and one White, as they talk about the shooting of a Black man by a police officer.

Sometimes People March by Tessa Allen. This picture book is written for older preschool-age children and young elementary school–age children and, in simple text, explains to them the power of coming together for change. The illustrations depict as much story as the text, with rich representations of diverse people.

Gun Violence and Terror Events

Gun violence and terror events can occur anywhere—in homes, neighborhoods, malls, restaurants, and schools. There are few if any greater fears for adults than to think of their child being at risk of violence within a school or care setting. And news of terror events, wherever they occur, touches us all. Fear and anxiety over the loss of control define how most adults react to terror events. People may avoid discussing terror events to divert the intense emotions, or they may begin to feel desensitized to such events as these happenings become increasingly frequent.

Terror events and gun violence are unfathomable for a young child—such events inherently lack a concrete or simple explanation. The vocabulary used to talk about these attacks—words like *terror, extremist, shooter, massacre, bomb, motive, casualties*—are unknown to a young child and add to the anxiety. Children may hear brief references about what occurred, see an image or part of a video clip without context, notice grown-ups talking in hushed whispers, or witness emotional reactions among adults. To add to the confusion, children and teachers often participate in routine safety drills, the purpose behind which is, appropriately, not fully explained to young children. All of this adds to the mystery and sense that asking questions may be taboo.

When young children are exposed to or learn of shootings and other terror events, it is highly likely that they will exhibit physiological and psychological symptoms. Children may report new fears or show increased emotional reactions such as crying. They may start to have unsettling dreams or night terrors. Exposure to any element related to the event (such as seeing a train go by after a child has heard about a terrorist attack on a train, or hearing a car backfire after exposure to gunfire) may generate a fear response. Children need to be reassured that they are safe and reminded that it is okay to talk about anything that scares them.

Talking with Family Adults About Terror Events

If possible, conversations with parents should take place following terror events that are in the news to understand what, if anything, a child knows about the event's occurrence. Provide any resources your school or program has available as well as the handout "Talking with Your Child About Gun Violence and Terror Events" (page 204).

Talking with Children: Conversation Starters

Difficult conversations are inevitable when working with young children, but the emotional charge of such conversations can be lessened by being prepared and by being mindful of your own emotions. The examples of responses here offer some language you might use.

> **Johnny, to Birdie (while playing):** "I drove my car in and blowed up the building just like those bad guys did to the building in the desert! Boom!"
>
> **Teacher, Ms. Parker, to Johnny (later):** "I heard you talking to Birdie about blowing up a building like some bad guys did. Did you see something about a building blowing up in a desert?"
>
> **Johnny:** "I saw it on YouTube—my uncle was watching it."
>
> **Ms. Parker:** "That was a scary thing that happened. How did that feel to see that on YouTube? Would you like to talk with me about it?"

The goal is to ascertain what the child has seen or heard and offer support. Ms. Parker does not criticize Johnny for his way of playing. Instead, they ask him about what he saw. This is important as it prevents the teacher from sharing additional information about an event beyond what the child knows. Ms. Parker then asks him about his feelings and lets him know they are available to talk. This response from his teacher reassures Johnny that it is acceptable to talk about the event and that Ms. Parker is a safe person who will listen.

> **Dori, to Aaditya:** "Is your brother a teenager? Two teenagers shooted up a bunch of other teenagers at a school. I saw it on the TV!"
>
> **Ms. Parker, to Dori (later):** "I heard you talking to Aaditya about teenagers shooting at a school. That was a very scary thing that happened, and it makes me feel very sad. If you want to talk to me, I am here. I need you to know that you are safe here at our school, and my job is to keep you safe. Would you like a hug?"

The goal is to reassure the child that it is acceptable and safe to talk with the teacher about the event she witnessed. Here Ms. Parker acknowledges objectively what they overheard. The teacher does not negate what was discussed, since clearly Dori had exposure to the news of the school shooting. Ms. Parker assures Dori that the school is a safe place to be, and pairs this with a physical comfort by offering a hug.

In this example, the teacher will also need to speak with Aaditya, who may not have known about the school shooting and now may also have questions.

> **Ms. Parker, to Aaditya (privately):** "I heard Dori talking to you about teenagers shooting at a school. That was a very scary thing that happened, and it makes me feel very sad. I need you to know that you are safe here at school, and my job is to keep you safe. How do you feel about what Dori told you? Would you like to talk with me about this?"

Here the teacher's goal is to learn how Aaditya was affected by hearing about the shooting and to reassure him that he is safe. Ms. Parker invites Aaditya to share his emotions about what his friend told him and then offers themselves as a safe person to talk to.

> **Peter, to Ms. Parker:** "My synagogue has a police guard now. Is someone going to shoot people in my synagogue like happened at that other one?"
>
> **Ms. Parker:** "That is a big question. The guard at your synagogue is a helper who is there to keep everyone safe. There are lots of helpers in our community who work to keep us safe every day—police, firefighters, teachers, and our families too. You are safe here at school and safe here in our classroom. The guard at your synagogue is there to keep you safe there too. How do you feel to have the guard there?"

The goal again is to emphasize safety. Note that the teacher uses very concrete language. They do not silence the question, but they do help shift Peter's focus away from the violent act and toward the community helpers. Ms. Parker then asks about how Peter feels, allowing him to identify and express his emotions further.

> **Lucia, to Ms. Parker:** "Someone got shot across the street from my house last night. The police and ambulances all came."
>
> **Ms. Parker:** "I did not know that happened. How did it feel for you to have all of that happening? Can I give you a hug?"

Connect first with the emotion. The child may not know how she feels, or is supposed to feel, with regard to what happened. Mixed with the likely fear may be excitement over seeing all of the emergency vehicles. Ms. Parker has opened the dialogue for Lucia to talk more about how she is feeling. In listening and following through, the teacher should be open and accepting of any emotion the child brings up.

Following Up

Following any conversation with a child about terrorism, shootings, or other violence, it is appropriate and strongly advised that you connect with the family or families of the children involved in the conversation. Share with the family what the child said or asked and how you responded. Ask the family how they would like the conversation handled if their child asks another question or further discussion takes place. This forges a partnership between school and home and also gives families appropriate notice to prepare for follow-up conversations the child may wish to have with them. Offer the family handout "Talking with Your Child About Gun Violence and Terror Events" (page 204). Here are three examples; for more ideas, see "Framework for Parent Conversation Starters " in Part I, page 12:

▶ "Dori was talking today about the school shooting reported on TV last night. I talked to her one-on-one and assured her she is safe here at our school. She seemed keyed up and wanted a hug. You may want to check in with Dori about this to see if she has questions or worries. If she brings this up again, is there something particular you would like me to tell her?"

▶ "Aaditya heard from another child today about the school shooting that just happened. I checked in with Aaditya to let him know we're safe here at school and ask how he's feeling. He seemed upset that a teenager would do that. I thought you should know so you can talk more with him about this at home."

▶ "I wanted you to know that Lucia shared with me today about someone getting shot near your home last night. I asked her how she was feeling and she seemed agitated and not really sure how to feel. I have an information sheet that might help you talk with her about this more at home. Would you like me to give you a copy?"

A child may also approach you for further discussion. If a child seeks you out again, allow them to lead the conversation and try to keep it focused on how they are feeling. For example:

Aaditya, to Ms. Parker: "Is someone going to hurt kids at our school like that teenager did at (name of school)?"

Ms. Parker: "That is a big question. What happened at (name of school) is very sad and was very scary. The teachers and the police and rescue workers worked fast to stop the shooting and keep everybody else there safe. You are safe here at our center and safe here in our classroom. My job and the job of all the grown-ups here is to keep you safe so that nothing like that will happen to us. Can you draw a picture with me of how you are feeling and what things make you feel safe?"

The goal is to calm the child's worries and affirm his safety. The teacher uses very concrete language. Because Aaditya states the name of the school where the shooting occurred, Ms. Parker acknowledges the school by name too. They do not silence the question but do help shift the child's focus away from the violent act and toward the community helpers. The teacher then responds with an open-ended question that allows Aaditya an opportunity to further explore and share his feelings and what makes him feel safe.

Lucia: "My grandpa said no one's safe anymore, but my daddy said that's not true. He said he'll always keep me safe. I'm glad my daddy knows how to keep me safe."

Ms. Parker, to Lucia: "Your daddy loves you, and I know he will keep you safe. You are safe here at school too. What is your favorite place to be in our classroom?"

Safety needs to be reiterated. Children need to know that when bad things happen in the world, there are always people near them who are there to keep them safe.

Talking with Your Child About
Gun Violence and Terror Events

Terror events and gun violence are sudden and shocking, and impossible for a young child to conceptualize or understand. The words used to talk about terror attacks—*terrorist, extremist, shooter, massacre, bomb, motive, casualties*—are mysterious to a young child, adding to the level of stress and anxiety. Children may overhear news reports or see images of what occurred, hear adults talking in hushed whispers, or witness emotional reactions among adults. All of this adds to the mystery and the sense that asking questions may be taboo.

When young children are exposed to or learn of shootings or terror attacks, it is highly likely that they will exhibit physiological and psychological symptoms. Your child may talk about new fears or show increased emotional reactions such as agitation, crying, unsettling dreams, or night terrors. Exposure to anything related to the event (such as seeing a train go by after a child has heard about a terrorist attack on a train, or hearing fireworks or a car backfire after exposure to gunfire) may arouse a fear response. It's critical that you reassure your child that they are safe and remind them that it is okay to talk about anything that scares them.

We all want and need to protect children from knowing about terrorism and gun violence, and it's important to do all you can to shield your child from news coverage, conversations, and visual images related to these events. Despite your best efforts, your child might learn about shootings or terrorism far away or close to home. If you suspect your child is aware of a violent event, it's important to bring the subject out into the open. It's especially important to do this in situations where you're not sure how much your child has seen or heard about what happened. They may ask a question, or you may need to start with a simple prompt, signaling that it's okay to talk about the topic. For example:

▶ "I saw you looking at the big TV screens while we were in the store today. They were showing pictures of something very sad and scary that happened in a place far away called (name of place). I don't think you have ever seen pictures like those before. How did it feel when you saw them?"

This statement tells your child that you know what they saw and that it's okay to talk about it. It gives them a platform to share how they felt in seeing the images, and it also provides a safe place if they have other questions. It is helpful to say how you are feeling—this can reassure your child that their own feelings are acceptable. Here, the parent notes that the images on the screen were scary and sad and then offers only one new detail—that the event took place far away. If it is possible to make the point that it happened far way (or in another town, or in another neighborhood), be sure to say so. This reassures the child that they are in a safe place. Equally important is to offer no more details. Your child may not know much, and you do not want to create anxiety or fear by providing information they may not need to learn. Asking about your child's feelings opens a window for you to discover more.

▶ "I think you may have been looking at the computer with your big sister. She told me she watched a news report to learn about something that happened far away. I do not know what you saw or heard. Can you tell me what you heard and how you are feeling?"

The goal is to learn how much the child saw and heard and how they are feeling about it. This example acknowledges that the parent learned about something the child might have seen and heard. The parent asks the child to share what they saw. In this situation, your child may have seen and absorbed very little or may have taken in the entire story of a terrorist attack. Again, you do not want to volunteer more than is necessary. Next, ask how your child is feeling. Besides giving you a chance to gain insight into how they interpreted what they saw or heard, your question allows your child to consider and express emotions they are experiencing.

▶ "Your teacher told me your friend Carina told you about something that happened at a high school. Can you talk to me about what you and Carina said? I want to help you understand as best I can and answer any questions you might have. You can always talk with me."

The goal is to open dialogue and let your child know it is okay to ask questions. Do not explain or offer any additional information until your child shares what they were told. After listening, you can confirm or clarify what your child understands. This also allows you, as the adult, to gauge how much support, probing, and guidance your child may need or be seeking. Always affirm your willingness to listen, so your child knows they did not do something wrong in knowing or wondering about something they've overheard or been told.

Next, it's important to pause. The images and words are new, there is a lot of emotion to understand, and it may take your child a few moments to process what was said.

If your child's response is silence, that's okay. A simple follow-up question— "Are you okay? Do you have any questions for me?"—allows them to respond if they wish.

Additional Questions and Answers to Consider

Your child may have questions, in the moment or later, that you will want to be prepared to answer.

Question: "Did people die from that bomb (or "at that school")?"

Answer: "Yes. People did die, although many people were saved or got away. There were lots of helpers there to help people—people nearby who helped right away, and other helpers like rescue workers, firefighters, soldiers, and doctors and nurses. I am very sad that some people died. I am also glad that people were there to help. How do you feel?"

This question likely reflects a child's anxiety and fear regarding what they saw. The child needs an honest response paired with reassurance that adults were present to intervene and help. Tell the truth, briefly and with no unnecessary details. Focus on and emphasize the helpers to ease your child's anxiety. Share your own sadness or fear over what happened, but pair this with an expression of gratitude for the adults who helped. This allows your child to see that both sets of feelings are accepted and expected.

Question: "Who did that?"

Answer: "The person was called (name of person), and they made a very bad choice. It's over now, and I am thankful so many people were there to help. I am also thankful we have lots of helpers here in our town working to keep us safe. Would you like to make a card or a picture for one of our community helpers?"

The heart of this question may be curiosity or a concern about safety. This is not a time to talk about extreme views, religious hostilities, military conflict, or mental illness. In this example the adult knows and therefore gives the name of the perpetrator, to answer the child's direct question. If you don't know, simply say "I don't know who did it, but they made a very bad choice." Then it is important to shift the focus to laypeople and professionals who were there to offer aid, assistance, and recovery. Always emphasize the helpers and the safety in your own community as well. This reassures your child that they're safe and that there are helpers to assist in unknown or known places and in your child's own world. The invitation to make a card or picture helps direct your child to something concrete and positive they can do.

Question: "Could that happen at my school?"

Answer: "That is a very big question. Bad things *could* happen anywhere, but I think you are safe at your school. The principal, teachers, and security guards work to keep you and the other children safe every day. You are safe at your school, and you are safe at home. Can you draw a picture to show me how you are feeling and what things help you feel safe?"

This question shows that your child is worried about their own safety. Do not silence a question like this. It is important to be honest and affirm that it is possible for bad things to happen anywhere. Then quickly shift the focus to calm and reassure your child. Emphasize your own belief that the school is a safe place. Children need to know they are safe at school and at home and that adults around them are working to ensure their continued safety. Drawing and sharing a picture can help your child process their feelings and open up more discussion about safety and helpers.

Preparing for Unexpected Responses

Young children are not always aware of what "should" and "should not" be said. This lack of life experience can lead them to make statements that are unexpected and may feel hurtful. Preparing for such remarks and considering why a young child might respond this way can help you support your child and buffer yourself from emotional reaction.

> **Child:** "I want to blow something up too!"
>
> **Adult:** "There are fun things we can think of like fireworks, knocking our blocks down, and making slime. What happened there is not fun. It is very sad and scary for those people. Let's play something different so we can think of something that is happier."

A young child responding this way does not understand what they have seen. There is some comfort in the naïveté of childhood, and a child should not be scolded for this kind of remark. The most appropriate response is to acknowledge what really is fun (fireworks, knocking down block towers, playing with slime), and explain that what the child saw or heard is not fun and is not okay. Young children often look to adults to model how to express emotion. It is perfectly acceptable and appropriate to share with a young child the alarm or sadness people felt, as well as your own feelings about it. However, this is not a time to tell your child more about the event or to try to prompt or kindle sadness in your child.

> **Child:** "Let's kill the bad guys."
>
> **Adult:** "Those are very violent words. It is never okay to hurt other people. I am sad about what happened but I am also very happy and proud that safety officers and firefighters were able to help."

This response probably reflects a child's desire to delineate good from bad. The child may also be keyed up and seeking to release emotional energy. Do not scold. Instead, remind your child that it is never okay to harm other people. Shift the focus to the rescue workers and responders present to offer aid, assistance, and recovery. Help your child see that the good actions are those of the people who work to help others.

> **Child:** "I want to see what happened."
>
> **Adult:** "I know you are curious, but seeing pictures of sad, scary things makes *us* feel sad and scared. I don't want to do that. Can we think of something else that we can look at or something else that we can do that will be a happy thing instead?"

This response reflects a child who does not fully understand what has occurred and has natural curiosity. Affirm your child's curiosity, and then redirect them to think of something uplifting and happy to focus on instead.

> **Child:** (silence)
>
> **Adult:** "Would you like a hug?"

Silence may denote that your child does not understand and therefore is not reacting, or it might mean they're still processing what they've seen or been told and how they feel about it. Respect this silence. Any exposure to terror attacks and gun violence is difficult for adults to handle and can be overwhelming for young children. Give your child a few moments to think and be still and then reassure them that you are here if they want to talk. Offer a hug, snuggle, or some cozy time together. This will remind them that they are loved and will allow some space for your child to feel whatever they are feeling. Even if your child does not understand what has happened, they will sense your emotion, and the extra dose of comforting will ease any anxiety they may be feeling.

In discussing terror and violence, your most critical goals are to understand what your child knows and feels and to help them feel safe and secure. You know your child. Use that understanding, always taking care to listen and observe and not jump to conclusions about what they may know or not know or how they may feel. Talking together is the key to understanding and supporting your child.

Additional Resources for Families

Come with Me by Holly M. McGhee, illustrated by Pascal Lemaître. This children's book does not address terror events directly, but it focuses on a child who knows of news reports about fearful and violent events and whose family helps her see how goodness occurs in her everyday life. Children learn the impact of showing friendship and giving to others through kind deeds and words.

Safe and Sound: A story about a little girl who overcomes fear by Paul North and Lydia So. This children's book tells the story of a young girl who fears loud noises and scary thoughts. She learns to overcome her fears, feel safe, and feel loved and secure.

Something Happened in Our Park: Standing Together After Gun Violence by Ann Hazzard, Marianne Celano, and Marietta Collins, illustrated by Keith Henry Brown. In this book for kindergarten and early-elementary students, a young boy's sister is injured in a shooting and the boy learns he can cope with his fears and that people can work together to lessen or stop violence in their neighborhoods or communities.

A Terrible Thing Happened: A Story for Children Who Have Witnessed Violence or Trauma by Margaret M. Holmes, illustrated by Cary Pillo. This children's book talks about the main character seeing something terrible that is making him nervous and giving him bad dreams. The character learns that by talking to someone that he can begin to feel better. The book was written to help children who have witnessed violent events. However, because it never states what the terrible thing was, it is also helpful for children aware of different types of occurrences who have not been present to see them.

References

American Academy of Pediatrics (AAP). 2009. "Talking to Your Young Child About Sex." HealthyChildren.org. Last updated November 12, 2009. healthychildren.org/English/ages-stages/preschool/Pages/Talking-to-Your -Young-Child-About-Sex.aspx.

———. 2019. "Sexual Behaviors in Young Children: What's Normal, What's Not?" HealthyChildren.org. Last updated April 1, 2019. healthychildren.org /English/ages-stages/preschool/Pages/Sexual-Behaviors-Young-Children.aspx.

American Psychological Association (APA). 2014. "Transgender People, Gender Identity, and Gender Expression." Psychology Topics: LGBTQ. Accessed August 25, 2021. apa.org/topics/lgbtq/transgender.

———. n.d. "Marriage & divorce." Psychology Topics: Divorce. Accessed August 25, 2021. apa.org/topics/divorce-child-custody.

Bauer, Lauren. 2020. "About 14 million children in the US are not getting enough to eat." Up Front (blog), Brookings Institution. July 9, 2020. brookings.edu/blog /up-front/2020/07/09/about-14-million-children-in-the-us-are-not-getting -enough-to-eat/.

Beacham, Barbara, and Janet Deatrick. 2015. "Children with Chronic Conditions: Perspectives on Condition Management." *Journal of Pediatric Nursing* 30, no. 1 (January 1, 2015): 25–35. doi.org/10.1016/j.pedn.2014.10.011.

Boelen, Paul A., Mariken Spuij, and Albert H. A. Reijntjes. 2017. "Prolonged grief and posttraumatic stress in bereaved children: A latent class analysis." *Psychiatry Research* 258 (December 2017): 518–524. doi.org/10.1016/j.psychres.2017.09.002.

Bonanno, Caitlin M., and Richard L. Levenson, Jr. 2014. "School Shooters: History, Current Theoretical and Empirical Findings, and Strategies for Prevention." *SAGE Open* January–March 2014: 1–11. doi.org/10.1177/2158244014525425.

Children's Health Policy Centre. 2014. "Alcohol and drugs don't mix with parenting." *Children's Mental Health Research Quarterly* 8, no. 1 (Winter 2014): 3. childhealthpolicy.ca/wp-content/uploads/2014/01/RQ-1-14-winter.pdf.

Clayton, Gina, Endria Richardson, Lily Mandlin, and Brittany Farr. 2018. *Because She's Powerful: The Political Isolation and Resistance of Women with Incarcerated Loved Ones*. Los Angeles and Oakland, CA: Essie Justice Group. hbecausesshespowerful.org /wp-content/uploads/2018/05/Essie-Justice-Group_Because-Shes-Powerful- Report.pdf.

Copple, Carol, and Sue Bredekamp, eds. 2009. *Developmentally Appropriate Practice in Early Childhood Programs Serving Children from Birth Through Age 8*, 3rd. ed. Washington, DC: National Association for the Education of Young Children (NAEYC).

Cutchlow, Tracy. 2015. "Why Reality Slides Into Fantasy for Preschoolers." Child Development Institute. March 2, 2015. childdevelopmentinfo.com/development /reality-slides-fantasy-preschoolers/#gs.9snk7m.

Deczynski, Rebecca. 2015. "17 TV Shows that Celebrate Non-Traditional Families." Cafemom (blog), Wild Sky Media. December 10, 2015. cafemom.com /entertainment/193443-17_tv_shows_that_celebrate.

Derman-Sparks, Louise, and Julie Olsen Edwards. 2019. "Understanding Anti-Bias Education: Bringing the Four Core Goals to Every Facet of Your Curriculum." *YC Young Children* 74, no. 5 (November 2019): 6–13. jstor.org/stable/26842300.

Enns, Peter K., Christopher Wildeman, Youngmin Yi, Megan Comfort, Maria Fitzpatrick, Alyssa Goldman, Hedwig Lee, Christopher Muller, Sara Wakefield, and Emily A. Wang. 2018. *Family History of Incarceration Survey* (FamHIS) - Release 3. NORC at the University of Chicago. Cornell University, Ithaca, NY: Roper Center for Public Opinion Research [distributor]. doi.org/10.25940/ROPER-31115615.

Erdman, Sarah, Laura J. Colker, and Elizabeth C. Winter. 2020. *Trauma and Young Children: Teaching Strategies to Support and Empower*. Washington, DC: National Association for the Education of Young Children (NAEYC).

Gallup-Sharecare Well-Being Index. 2018. "State of American Well-Being: 2017 Community Well-Being Rankings." March 2018. wellbeingindex.sharecare.com /wp-content/uploads/2018/03/GallupSharecare-State-of-American-Well-Being _2017-Community-Rankings_vFINAL.pdf.

Gates, Gary J. "Marriage and Family: LGBT Individuals and Same-Sex Couples" *The Future of Children* 25, no. 2 (Fall 2015): 67–87. jstor.org/stable/43581973.

Generations United. n.d. "Multigenerational Households." Accessed August 25, 2021. gu.org/explore-our-topics/multigenerational-households/.

Gotsch, Kara. 2018 "Families and Mass Incarceration." The Sentencing Project. April 24, 2018. sentencingproject.org/publications/6148/.

Grosemans, Ilke, Karin Hannes, Julie Neyens, and Eva Kyndt. 2020. "Emerging Adults Embarking on Their Careers: Job and Identity Explorations in the Transition to Work." *Youth & Society* 52, 5: 795–819. doiorg/10.1177 /0044118X18772695.

Harms, Thelma, Richard M. Clifford, and Debby Cryer. 2014. *Early Childhood Environment Rating Scale*, 3rd ed. (ECERS-3). New York: Teachers College Press.

Harms, Thelma, Debby Cryer, Richard M. Clifford, and Noreen Yazejian. 2017. *Infant/Toddler Environment Rating Scale*, 3rd ed. (ITERS-3). New York: Teachers College Press.

Holloway, Holly. 2018. "How Substance Abuse Affects Children." MedMark Treatment Centers. August 29, 2018. medmark.com/how-substance-use-affects -children/.

Kübler-Ross, Elizabeth, and David Kessler. 2014. *On Grief and Grieving*. London: Simon & Schuster.

Lipari, Rachel N., and Struther L. Van Horn. 2017. "Children Living with Parents Who Have a Substance Use Disorder." The SBHSQ Report. August 24, 2017. Rockville, MD: Center for Behavior Health Statistics and Quality, Substance Abuse and Mental Health Services Administration (SAMHSA). samhsa.gov/data /sites/default/files/report_3223/ShortReport-3223.html.

Military.com. n.d. "Deployment: An Overview." Accessed August 25, 2021. military.com/deployment/deployment-overview.html.

National Association for Children of Addiction (NACoA). 2021. nacoa.org.

National Association for the Education of Young Children (NAEYC). 2019. *NAEYC Early Learning Program Accreditation Standards and Assessment Items*. Washington, DC: NAEYC. naeyc.org/sites/default/files/globally-shared /downloads/PDFs/accreditation/early-learning/standards_assessment_2019.pdf.

———. 2020. "Crosswalk for Using *Developmentally Appropriate Practice* (3rd ed.) with NAEYC's 2020 DAP Position Statement." Washington, DC: NAEYC.

Newport, Frank. 2018. "In U.S., Estimate of LGBT Population Rises to 4.5%." Gallup News. May 22, 2018. news.gallup.com/poll/234863/estimate-lgbt -population-rises.aspx.

Nolan, Ian T., Christopher J. Kuhner, and Geolani W. Dy. 2019. "Demographic and temporal trends in transgender identities and gender confirming surgery." *Translational Andrology and Urology* 8, no. 3 (June 2019): 184–190. doi.org/10.21037 /tau.2019.04.09.

Poole, Carla, Susan A. Miller, and Ellen Booth Church. n.d. "Ages & Stages: How Children Develop a Sense of Time." Early Childhood Today from Scholastic. Accessed September 8, 2021. scholastic.com/teachers/articles/teaching-content /ages-stages-how-children-develop-sense-time/.

Rafferty, Jason. 2018. "Gender Identity Development in Children." HealthyChildren.org, American Academy of Pediatrics (AAP). September 18, 2018. healthychildren.org/English/ages-stages/gradeschool/Pages/Gender -Identity-and-Gender-Confusion-In-Children.aspx.

Sepulveda, Kristin, and Sarah Catherine Williams. 2019. "One in three children entered foster care in 2017 because of parental drug abuse." Child Trends. February 26, 2019. childtrends.org/blog/one-in-three-children-entered-foster-care-in-fy -2017-because-of-parental-drug-abuse.

Sexuality Education Resource Centre (SERC). n.d. "Gender Identity." Teen Talk. Accessed August 25, 2021. teentalk.ca/learn-about/gender-identity/.

Strasser, Janis. 2019. "Conversations with Children! Asking Questions That Stretch Children's Thinking." *Teaching Young Children* 12, no. 3 (February/March 2019). naeyc.org/resources/pubs/tyc/feb2019/asking-questions-stretch -children%27s-thinking.

Tarasuk, Valerie, and Andy Mitchell. 2020. "Household Food Insecurity in Canada, 2017–18." PROOF. March 12, 2020. proof.utoronto.ca/resources /proof-annual-reports/household-food-insecurity-in-canada-2017-2018/.

Index

Conversations with family adults, 5, 13. *See also*
Following up with family members
about a child's major illness or medical condition,
75–76
about a miscarriage, 84
about a natural disaster, 183–184
about child's response to social upheaval, 192
about death of a family member, 99
about death of a friend or classmate, 107–108
about family structure, 155–156
about food insecurity, 138–139
about gender and gender expression, 173–174
about incarceration, 58–59
about major illness of an adult, 67
about military deployment, 51–52
about physical and cognitive differences, 146–147
about race and culture, 128–129
about separation and divorce, 43
about sex and sexuality, 164–165
about substance abuse/addiction, 34–35
about terror events, 200
about the death of a pet, 91
about unemployment, 26–27
introductory letter for families, 6
mode of, 19–20
occurring before conversations with young children,
13–14
Counselors, 18
COVID-19 pandemic, 192, 197
Curfews, 192

D

Deafness, 152
Death (conversations about), 6
child's limited understanding about, 97, 105, 114, 123
child's questions about, 68, 71
child's understanding/concept of, 65–66, 94, 102
child's unexpected responses about, 72–73
conversation starter for, 12
explaining, 72, 91, 99, 107, 111, 120–121
of a family member, 99–106
focusing on care when child asks about, 72, 80, 81
of a friend/classmate, 107–115
miscarriages, 84–90
of a pet, 12, 91–98
of a teacher or caregiver, 116–124
using concrete terminology for, 94, 102, 107, 111, 120
Developmental appropriateness, 17–18
when talking about death, 113
when talking about food insecurity, 140
when talking about incarceration, 61
when talking about sex and sexuality, 168
Diabetes, 76, 77, 79, 81
Disabilities, talking about physical and cognitive, 146–
154. *See also* Cognitive differences, conversations
about; Physical differences, conversations about
Divorce and separation, 43–50, 155
Doctors, 65, 70, 72, 78, 80, 166
Downs syndrome, 148, 151, 153
Drawing or painting pictures, 15, 16, 44, 49, 52, 59, 60,
63, 68, 79, 92, 93, 101, 186, 206
Dreams, bad, 51, 54, 61

E

Educators. *See also* Teachers
addressing food insecurity, 139
being prepared for tough questions, 3–4
comfort level with conversation topic, 19
Email, communicating with family by, 19–20
Emotional vocabulary, 35–36
Emotions. *See also* individual emotions
acknowledging child's, 42, 52
adults labeling and expressing their own, 54, 61, 62,
71, 78, 79, 97, 98, 105, 206
educators reflecting on their own, 4
labeling, 28, 79, 87, 123–124
related to divorce and separation, 43, 46
related to gun violence and terror events, 200, 204
related to incarceration, 58
related to military deployment, 51, 54
related to miscarriage, 84
related to serious illnesses, 67
teacher not labeling a child's, 41, 48, 64
Emotions, encouraging child to identify and express,
14–15
about childhood illness/medical condition, 81
about death of a classmate, 109
about death of a family member, 100, 101
about death of a pet, 96
about death of a teacher or caregiver, 118
about divorce/separation, 45, 48, 49
about gun violence and terror events, 202, 205
about immigration, 193–194
about incarceration, 60
about military deployment, 52, 53, 54
about miscarriage, 85
about natural disasters, 185
about race and culture, 130, 136
about serious illness, 69, 73, 76
about social upheaval, 194
about substance abuse, 36, 37
about their own medical condition/illness, 76, 81
about unemployment, 28–29, 30
Empathy, 31, 73, 82, 144, 145, 153, 186

F

Face-to-face conversations, 19
Faith-based responses, 71, 80, 113, 123
Families, conversations with children
about a major childhood illness or medical condition,
78–82
about an adult's illness, 70–74
about death of a family member, 102–106
about death of a friend/classmate, 111–115
about death of a pet, 94–98
about death of a teacher or caregiver, 120–124
about family structure, 159–162
about food insecurity and hunger, 142–145
about gender and gender expression, 177–180
about gun violence and terror events, 204–208
about incarceration, 61–64
about military deployment, 54–56
about miscarriage, 87–90
about natural disasters, 187–191
about physical and cognitive differences, 151–154
about race and culture, 131–136
about separation and divorce, 46–47
about sex and sexuality, 168–171

Incarceration, 12, 58–64
Inclusiveness, encouraging, 148, 151
Intellectual developmental disorder/disabilities, 153
Introductory letter for families, 6. *See also* Conversations with family adults; Family

K

Kindness for others, 38, 130, 131, 132, 133, 134, 136, 137, 144–145, 149–150, 152, 153, 174, 198
Kosher, eating, 134

L

Language. *See* Terminology
Leg braces, 147–148
Lesbian parents, 155, 158, 161

M

Mandatory reporting, 19, 35, 141, 164
Marriage, 43, 162. *See also* Divorce and separation
Masks, wearing, 193
Media, news. *See* News media/stories
Media portrayals, family structure and, 155
Medical concepts, explaining, 70–72, 78–79
Medical professionals, 70, 78, 80, 113. *See also* Doctors
Military deployment, 51–56
Miscarriages, 84–90
Mother's Day, 158
Multigenerational households, 155

N

Name-calling, 37–38
National Center on the Sexual Behavior of Youth (NCSBY), 165
National Child Traumatic Stress Network (NCTSN), 165
Natural disasters, 12, 183–191
News media/stories
    on food insecurity, 140, 141, 142
    gun violence/terror events on, 204
    natural disasters on, 184, 188
    on social upheaval, 196
    young children seeing the, 2
Nonbinary teachers, 178
Nonverbal communication, 2, 14

O

One-parent families, 155, 156, 157
Open-ended questions, 14–15, 28, 36, 44, 68, 76, 92, 109, 118, 129, 185

P

Painting pictures. *See* Drawing or painting pictures
Parents. *See also* Conversations with family adults; Families, conversations with children; Family
    affirming their love for their child, 41, 47
    divorced. *See* Divorce and separation
    following up conversations with. *See* Following up with family members
    incarceration of, 58–64
    influence on racial/cultural attitudes, 128
    labeling and expressing their feelings, 96–97, 98, 105, 111–112, 114, 123, 206
    military deployment of, 51–56
    response to miscarriage, 84
    unemployed, 26–32
Pauses, in conversations, 15
Pets, death of, 12, 91–98
Phone, communicating with family by, 19

Photos, 53, 54, 58, 61
Physical comfort, offering, 35, 44, 59, 69, 85, 184, 201
Physical differences, conversations about, 146–154
Pictures, drawing. *See* Drawing or painting pictures
Picture story, about a friend/classmate who has died, 109, 110
Planned conversations, 9
Pregnancy. *See* Babies and pregnancy
Preschoolers, understanding of time and future events by, 18
Prison. *See* Incarceration
Privacy
    body privacy, 164
    conversing with an individual child *versus* a group and, 13
    honoring a family and child's, 18–20
Protest marches, 192, 194–195

Q

Questions
    about a child's medical condition or serious illness, 79–80
    about death, 92–93, 103–104, 112–113, 121–122
    about death of a pet, 95–96
    about divorce and separation, 47
    about family structure, 160–161
    about food insecurity and hunger, 143–144
    about gender and gender expression, 178–179
    about gun violence and terror events, 206–207
    about incarceration, 62–63
    about major illnesses/death, 71
    about military deployment, 55
    about miscarriage, 88
    about natural disasters, 188–189
    about physical and cognitive differences, 147–148, 152
    about race and culture, 134–135
    about sex, sexuality, and babies, 169–170
    about social upheaval, 197–198
    about substance abuse/addiction, 40–41
    "acknowledge, affirm, ask, and be there" response to, 16
    general family check-in, 11
    responding to a child's questions with open-ended, 14–15

R

Race and culture, conversations about, 127–137
Racism, 133, 134
Real-life events, children's anxieties exacerbated by fears from, 2
Reassurance, offering to child
    death and, 109–110, 114, 118, 123
    divorce/separation and, 44, 47, 49
    food insecurity and, 140
    gun violence/terror events and, 206
    incarceration and, 59, 60
    major illnesses and, 69, 70, 78
    military deployment and, 53, 56
    miscarriages and, 88
    natural disasters and, 189
    substance abuse and, 39, 40
    unemployment and, 30, 31
Reincarnation, 104, 113, 122
Religious teachings/practices
    cultural practices and, 134
    explaining death and, 113, 122–123
    knowing the family's, 20–21

Digital versions of all family take-home pages can be downloaded at
freespirit.com/big-forms. Use password **4children**.

About the Author

Early childhood education expert **Dr. Lauren Starnes** has completed dual-doctoral programs in both child development and educational leadership. She currently holds the position of vice president of early childhood education for Primrose School Franchising Company, where she supports curriculum development, implementation, and evaluation. Previously she served as the company's executive director of professional development, leading and facilitating instructor-led and eLearning professional development for all stakeholders in the over 420 Primrose Schools. Prior to that she led the early childhood education department for a private  education company, authoring their proprietary early childhood curriculum and leading professional development creation and delivery. Lauren has worked at every level of early childhood education. While she began her formal career teaching at the university level, she has prior experience teaching within preschools, consulting and serving as a support professional for children with autism, and serving as an embedded instructional coach for preschool teachers. She has worked as a school principal for multiple schools and remains actively involved as a voice for early childhood education in various professional associations. When not working, Lauren enjoys spending time with her family, traveling, and cheering on her two sons in sports. She lives in Marietta, Georgia, near Atlanta.

Visit Lauren at **drlaurenstarnes.com**.

More Great Resources from Free Spirit

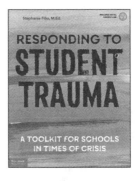